WOMEN at WAR

The Women of World War II—At Home, at Work, on the Front Line

BRENDA RALPH LEWIS

Reader's Digest

The Reader's Digest Association, Inc.
Pleasantville, New York/Montreal

A READER'S DIGEST BOOK

This edition published by The Reader's Digest Association, Inc., by arrangement with Amber Books Ltd.

Editorial and design by
Amber Books Ltd
Bradley's Close
74–77 White Lion Street
London N1 9PF

FOR AMBER BOOKS
Project Editor: James Bennett
Design: Zoë Mellors
Picture Research: Lisa Wren

FOR READER'S DIGEST
Project Editor: Robert Lockwood Mills
Canadian Contributing Editor: Robert Ronald
Project Designer: George McKeon
Executive Editor, Trade Publishing: Dolores York
Senior Design Director: Elizabeth Tunnicliffe
Editorial Director: Christopher Cavanaugh
Director, Trade Publishing: Christopher T. Reggio
Vice President & Publisher, Trade Publishing: Harold Clarke

Library of Congress Cataloging in Publication Data

Lewis, Brenda Ralph.
Women at War : the women of World War II, at home, at work, on the Front Line /
Brenda Ralph Lewis.
p. cm.
Includes bibliographical references and index.
ISBN 0-7621-0392-2
1. World War, 1939-1945--Women. 2. Women and war. 3. Women and the military. 4.
Women–History–20th century. I. Title.

D810.W7 L47 2002
940.53'082–dc21

2002024838

Address any comments about *Women at War* to:
The Reader's Digest Association, Inc.
Adult Trade Publishing
Reader's Digest Road
Pleasantville, NY 10570-7000

For more Reader's Digest products and information,visit our website:
www.rd.com (in the United States)
www.readersdigest.ca (in Canada)

Printed in Italy

10 9 8 7 6 5 4 3 2 1

CONTENTS

WOMAN'S PLACE IN WAR

The Army of the United States has 239 kinds of jobs for women

THE WOMEN'S ARMY CORPS

Introduction

'A woman's place is in the home' was an old adage, but it still held true at the start of World War II. Even though millions of women worked, home and family were considered the focus of their lives.

After working a seven-hour shift at Pearl Harbor's Naval Hospital the day before, Lieutenant Ruth Erickson of the U.S. Navy Nursing Corps awoke on Sunday morning, December 7, 1941, looking forward to her day off. Hawaii was a 'paradise' posting and off-duty days were uniquely enjoyable – dating, a game or two on the tennis courts, beach parties and picnics or just simply lazing around, followed by evenings spent dancing under the starlit Pacific skies or listening to lilting Hawaiian melodies.

On this particular Sunday, though, Erickson's relaxing day off ended at breakfast time.

'Two or three of us were sitting in the dining room having a late breakfast and talking over coffee,' Erickson later recalled. 'Suddenly we heard planes roaring overhead and we said, "The fly boys are really busy at Ford Island this morning." '

RISING SUN OVERHEAD

'We no sooner got those words out than we started to hear noises that were foreign to us. I...dashed to the nearest window.... Right then, there was a plane flying directly over the top of our quarters.... The Rising Sun under the wing of the plane denoted the enemy....

The demands imposed by World War II meant that traditional ideas about female roles had to be set aside, as women embarked on work they had never done before.

2 CENTS Chicago Daily Tribune FINAL

U.S. AND JAPS AT WAR

BOMB HAWAII, PHILIPPINES, GUAM, SINGAPORE

Despite isolationists who wanted to stay out of it, the Japanese sneak attack on the U.S. Pacific fleet at Pearl Harbor forced the United States into World War II.

One could almost see [the pilot's] features around his goggles. He was obviously saving his ammunition for the ships. Just down the row, all the ships were sitting there – the *California,* the *Arizona,* the *Oklahoma* and others.... The telephone was ringing – the chief nurse, Gertrude Arnest, was saying, "Girls, get into your uniforms at once. This is the real thing." '

Within minutes, smoke billowing into the air from the burning ships on Battleship Row dulled the sunny Pacific morning into a surreal dusk. The first patient came into the Naval Hospital at 0825 hours, bleeding unstoppably from a gaping wound in his abdomen. Within the hour, he was dead. He was among 2,043 casualties suffered at Pearl Harbor, where 18 warships and 188 aircraft were also lost. Next day, the United States declared war on Japan.

The rest, as they say, is history – at its most profound. Erickson's lost day off in Hawaii was a definitive moment that changed the world, as well as the lives and futures of Americans, both immediately and forever. Sixty years would pass before the terrorist attacks of September 11, 2001, on the World Trade Center in New York and the Pentagon in Washington gave the United States a comparable wake-up call to heed the fearful realities of the wider world.

ISOLATIONISM DROPPED

Before Pearl Harbor, the dominant mood in America had been strongly isolationist, a reaction to what many saw as the forced entry of their country into the First World War in 1917. Much better, it was thought, to leave the Old World to its own destructive devices – an attitude reflected in the refusal of Congress to ratify the Treaty of Versailles, which had formally concluded the war in 1919, or to join the League of

The spectacle of U.S. ships sunk, crippled and on fire at Pearl Harbor produced in Americans an iron resolve to avenge themselves and make the Japanese pay.

Nations, so dear to the heart of President Woodrow Wilson.

This attitude altered, however, in a mere two hours – the duration of the Japanese attack on December 7, 1941. Pearl Harbor demonstrated a new and sobering truth: Americans were no longer safe from the upheavals that had already convulsed Europe, where World War II had begun two years earlier. In particular, this situation brought into focus the new and unusual demands that were going to be made on women. With most of the men called up into the armed services, there were factory jobs to be filled and new war industries to be supplied. Transport networks – trains, buses – needed new personnel. These and other vital wartime tasks were going to make women's lives and work as different as possible from those they had previously known. For all this, a revolution in their thinking would be required.

PROPAGANDA SUCCESS

In the United States, a powerful programme of propaganda, featuring carefully designed posters, was organized to encourage women to see themselves as directly involved in the war effort, capable of an independence they had never known before and a physical strength no one imagined they possessed. In Britain, where official schemes to encourage volunteers produced disappointing results, women were conscripted for war work, for the first time in history, in 1941. It may have required prompting, but the response of women to their new tasks proved to be a major factor in the war effort. The effort came from all over the world, not only from Britain, the United States and Canada, but also from Australia, New Zealand, South Africa and other countries of the British Commonwealth and Empire, which all sent troops to help fight the war. In addition, Canada, New Zealand and other countries outside of Europe had the advantage of being out of reach of Nazi or Japanese air attacks and were therefore free of the risk of invasion. This also applied to Australia, although later in the war the north coast of the country was raided and threatened with invasion by the Japanese, a threat that fortunately never became reality.

In practical terms, their faraway location meant that women and men in Canadian and other factories were able to continue their work uninterrupted by the air raids that hampered their counterparts in Britain. Farms, too, were left in peace to produce food to supply the beleagured 'home country', although delivery could involve their ships in long and dangerous voyages. Canada also proved the ideal place for the 151 flying schools of the British Commonwealth Air Training Plan (BCATP) which were sited all over the country. Between 1940 and 1945, 131,553 pilots, wireless operators, air gunners and navigators of several nationalities were trained in these schools for the air forces of Britain, Australia, New Zealand and Canada

American families united behind their fighting men – note the photograph on the mantelpiece – typified the propaganda initiatives which roused feelings of patriotism and harnessed popular enthusiasm for the war effort.

Europeans living under Nazi rule kept their ears pressed close to their radios and listened with the volume turned down to near inaudibility while someone watched at the window in case any Germans came by. The Germans, of course, knew about these secret radios and were always on the lookout for them.

itself. The BCATP, which British Prime Minister Winston Churchill regarded as Canada's most prestigious contribution to the Allied war effort, used the skills of 104,113 men and women.

In this context, women, who held all ranks up to and including Section Officer, the equivalent of Squadron Leader, did a remarkable number of jobs. They performed the same functions as the male ground crew – as clerks in accounting, uniform and aircraft parts stores, parachute packers, aero-engine mechanics, riggers and fitters, armourers, both ground and air photographers, wireless and vehicle operators and mechanics. They refuelled and oiled aircraft and worked as drill instructors.

Leading Airwoman R. B. Cutliffe was assigned to the BCATP school at Toronto, where she became the first woman to operate a refuelling tender.

'The looks on the faces of the hangar crew were something to behold,' Cutliffe later recalled. 'Surprise and maybe a look of horror.'

Although she had only a 20-minute lesson in refuelling tenders, Cutliffe obviously did the job well. 'It wasn't long before I was being treated as one of the crew,' she remarked.

On another occasion, Cutliffe, now employed as a truck driver, was ordered to pick up a Sergeant and two airmen, plus a 40-gallon drum of aviation fuel.

'Then I was to pick up an officer, complete with his parachute, at one of the hangars. After I had done this, I was to go to the town of Mount Forest, where a student had put a Harvard aircraft down in a farmer's field. All the way there, the officer kept on complaining about the truck, how slow it was, the reek of gasoline and the fact that one of his students had made a forced landing.'

The Harvard was quickly found, inspected and refuelled, but the officer refused to allow the student to fly the plane back to the airfield.

'No,' he was told. 'You can ride home in that damned stinking truck!'

With an empty fuel drum in the truck, Cutliffe had to drive back with all the truck windows open because of the fumes.

These young Polish children arrived in London on August 29, 1939, three days before their country became the first to come under attack from Nazi Germany in World War II.

FAMILY LIFE CHANGED

Family life, however, was never so easily removed from the war zone as the BCATP. In all the combatant countries, in millions of homes, fundamental changes were unavoidable. Women trying to preserve a semblance of family life faced a daunting barrage of restrictions and, in Britain and mainland Europe, dangers never before imagined. Rationing of food, clothes and gasoline was introduced, and women found themselves struggling to balance their work and home lives.

War work did not necessarily involve factories. American women put a great deal of time into raising funds for the war effort, selling U.S. war bonds, and tending the Victory Gardens which produced a total of 8 million U.S. tons (7.25 metric) of food for home consumption. Canadian women had their own Victory Gardens and Victory bonds to sell and, like the Americans, collected scrap metals and other useful materials and provided comforts for the troops.

BRITAIN IN PERIL

British women at home made similar efforts, but, of course, their situation was very different from that of their counterparts on the home front across

A British Family's Story

On September 3, 1939, when Britain and France declared war on Nazi Germany, Esther Albert, mother of two daughters aged 7 and 10 months, packed up her home and left London for Amersham, a town in the Buckinghamshire countryside 30 miles northwest of the British capital. She had good reason. The London suburb where Esther and her husband, Simon, lived with their family was too dangerous. Only a quarter of a mile (400m) from their home were several factories, natural targets for German air raids.

An Unsettling Existence

Esther was catapulted from her comfortable, quite affluent pre-war life into an unfamiliar, sometimes unsettling, existence. Nannies for the children, an expensive social round, a stylish wardrobe, trips abroad – all that had to go. Now, in wartime Amersham, Esther was issued ration books with strictly controlled allowances of food and clothing. The food ration included one egg per person per month. Esther increased this miserly portion by buying hens and giving them to a farming family who looked after the hens and gave her their eggs. To complement the coal ration, Esther's elder daughter, Patricia, often went into the nearby forest with friends to collect wood for fuel.

When the Alberts took their daughters away from London, this was why: they could have been left like this dejected family, sitting among the rubble of their home after an air raid.

Family under Fire

The family slept on the ground floor. When the air-raid siren sounded, Esther turned off all lights, opened the back doors and ushered her children into the family's garden shelter. Once, Patricia looked up and saw the distinctive black crosses on the wings of a German bomber, illuminated in the pale moonlight. It was an image she has not forgotten to this day.

When at last, in 1945, the war ended, the family was able to return to London. Though they had spent the war years in relative rural safety, their minds had been marked – so much so that it was 1948, when Patricia was 16, before she realized that peace was the normal state of affairs and war an aberration.

the Atlantic. In 1940, the forces of Nazi Germany stormed from one European conquest to another in just three months – April, May and June – leaving Britain the only combatant in Europe still free to oppose them. However, when the British Expeditionary Force was evacuated from Dunkirk in northern France between May 26 and June 4, 1940, they had to leave their heavy equipment and vehicles behind; at that juncture only divisions stationed in Britain were fully equipped, one of which was Canadian.

Just how long Britain's freedom would last was in doubt throughout 1940. Women at home found their days punctuated by urgent calls of air-raid sirens and a rush to the shelters where, crowded together with others, they remained for as long as the Luftwaffe bombing continued. Even after October 1940, when the Luftwaffe was finally defeated by the Royal Air Force in the Battle of Britain and Hitler postponed his cross-Channel invasion 'indefinitely', the bombing raids continued to lay waste to large areas of cities like London and Liverpool.

Across the English Channel in Nazi-occupied Europe, a sombre pall fell over everyday life as the presence of the conquerors pervaded cities, towns and villages. Tension was ever present. An unwary word or gesture – even a look that could be interpreted as unfriendly – meant trouble, perhaps a prolonged Gestapo questioning: even if released, a man or woman was henceforth marked, always under scrutiny for some other infraction of the harsh new rules.

General office work continued in wartime, and many women, like this CWAC working on the Kardex filing system at Canadian Military HQ, did many of the same jobs as in peacetime.

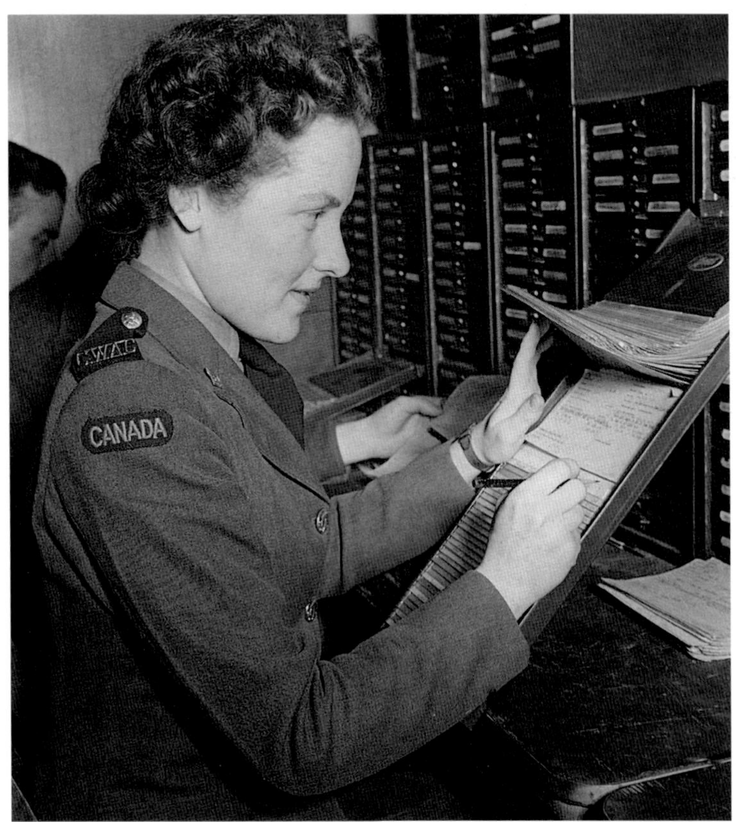

UNDER SUSPICION

Once the exhilaration of their speedy success had faded and the Germans got down to the mundane task of guarding their gains, they grew nervous. In the early days of the Occupation, they were well aware that resistance against them was being organized. As a result, they suspected spies and saboteurs everywhere. No one knew whether she might be the next to hear the dreaded knock on the door and open it to face Gestapo standing there, demanding to search the house. All too often, the Gestapo came for Jews, whose extermination had been decreed by Adolf Hitler. It was not unknown for Jewish children to return from school only to discover that one or both of their parents were no longer there: they had been snatched away by the Gestapo and sent off to a concentration camp, never to be seen or heard from again.

It was a furtive existence permeated by fear. Most people kept their heads down and tried to stay out of trouble.

Some, more defiantly, risked listening to the broadcasts put out in 19 languages by the British Broadcasting Corporation in London.

Living in fear meant considerable nervous strain, but some women, such as trained nurses, were already geared for war situations. On the Pacific front, being taken prisoner by the Japanese, as many nurses were, was an occupational hazard. That risk also applied to civilians, the wives of colonial administrators or servicemen stationed in Singapore, Hong Kong and other Japanese occupation sites after 1941.

WOMEN WHO VOLUNTEERED

Intrepid types like women aviators, journalists and photographers found an outlet for their energies in war service. So did women who worked as spies and agents or volunteered for the women's military services. Likewise, film and stage stars, singers and other performers offered their talents to keep troops entertained. In occupied countries, many women were willing to run extraordinary risks in movements that resisted German invaders. Russian women, more accustomed to hardship than most others, were drafted directly into the armed services and flew as pilots or fought land battles.

AFTER THE WAR

When it was all over, in 1945, wartime jobs disappeared, especially in industry. Large numbers of women literally and metaphorically returned home. However, the war years had allowed them new insights into their own capabilities and importance. This book is therefore the story not only of the enormous contribution women made to World War II, but also of the medals for bravery they earned, the new skills they developed, and the depredations they survived. It also tells of a new self-image, which may have taken its time to filter into the liberation movements of the 1960s, but which still laid the foundations for the positions so many women have attained today.

I'm Proud... my husband wants me to do my part
SEE YOUR U. S. EMPLOYMENT SERVICE
WAR MANPOWER COMMISSION

After fighting hard against the idea at first, the authorities were eventually forced to recruit women for war work and even encouraged them to volunteer with emotionally appealing posters like this one.

CHAPTER 1

Gearing Up For War

The outbreak of World War II – in 1939 in Europe, in 1941 for the United States – was not entirely unexpected. Anticipating the event was, however, quite different from experiencing it and the war meant upheaval as millions geared up to cope with its demands.

Privately, Admiral Isoruku Yamamoto, architect of the Japanese surprise attack on Pearl Harbor, had never wanted war with the United States. Yamamoto had spent time studying in the United States before the war, and he had learned enough during his stay to judge the American people well. He perceived that beneath the laid-back pre-war image of the U.S. Navy was a brand of strength and determination to avenge the insult they had suffered and throw it back, with interest, into the face of the enemy.

'All we have done,' said Yamamoto, 'is to waken a sleeping giant and fill him with a terrible resolve.'

AMERICAN WOMEN AT WAR

The giantess awoke as well. The women of America went to war with a high sense of patriotic resolve. By 1944, more than 2.3 million were working in new war industries in the United States, building ships, aircraft, vehicles and weaponry. By the summer of 1945, 57,000 Army nurses and 11,000 Navy nurses were on duty, together with 100,000 in the Women's Auxiliary Army Corps (WAAC), 86,000 Women Accepted for Volunteer Emergency Service (WAVES), 1,800 women Marines, and 11,000 in the Coast Guard Reserve (SPARS).

In wartime, both British and American women joined the navy. These two were U.S. Navy nurses. The British WRNS, formed in 1939, did a wide variety of jobs, including technical work.

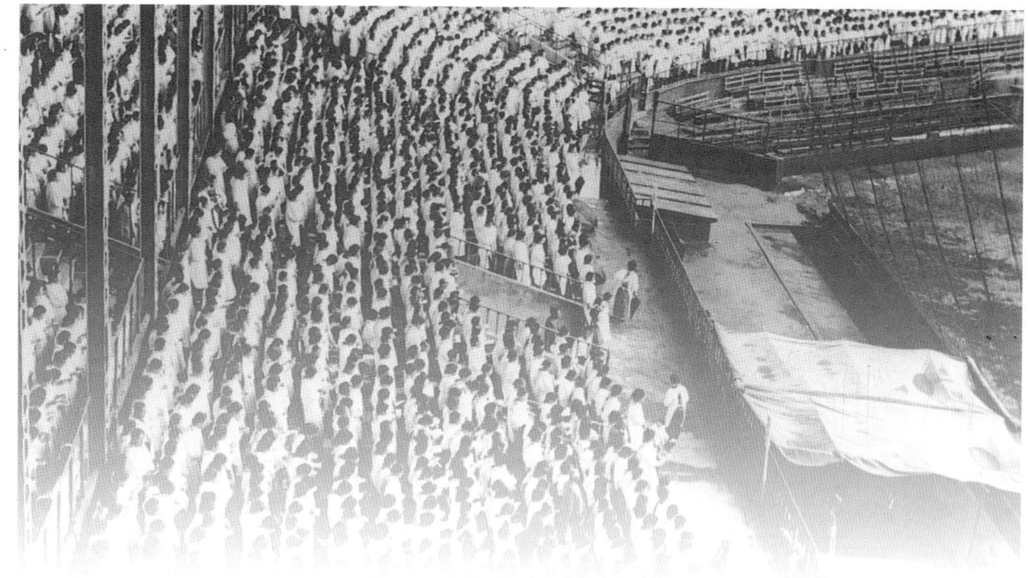

Huge rallies, like this Women Behind the Guns meeting in Osaka, Japan, were designed to create mass excitement and near-hysterical patriotism: the same high emotion informed Nazi rallies in Germany.

American WAVES on parade. The sense of belonging to the military and sharing an important purpose – to win the war – was reinforced by marching on parade and following the flag.

CANADIAN WOMEN AT WAR

Canadian women were hardly less enthusiastic and 1,331,383 became engaged in working for the war effort. Of these, 43,383 volunteered for the military services alone: 20,497 joined the Canadian Women's Army Corps (CWAC), 16,221 went into the Canadian Women's Auxiliary Air Force (CWAAF) and 6,665 into the Women's Royal Canadian Naval Service (WRCNS). The three services combined to send 4,439 of their members to the health services. In addition, there were 261,000 Canadian women who were engaged in war production, 31,000 in communications and another 996,000 in other work vital to the war effort, including the service sector, general manufacturing, finance and construction.

BARRIERS

Ultimately, American and Canadian women, like those in other countries, scored a level of success few, if any, had thought to be within their compass. For mobilizing the women of North America was not a straightforward task. There were many barriers – of gender, colour, class and tradition.

In both countries, there was a traditionalist backlash – fierce resistance to the very idea that women should go to war in any capacity, and that resistance came not only from men, but from women as well. The United States had a particular problem. It took Americans a quantum leap in thinking to accept black women and black men as equals in the war effort. It took a catastrophe like Pearl Harbor to shift traditional thinking about what was and was not 'women's work', beginning a new era in which American women participated in national life as never before.

However, if the attack itself came as a fearful shock, the notion of America at war was not as unimaginable as has often been made out. There was, after all, plenty of evidence in the 1930s that this would be the outcome of world events.

Mabel Smith of Matunuck, Rhode Island, who married in January 1939 and spent the war raising three children on her own, saw some of this evidence first-hand when she travelled to Europe in 1937. Already, fear of war was rife. In Austria, Mabel witnessed some of the reasons.

'Hitler encouraged young people to have great pride in the Aryan race and the German nation...the great, strong German master race, he called it. It was a little scary....'

'[The Austrian] people were very enthusiastic about Adolf Hitler.... Oh, they were for Hitler, they were! He encouraged young people to have great pride in the Aryan race and the German nation...the great, strong German master race, he called it. It was a little scary even then. I didn't know too much about anti-Semitism, hatred of the Jews, but...I knew it was part of Hitler's build-up and his policy.'

MABEL SMITH IN AUSTRIA

The time Mabel spent in Austria gave her a special insight into the significance of the Munich Crisis of 1938, when the British and French leaders virtually handed over to Hitler the Sudetenland region of Czechoslovakia.

'That made a great many people uneasy. They said it would be "peace in our time," but you felt it couldn't last.'

Mabel was right. Peace in Europe broke down in 1939, when Hitler's Germany invaded and quickly conquered Poland. The following year saw the Germans triumph across Western Europe as Norway, Denmark, Belgium, the Netherlands and France were defeated in turn and absorbed into a new Nazi empire. Only Britain was left to be conquered – and in 1940 no one knew how long it would remain free.

JAPAN, THE POTENTIAL ENEMY

If the rumblings of a coming war could be heard in Europe before the actual outbreak, it was the same in the Pacific, where Japan was becoming a potential enemy of the United States.

The Japanese had already gone to war, invading Manchuria in 1931 and

German women were destined to produce and rear the next generation of the 'Aryan' master race. To this end, these girls, seen here meeting Hitler, were strictly trained and disciplined.

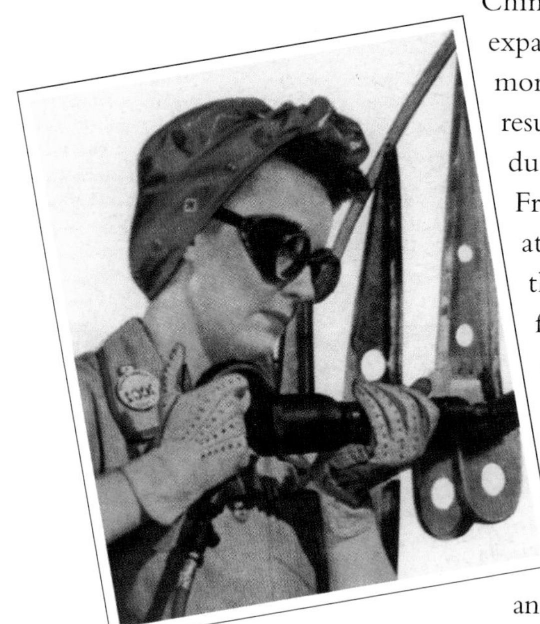

The tough, feisty Rosie the Riveter, created to inspire American women to join the war effort, was one of the most successful fictional female characters ever devised.

China in 1937. Their expansionist aims became more and more evident, resulting in diplomatic duelling as President Franklin D. Roosevelt attempted to curb their ambitions by freezing Japanese assets in America and placing an embargo on Japanese trade.

By 1939, tension in the Pacific was building up fast, and Navy nurse Ruth Erickson was well aware of it. In April of that year, she thought she was on her way to help out at the opening of the World's Fair at Flushing Meadows, New York. She never got there.

'Japan was rattling the saber,' she later recalled. All ships, including Erickson's vessel, *Relief,* were ordered to refuel, take on provisions and immediately return to the West Coast. 'When we reached the Panama Canal, the locks operated around the clock to get the ships through. *Relief* was the last ship, and we remained on the Pacific side for two or three days and then continued to our home port, San Pedro, California.'

Late that summer, fleet manoeuvres were ordered to take place off the coast of Maui, Hawaii.

Erickson was detached to report to the Naval Hospital at Pearl Harbor when the manoeuvres were complete.

At this stage she and her fellow nurses couldn't quite decide whether war was imminent or not, but – as she soon discovered once stationed at Pearl Harbor – Hawaii was already in a state of high alert.

'We're on alert again, only this time they say it is the real thing.... There are guards all over the place and everyone is running around with guns on.'

GINGER'S DIARY

Ginger, the 17-year-old daughter of an Army family stationed at Hickam Field, Oahu, recorded the increasing tension in her diary. On Friday, November 28, 1941, Ginger wrote:

'Boy, the atmosphere is getting tense! We're on alert again, only this time they say it is the real thing instead of just practice.' Two days later, Ginger recorded: 'This alert is sure queer. There are guards all over the place and everyone is running around with guns on. The sirens keep blowing on all sides of us.... '

Before November was out, Ginger's curiosity had turned to near certainty: 'Wonder if we'll be at war by this time next month.... I certainly do hope not. Especially not with the Japs!' The state of emergency in Hawaii had heightened by Tuesday, December 2. 'It's really going to be a battle, then,' Ginger wrote that day.

ON THE MAINLAND

On the North American mainland, these realities seemed less immediate. As Eileen Hughes of Narragansett, Rhode Island, put it:

'Before Pearl Harbor, I didn't realize how serious the war in Europe was. I think it seemed very, very far away. We were also far away from Japan as well as Germany. It was horrible what was going

Women in the military had image problems – as shown in the glamorized scene on the opposite page. They were seen as femmes fatales; their role was trivialized or they were dubbed 'unfeminine' for deserting their proper place, the home.

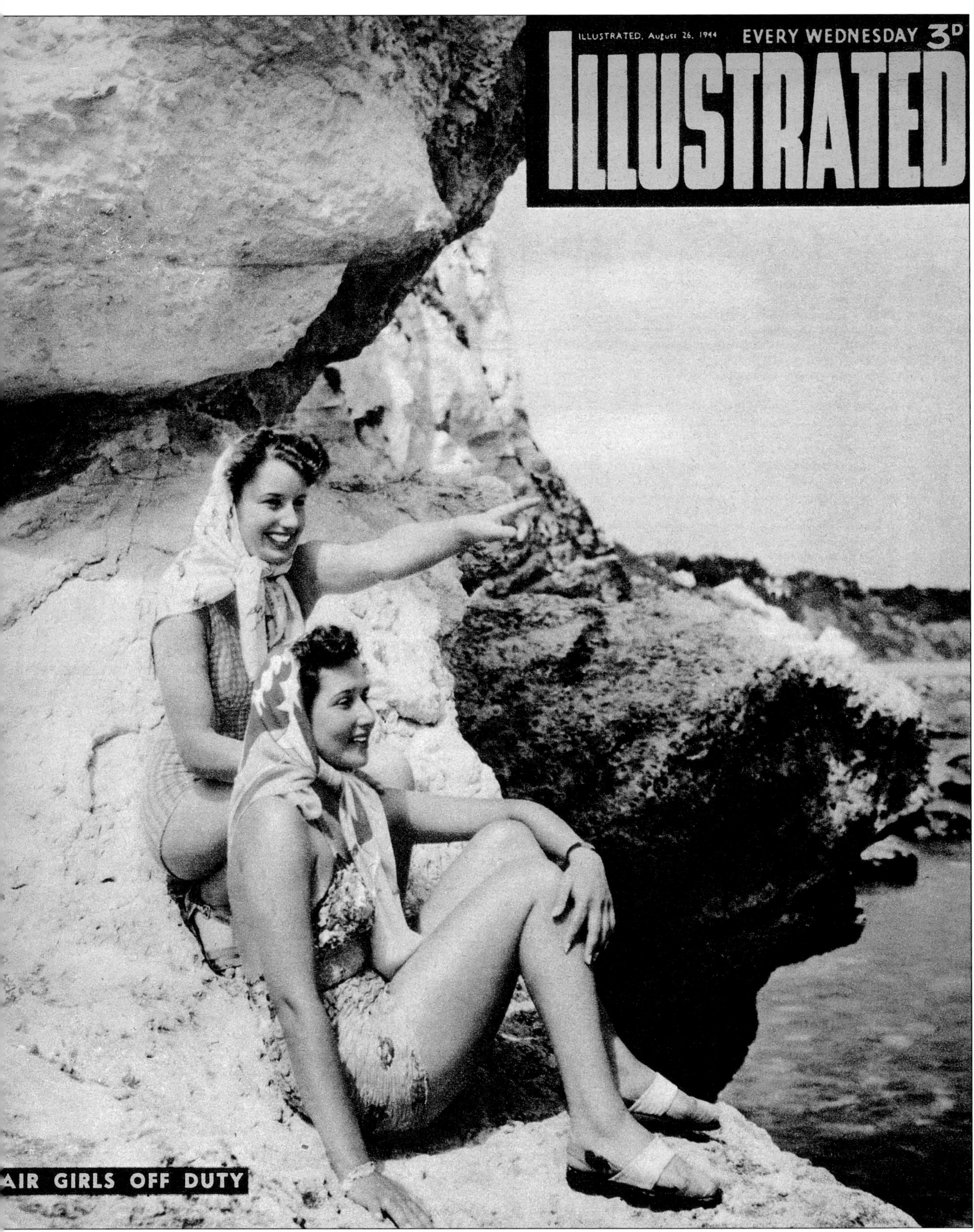
ILLUSTRATED, August 26, 1944
EVERY WEDNESDAY 3D
ILLUSTRATED
AIR GIRLS OFF DUTY

on in Europe, but I don't think I realized how close it was going to hit us until Pearl Harbor.'

Eileen and her family had just finished lunch on that fateful Sunday. She heard her mother call out from the kitchen, 'Oh, dear God. They have bombed Pearl Harbor!' 'I said, "What?" and she said, "Pearl Harbor. That's Hawaii. Do you know how many troops we have over there?" and I said, "No!" '

Still in school then, Eileen soon found the war affecting her family life when her brother left school to join the Army. Many boys in Eileen's class didn't bother to graduate. They, too, left to enlist. 'Everybody was very patriotic,' Eileen commented.

Eileen herself intended to join the Army, and longed to reach age 18 when she would have been eligible, with parental permission, for the Women's Auxiliary Army Corps (WAAC). Unfortunately, before she did, the age of eligibility was changed to 21. Eileen was so furious that she wrote to President Roosevelt complaining of this unfairness. The President failed to come across, though, and Eileen joined the Civilian Defense instead.

RESISTANCE

However, it was not as easy for a woman to enlist in the military as Eileen Hughes may have supposed. There was a lot of resistance, not necessarily to women's entering a 'man's world' but to protect them from doing so. In this, the old 19th-century belief that women were too refined and sensitive to endure the rough and tumble of the world outside the home was still commonly held in the middle of the 20th century.

On the face of it, popular wartime polls supported the principle that women should be allowed to serve in non-combat roles. The face of it was, however, deceptive. Closer examination of the polls showed that women were far more in favour than men. Even among those men who approved of women in the military, many disliked the idea that their own mothers, sisters, wives or daughters might be included. In at least one instance, a man physically attacked recruiting personnel in charge of enlisting women.

The picture opposite shows two WAAFs enjoying time off by the seaside. It is a glamorous though deceptive image: many British beaches were cordoned off by barbed wire and other obstacles as a deterrent to invasion.

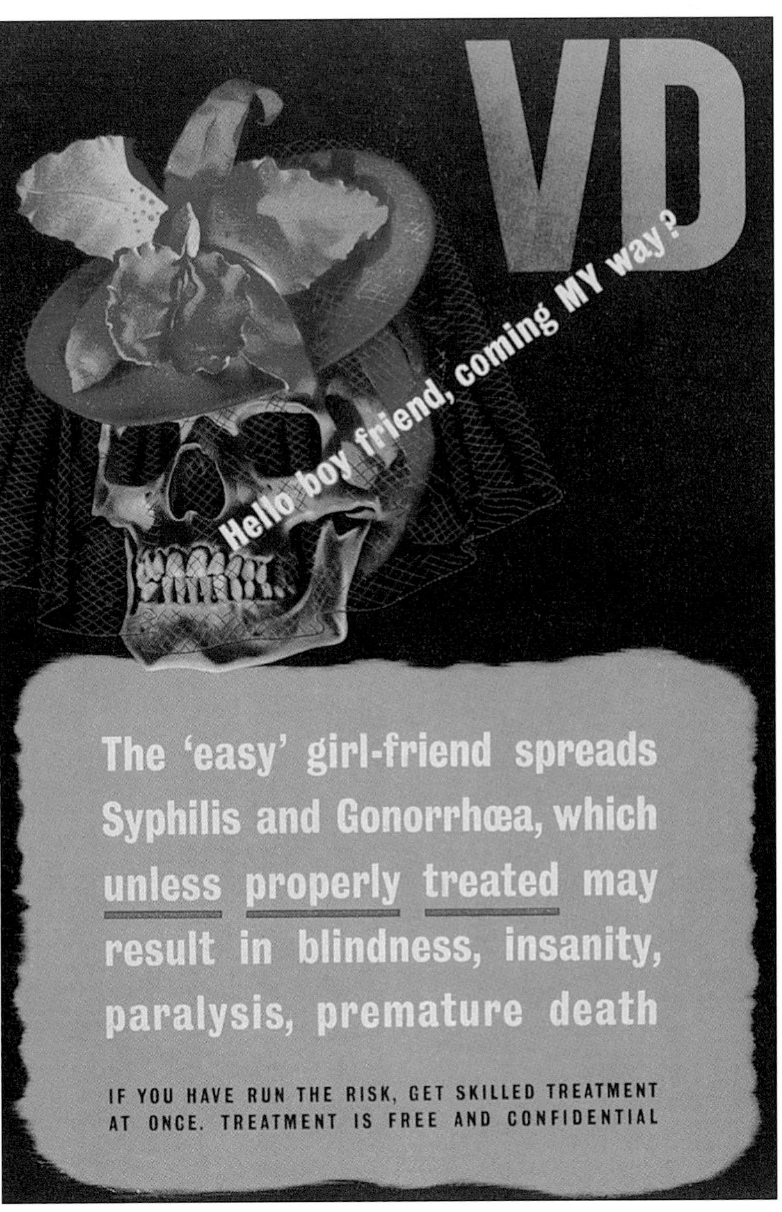

VD
Hello boy friend, coming MY way?
The 'easy' girl-friend spreads Syphilis and Gonorrhœa, which unless properly treated may result in blindness, insanity, paralysis, premature death
IF YOU HAVE RUN THE RISK, GET SKILLED TREATMENT AT ONCE. TREATMENT IS FREE AND CONFIDENTIAL

In war, disease – particularly venereal disease – was as much a danger as enemy action.

GI mail, read by censors, included numerous letters to female relatives objecting to their joining up. Some women were threatened with divorce or with being disowned by their families.

This was not all. Angry GIs and other men bombarded President Roosevelt, Secretary of War Henry Stimson, and members of Congress with letters and telegrams demanding the immediate release of their women from service.

American religious leaders also weighed into the argument. Catholics asserted that 'the amount of war work [a WAAC] might do no longer signifies, for the soul of our society will already be lost'. One Massachusetts bishop regarded women in the military as 'opposed by the teachings and principles of the Catholic Church'. In June 1942, a church in Brooklyn, New York, went even further, condemning WAACs as 'no more than an opening wedge, intended to break down the traditional American and Christian opposition to removing women from the home, and to degrade them by bringing back the pagan female goddess of de-sexed, lustful sterility'.

Unfortunately, this resistance gave rise to widespread rumours that equated military women with immoral women. There was even talk that 500 WAACs in North Africa had been 'guilty of sexual misconduct down to the last woman'. Several of them, it was whispered, had been shipped back to the United States because they were pregnant. The rumours were so vicious and persistent that, at first, a German propaganda campaign was suspected. The Nazi propaganda minister, Josef Goebbels, was after all a master of his nefarious art and perhaps the most cunning and successful of his breed. Investigations by the U.S. government, however, found Goebbels innocent. Most of the rumours, it was found, had originated with non-combatant U.S. Army personnel, most of whom had never worked with women in the military and feared that females would be foisted on them, like it or not. The press was also to blame for reporting unverified gossip as legitimate 'news'.

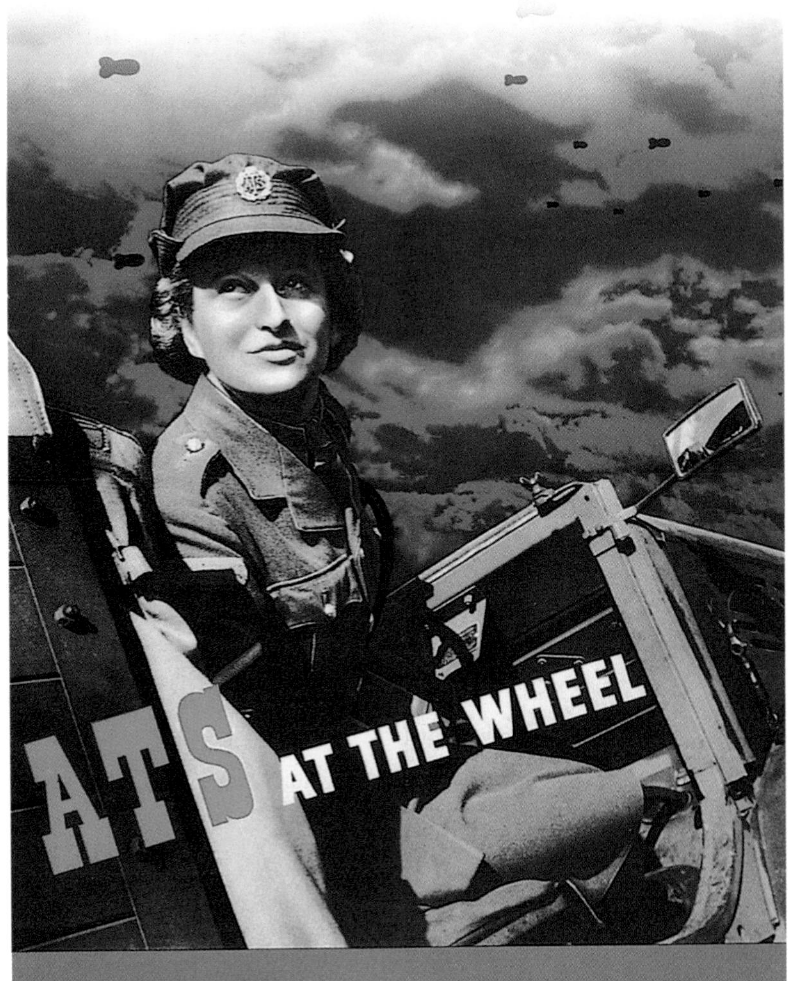

Despite the poor public image of women in the military, propaganda posters, like this one for the British ATS, emphasized the strength, dedication and nobility of purpose required by recruits.

RECRUITMENT MADE DIFFICULT

All this had a deleterious effect on efforts to fill the thousands of clerical,

British Women Go to War

In Britain, as in the United States, World War II began on a Sunday – September 3, 1939, two days after the German invasion of Poland. Nearly a year earlier – in October 1938, during the Munich Crisis when peace was in the balance – the Woman's Voluntary Service (WVS) had taken the precaution of evacuating children from cities liable to being bombed if and when war transpired. Another similar exodus occurred after September 1939. This wholesale shift of children into the shelter of the countryside involved thousands of households offering their homes as billets for the duration. Housewives across rural Britain who took in evacuees found their families greatly expanded, virtually overnight.

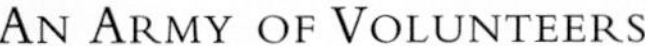

An Army of Volunteers

Thousands of British women volunteered for war work in 1939, and by 1943, 1.5 million of them were contributing to the war effort. On the home front, retired teachers came back to schools to fill the gaps left by men called up to fight in the war. Others worked in civil defence, as air-raid wardens searching for and rescuing survivors after air raids, as dispatch riders, in the Land Army, the NAAFI (Navy, Army and Air Force Institutes), which ran canteens, and in a variety of industries – munitions, light alloys, timber production, transport and vehicle maintenance, shipbuilding and aircraft production.

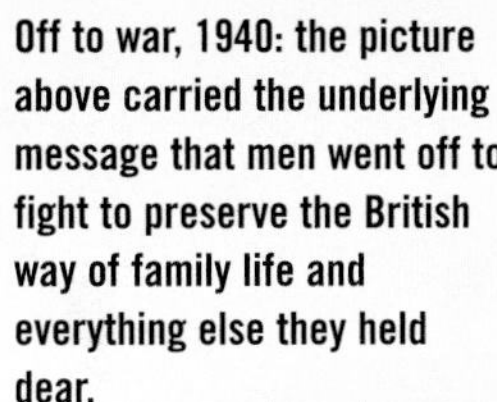

Off to war, 1940: the picture above carried the underlying message that men went off to fight to preserve the British way of family life and everything else they held dear.

Many British women took up engineering even before the war began. In wartime factory work, shown left, nimble female fingers proved an advantage.

Workers' Playtime

To help the morale of the women working long hours in the factories, the British Broadcasting Corporation put out a special programme called 'Workers' Playtime'. The broadcast was relayed to workers in their canteens and at their workbenches. At some time during the proceedings, the programme's presenter usually asked: 'Are we downhearted?', to which the answer was always a loud and definite: 'NO!!' It became a rhetorical question and a routine answer – but from the cheery atmosphere in the factories and their high output, it was clear that the women meant it.

The Home Front was just as much a part of the war as the battlefield. Despite wartime difficulties, women at home performed a vital task in the push for victory.

British female war workers were assessed for skills and assigned accordingly. Some joined the uniformed services, some the Land Army, and some went into factories. The mothers of young children were effectively exempt.

communications and other support functions vacated by the men who went off to war. It was not just a question of hiring workers. The recruitment of women for these tasks had to be done on a military rather than civilian basis. The peacetime freedom of working women to change jobs or to drop out of the employment market altogether had no place in wartime. What was needed were women willing to commit to military service so they could be assigned where they were needed without arguments.

Concern over the rumours went to the very top. President Roosevelt, Secretary of War Stimson, General George C. Marshall, General Dwight D. Eisenhower and Chief of the U.S. Army Air Forces Henry Arnold all thought them so serious that they went on record to refute them and denounce those who spread, publicized and believed them. Congress itself weighed in with special hearings which produced some potent statistics: it was found that, compared to women, male non-combatants were 89 times more prone to going absent without leave, 85 times more likely to get drunk, and 150 times more likely to breach military rules or commit a criminal offence. Venereal disease proved rife among men in the military, virtually non-existent among women.

Compared to women, male non-combatants were 89 times more prone to going absent without leave, 85 times more likely to get drunk and 150 times more likely to breach military rules.

At the same time, the rumours about WAACs in North Africa were scotched by evidence that only two of them had been shipped back home, one having been injured in an accident, the other because she was pregnant by her husband. There was a total absence of any kind of misconduct in reports from commanders in North Africa.

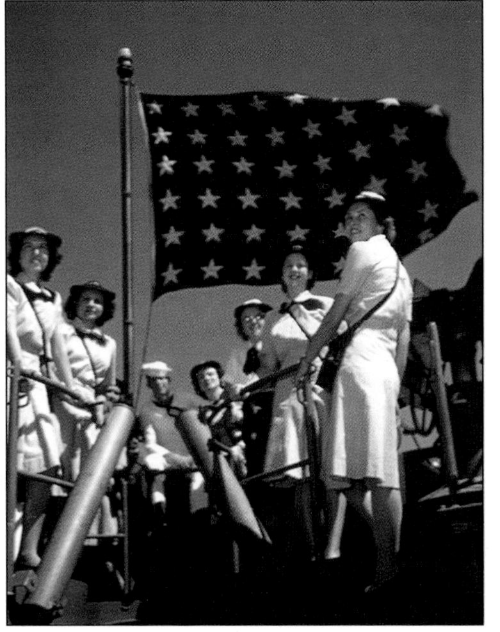

Happy, healthy, smiling, good-looking – these WAVES were visiting the USS *Missouri* in 1944 and represented the positive image of women in uniform which the U.S. government worked hard to promote.

REPUTATIONS AND REALITIES

The official campaign to clear the names of military women made the American press think twice about reporting unchecked rumours. However, turning over this particular new leaf was not helped by a tendency in some publications to trivialize the contribution of women with articles like 'WAACs Wiles Are Womanly' or overemphasis on uniform fashions as in 'Down to the Sea in Slips'.

But the mud, once slung, tended to stick. The basic irritant was a fact that could not be denied: war work meant that women had stepped out of their traditional role as wives and mothers. That was sufficiently unsettling for traditionalists to keep the slanders alive, and the problem was never really solved. It dogged the business of female recruitment throughout, and even beyond, World War II.

American women were not alone in facing such antipathy. The Women's Royal Naval Service (Wrens) suffered for years from the common notion that they were either frustrated lesbians or uniformed nymphomaniacs. In 1993, when the Wrens became an official section of the Royal Navy, the London *Times* commented on the fact that the women's service still had this same 'public image problem'.

To an extent, though, the U.S. military had itself to blame for its recruitment problems. Highly qualified women were hardly likely to come forward when stories – true, this time – began to circulate that their skills were being misused or ignored. In California, for instance, WAACs were employed by Army officers as servants and babysitters.

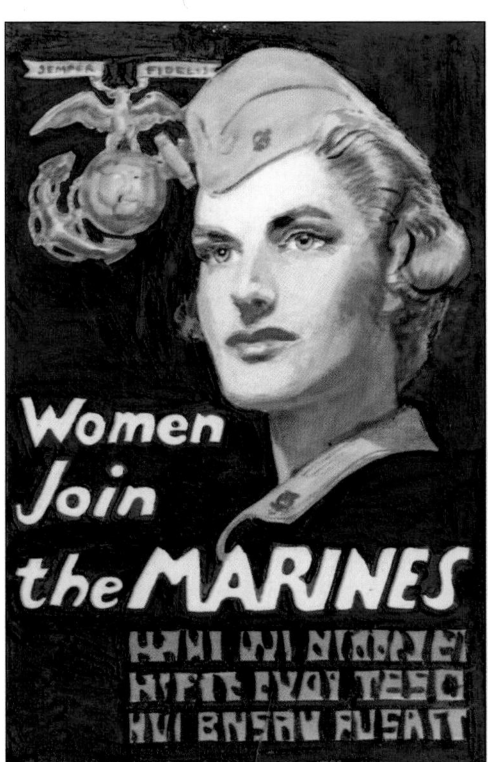

The Marines, the most 'macho' of all the American armed services, used this square-jawed, steely-eyed and slightly unfeminine image to persuade women to join up for tough, demanding non-combatant roles.

The Dame of Sark

The islands of Jersey, Guernsey, Alderney and Sark, lying in the English Channel only 25 miles (40 kilometres) off the coast of France, comprised the only part of Britain's home territory to be occupied by the Germans during World War II. Sark, with an area of only 2 square miles (5 square kilometres), is the smallest of the main islands. It was also, and still is, the only feudal state still extant in Europe.

Sibyl Hathaway, hereditary Dame of Sark, had become the island's ruler in 1927. Thirteen years later, the Germans conquered France in little more than six weeks. On July 3, 1940, they arrived in the Channel Islands.

Sibyl Hathaway, the hereditary Dame of Sark, was the right woman in the right place at the right time: formidable and imposing, she gained considerable respect from Sark's German invaders.

Staying Put on Sark

The British government had already offered Channel Islanders a haven in mainland Britain. More than 20,000 people from Jersey and Guernsey accepted the offer, but not the 471 inhabitants of Sark. Led by Dame Sibyl, they voted to remain on their tiny island for as long as the German occupation lasted.

Dame Sibyl, a strong-minded, imposing woman of 56, made Sark's official attitude toward the occupiers very clear from the start – and her private attitude was the same. Instead of simply waiting for Major Albrecht Lanz, the new commandant of Guernsey, and his chief of staff and interpreter, Dr. Maas, to arrive at her home, the Seigneurie, she summoned them into her presence. They arrived and found Dame Sibyl and her husband, Robert Hathaway, sitting in high-backed chairs at the far end of the room. The couple might have been waiting to bestow a royal audience on their visitors. The Germans had to walk the length of the room, after which Dame Sibyl received them with a great show of regal dignity.

Dame Sibyl in Charge

This introduction to Sark set the tone for the occupation, which lasted until 1945. The Germans largely behaved themselves, although Robert Hathaway was interned in Germany. Dame Sibyl, left alone, was friendly but not too friendly, and her regal bearing led some of the Germans on Sark to refer to her as *Königin* – queen. Some of the more belligerent Sarkese would have preferred outright resistance, even though this was impractical on such a small island. Dame Sibyl therefore came in for some criticism from her subjects, but her slightly aloof, rather patronizing stance, which never went as far as full collaboration with the invaders, helped preserve her island realm during the war years.

When Robert Hathaway was being deported, he was asked by a friend, Louis Guillemette, how his wife would manage without him.

'Manage?' Hathaway replied. 'That woman? My dear Louis, she could manage the United States – and knit' [at the same time].

A woman journalist, who spoke fluent Japanese and had front-line experience from reporting the Japanese invasion of China, had been hired as a cook.

Mary McMillin was assigned work at Fort Benning, Georgia, rigging parachutes, yet she was a veteran of high-altitude parachute jumping, including a world-record jump from almost 25,000 feet. Before the war, McMillin had worked in an aerial circus which featured her jumping from one plane to another.

In these circumstances, it was not surprising that about one-third of the WAACs who re-enlisted in the Women's Army Corps (WAC) during the war resigned and returned to civilian life, driven out by hostility, disrespect, indifference to their abilities – and those scurrilous rumours about their sexual proclivities.

The U.S. military had itself to blame for its recruitment problems. Highly qualified women were hardly likely to come forward when stories began to circulate that their skills were misused.

DEMOCRACY AT RISK

There were also perceived difficulties about the impact of the new war situation that had to be targeted by government departments, especially the Office of War Information. The main problem was geography. North and South America, together with Australia and New Zealand, were *at* war but not *in* the war. A few Japanese balloons drifted over California. The West Coast became a military zone, with its Japanese-American population interned in camps far inland. However, except for Japanese attacks on Port Darwin, Northern Australia, in February 1942 and May 1943, there were no serious air raids or bombardments that directly threatened life and property.

It was therefore vital for the U.S. government to impress on Americans that the faraway war was not happening only to other people, but rather was a real threat to their homes, their way of life and, above all, their cherished freedoms. The principle was clearly laid down in the *Government Information Manual for the Motion Picture Industry* issued by the Office of War Information (OWI).

'Civilians,' it read, 'must have the war brought home to them. Every individual must be made to see the immediacy of the danger…[They] must be made to understand that [they are] an integral part of the war front, and that if [they lose] the war, [they lose] everything.'

This was, of course, a subtler way of waging war, using words and posters as well as Hollywood films as ammunition.

Hollywood evidently got it right. As Eileen Hughes later commented: 'As we got involved, I noticed that many of the movies I saw were

Unlike Western women in the war, Russian women were accustomed to a hard life. Familiar with strenuous physical work, they could be truthfully depicted, as here, without glamour or overt femininity.

geared towards the war, especially after Pearl Harbor. I liked the war movies because they always made it look like we were winning.'

POSTER PROPAGANDA

The war awareness campaign was not, of course, aimed solely at American women at home, but several government posters made pointed use of the female factor. For a start, they frequently featured images of women and children in danger in order to rouse emotions and get the point across. One poster showed a beautiful young mother and her baby, with a black hand, marked with a Nazi swastika, poised above her head and carrying the message 'Keep These Hands Off!'

Another, designed by Norman Rockwell and entitled 'Save Freedom of Worship – Buy War Bonds', showed men and women praying in church, the two most prominent figures being an old woman in the foreground and a young woman in the middle ground. A further Norman Rockwell poster, entitled 'Ours...To Fight for Freedom from Want', depicted a domestic scene with the woman of the house about to put a turkey on the table. It would have been impossible to display such an image in Britain, where the meat ration was so paltry that a whole turkey – if one could be found – would have lasted a family for a month or more. All the same, the message was clear.

Symbolism was particularly important in the propaganda war. For example, posters designed to rouse emotions and feelings of patriotism featured images of strength – clenched fists, bulging muscles, tools and weapons.

To be effective, images of Rosie the Riveter were made deliberately unfeminine: rolled-up sleeves, capable hands, flexed arm muscles, direct gaze, determined mouth made no concession to feminine 'frailty'.

'HOMES IN DANGER!'

U.S. wartime posters also made frank use of fear and insecurity. One of them, entitled 'Warning! Our Homes Are in Danger Now', showed a Japanese with a sword and Adolf Hitler with a machine gun looming over a globe turned to show the North American land mass.

Symbolism was particularly important in the propaganda war being waged by the OWI. For example, posters designed to rouse emotions and feelings of patriotism featured images of strength – clenched fists, bulging muscles, tools and weapons. The patriotic colours of red, white and blue were prominent.

The OWI paid special attention to posters connected with the employment of women in the war industries wherever they were likely to use muscles they never knew they had and lift loads or operate machines they never knew they could. In the mid-20th century, women were still being described as 'the weaker

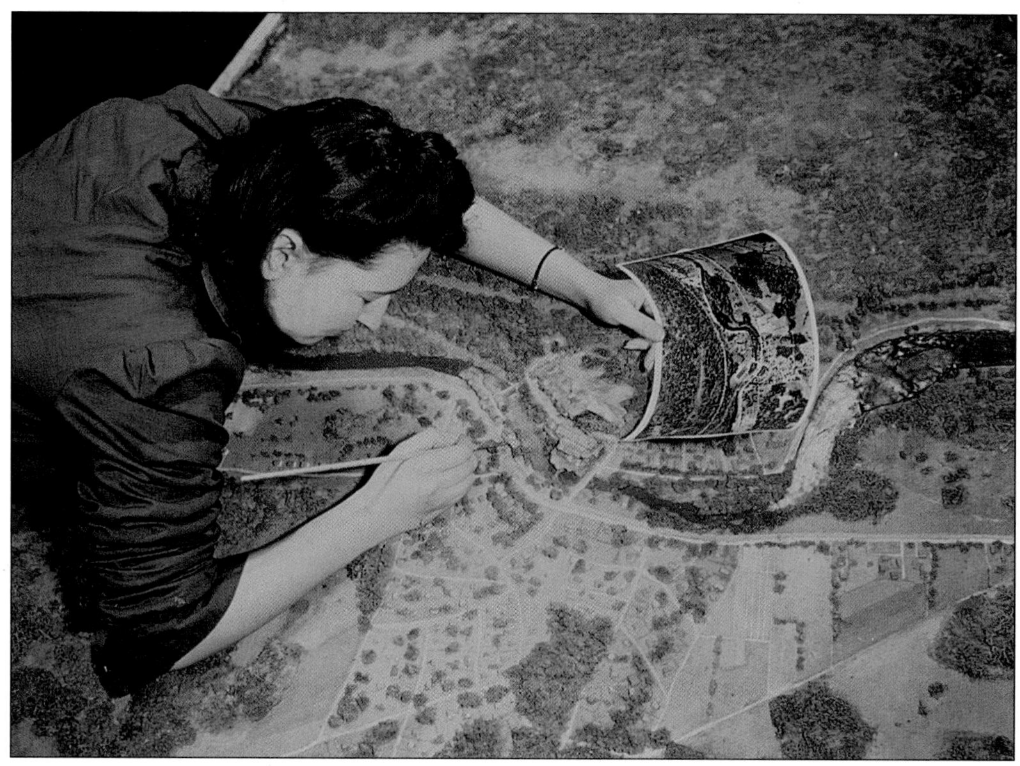

Patience, a steady hand and attention to detail were virtues women were able to bring to their war work – like this cartographer, seen updating a map from an aerial photograph.

sex', and many women themselves took the term literally. To them, and to most men, the physically strong woman was unfeminine, unattractive, even pseudo-male. Meanwhile, for the sake of the war effort, these ideas still had to be challenged and, if possible, overcome.

ROSIE THE RIVETER

Enter Rosie the Riveter, most famous of all American wartime poster images. Rosie, another Norman Rockwell design, first appeared on posters in 1943, and on May 29 that year adorned the front cover of the widely read *Saturday Evening Post.* Rosie was a pretty girl, but one with rolled-up sleeves displaying arm muscles prominently flexed, a big fist and a straight-jawed look that exuded willpower and determination. 'We can do it!' ran the message. One glance at the mighty Rosie was meant to convince women that they could could 'do it' too.

There were other, less muscle-bound images designed to draw women into factory work, using slogans like 'Women in the War: We Can't Do Without Them'. Rosie, however, was by far the most

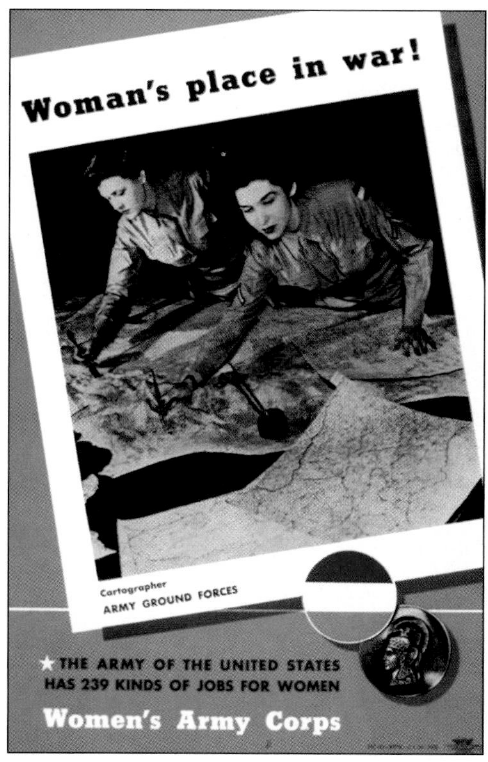

Cartographers at work in the Women's Army Corps: the headline countered the prevalent idea that a woman's place, even in war, was in the home, and only in the home.

Though it dismayed traditionalists, the Rosie the Riveter publicity encouraged American women, like this driller shown opposite, to come out of the home and undertake war work with confidence and enthusiasm.

potent – so potent, in fact, that she has since become part of American folklore. Her spirit is still invoked today as a symbol of patriotic, responsible American womanhood and as a tribute to the part played by women in World War II.

A 1980 documentary, *The Life and Times of Rosie the Riveter,* featured five real-life 'Rosies' who reminisced about their wartime experiences, with intercuts from recruitment films, stills, advertisements and a soundtrack featuring music from the 1940s.

In 1998, the American Rosie the Riveter Association was founded to honour the working women of the war. Two years later, Congress passed legislation authorizing the Rosie the Riveter World War II Home Front National Historical Park in San Francisco. Marina Park Bay in San Francisco has a Rosie the Riveter memorial, dedicated in October 2000 at a ceremony attended by one hundred real-life 'Rosies'.

The image that still has such power in the 21st century had no less impact 60 years ago as vast numbers of American

Leni Riefenstahl, Hitler's Filmmaker

After Adolf Hitler came to power in 1933, most German women, including university professors and other high achievers, were consigned to the home, where their task was to rear children to perpetuate the Nazis' 'Thousand-Year' Third Reich. There were exceptions, though, and one of them was the brilliant filmmaker Leni Riefenstahl, chosen by Hitler as director and producer of films for the Nazi Party.

Hitler confined German women to domesticity but had better uses for the talented Leni Riefenstahl, seen here wearing a white coat directing the filming of a parade at a Nazi rally.

Masterpieces

Born in Berlin in 1902, Riefenstahl had had a remarkable career even before she went to work for Hitler. She was a famous actress, film director and producer, and a magazine photographer. She worked as a dancer until suffering a knee injury, and she was a daredevil who did her own film stunts, including climbing mountain slopes in bare feet.

Riefenstahl produced two considerable masterpieces for Hitler, *The Triumph of the Will,* a record of the Nazi Party's Nuremberg Rally of 1934, and *Olympia,* her film of the Berlin Olympics in 1936.

Nemesis

Riefenstahl's work, which featured pioneering camera work conveying images of Nazi strength and resolve, won her many international awards but proved to be her ruin after the war was over. She was boycotted by the film world, and imprisoned for four years by the Allies. Riefenstahl never made another feature film, even though in 1952 she was cleared of committing war crimes. From 1972 until 1990, when she was 88, Riefenstahl turned to making undersea documentaries. Interviewed in 2000, when she was 98, Leni Riefenstahl expressed regret that she had ever made *The Triumph of the Will,* her nemesis even into extreme old age.

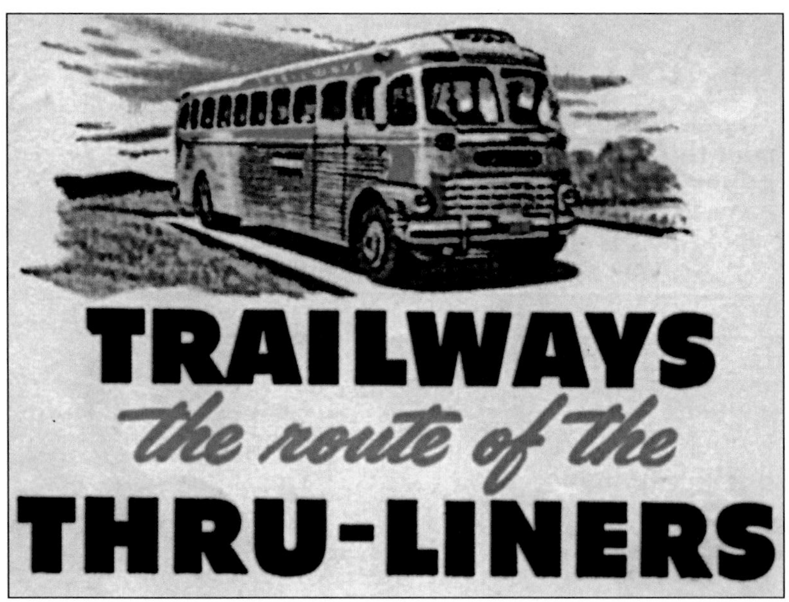

Getting war workers and war jobs together meant relocation for millions of Americans: as a bonus, they learned more about their own country and its people.

women responded to the call to war work. By 1943, American industrial production was outpacing that of the Axis powers, Germany, Italy and Japan. Japan, the weakest link, had only 10 percent of the industrial capacity of the United States.

RELOCATING

The shift of American women out of the home and into industry caused severe dislocation of family life, not least because of the need to leave familiar home towns and move to where the jobs were. The Great Depression following the Wall Street Crash of 1929 was still affecting the country, and in some areas jobs were scarce or non-existent. The only option for many was to relocate.

In all, some 40 million Americans were on the move in wartime, either to join the armed forces or to relocate for work. All but about 3 percent used the railroads for this purpose. The trains became crowded with civilians who, naturally, took second place to the movement of troops. Automobile travel, the most convenient means of transport, was limited by fuel rationing, thus many people were forced to reach their destinations any way they could. It was not unusual for travellers to start off sharing a car, go part way by train, board an aircraft for the next leg of the journey and finally arrive by bus.

LOUISIANA TO CALIFORNIA

One African-American woman, Annie Green Small, had to travel with her family from Louisiana to California to work in the Marinship shipyard.

'It took me from Wednesday night to Sunday night on the train,' Small later remembered. 'I had only $8 in my pocket when I got there.'

Small went to work in the welding section at the shipyard.

'We had to wear bandannas and hard hats and keep them on all the time, but most all the women in the shipyards would tie their hair up and then leave bangs [a fringe] in the front so it looked ladylike. So you could know the men from the women.' The men, however, didn't approve of this practice. Small recalls what they said: 'You're a woman, you'll always be a woman, and if you don't tuck that hair in, you'll have the damnedest permanent wave you've ever had because that weld is hot!'

There were compensations. Small made 'wonderful money', far more than she had earned in Louisiana. But she rarely saw her husband. She went to work in the morning. He went to work in the evening. It was not an uncommon arrangement in wartime.

TROOP TRAIN TO TACOMA

Jennie Fain Folan, 27 in 1942 and mother of four children, had endured hard times in Arkansas during the Depression, losing all the cattle and horses on her farm from disease or drought. By the time the war began, there was little left for her in her home state, so when she read of job opportunities in Tacoma, Washington, she leapt at the chance. It took Folan and her children three days and nights to reach Tacoma on a crowded troop train.

'We had to stand up part of the time,' Folan later recalled. 'There was no food on the train, and I took a big basket of food and then sometimes the soldiers

Under Fire in France

With four other British women, Patricia Moorhouse ran a canteen in the centre of Boulogne on the north French coast during the German invasion in 1940. She witnessed thousands of refugees crowding into the port, desperate to escape to England, and lived through several Luftwaffe air raids.

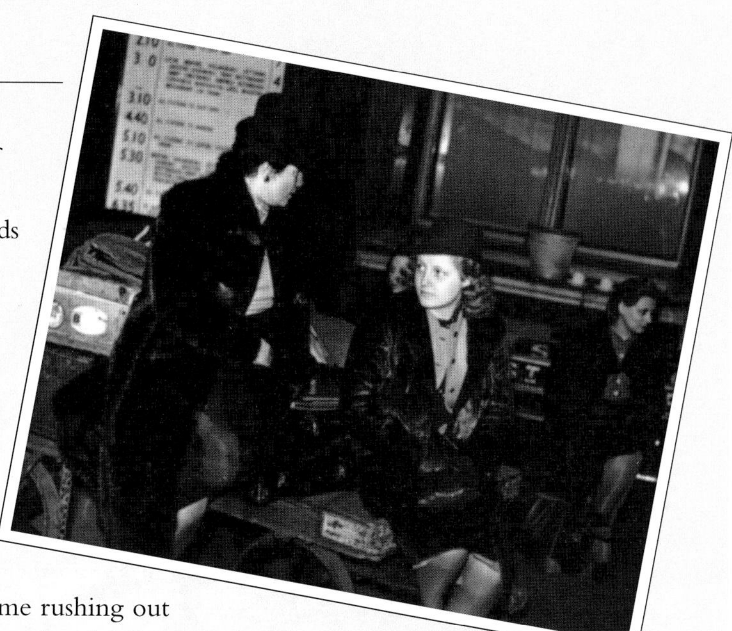

Unconquered Britain became a refuge for people from German-occupied countries, like these French women.

Machine Guns in the Streets

Later, Moorhouse recalled: 'The first raid was on a Sunday evening and lasted till early morning. We didn't realize they were coming till all the lights went out and anti-aircraft guns opened fire. Policemen were blowing whistles and you could hardly hear them for the gunfire. People came rushing out of their houses.... Many of them were hit by shrapnel and splintered glass from the windows. Many others stood gazing up into the sky till the Germans, flying low to get beneath the range of the guns, came in from the coast side of Boulogne and machine-gunned the streets.'

Refugees

Although Boulogne was bombed for the next three nights, Moorhouse and her companions fed the refugees and bandaged their wounds, often hand injuries sustained when they put them up to protect their heads.

'Most of the refugees,' Moorhouse remembered, 'were Dutch and Belgians who had travelled miles in ramshackle cars or farm wagons, on bicycles or on foot. One car drove into Boulogne with two little girls strapped to the running boards. There had been no room for them inside.'

British destroyers came alongside at Boulogne docks to pick up the refugees, but many of them never managed to get on board.

'During the shelling, women, children and wounded soldiers were...caught by German machine-gun fire while they were running the last 50 yards to the ships.'

Escape

At last, on May 21,1940, Patricia Moorhouse and the other four women had to board a ship and escape back to England themselves.

'When I left,' she said, 'fighting was still in progress. There must have been many killed.... I know hundreds were wounded.'

Last kiss, maybe last farewell: the British soldiers shown opposite were on their way to Egypt, where they were to face the brilliant German General Erwin Rommel and his crack Afrika Korps.

would get off and get some milk…It was a tough trip, but I was used to such a hard life that a lot of things didn't hit me like it hit a lot of people.'

At the Tacoma shipyard Folan helped to build ships, icebreakers and aircraft carriers. It was dangerous work. Folan and two male shipfitters once fell 30 feet to the ground when a bulkhead collapsed, taking the scaffolding with it. Folan, fortunately, was only bruised, but the men suffered broken ribs.

'When I came to work at Sandpoint Naval Air Station it was the first time I got to know blacks, and I can remember thinking that they're just like us.'

'JUST LIKE US'

For women like Small and Folan, moving across the country was the first really long journey they had ever made. Meeting new people opened their eyes to the great diversity of America and its various customs, lifestyles and ways of speaking.

One significant change concerned the relationship between whites and blacks. In 1941, President Roosevelt issued an executive order banning racial discrimination in war industries. This would require a complete reversal in contemporary social thinking. Black slaves may have been freed after the American Civil War 76 years earlier, but they were nowhere near equal with white Americans by the time of World War II. In Hollywood films, for example, they were still cast as servants, menials and underlings and the U.S. armed services were themselves strictly segregated. Needless to say, this mammoth weight of colour prejudice could not be shifted, even by presidential order, but for as long as this lasted, it enabled some blacks to meet whites on an equal footing.

This was something of a culture shock for some women, such as Betty Kirstine Gannon. Gannon was living in Seattle when she went to work at Sandpoint Naval Air Station, preparing aircraft for bringing home wounded personnel.

'We'd spent three or four years in the South, and before that I hadn't known any black people,' Gannon later recalled. 'When we were down South, the blacks worked for us. We had a woman who…cooked for us and did the ways…. She came and went and that was it.

'When I came to work at Sandpoint…probably every second person at the base was black. It was the first time I really got to know blacks, and I can remember thinking that they're just like us. It was an eye-opener for me.'

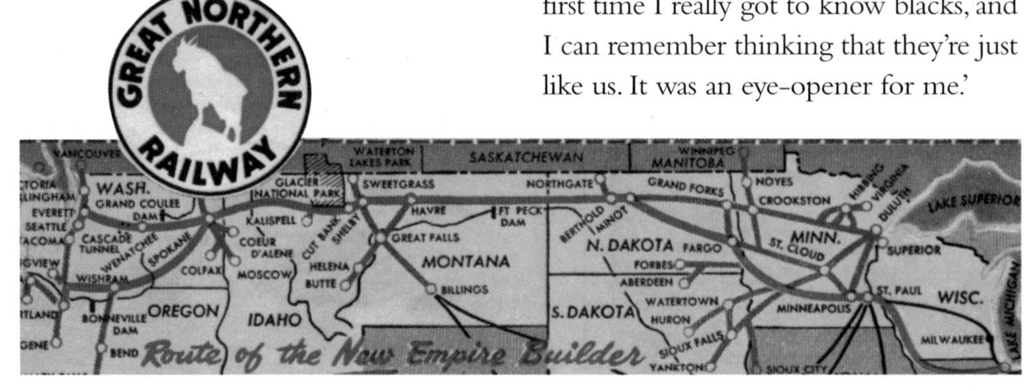

Long journeys on packed trains with little or no fresh food were a fact of life for many women who relocated to take up new jobs in the war industries.

Vogue
INCORPORATING VOGUE BEAUTY BOOK,
VOGUE HOUSE AND GARDEN BOOK
PARIS SPRING FASHIO
WITH VOGUE PATTERN BO
MARCH 1940 (3) • PRIC

CHAPTER 2

Life on the Home Front

A chief characteristic of World War II was that hostilities were no longer confined to the battlefield. Civilians, too, were in the front line. Women had to cope with rationing, air raids and the pressures of single parenthood.

The idea that there could be such a thing as a home front is a fairly recent one. Until the First World War, when German Zeppelin airships crossed the Channel (a feat in itself at the time) and dropped bombs on British cities, war had usually seemed a faraway event. However, the Zeppelins were only a first step toward shrinking the distance between civilians and warfare. By the First World War, weapons were already ten times more powerful than they had been a century earlier, in the Napoleonic Wars between Britain and France. By 1939, their power, linked with improved delivery capability, enabled them to reach easily into people's homes and nearby streets to deal out destruction to the very places that had always been considered the safest on earth.

DAILY BOMBING

In Britain after 1940, bombing raids were virtually a daily occurrence. Equally common were nights spent in public shelters, or in the Morrison and Anderson shelters built in back gardens, or on the deep-sunk platforms of the London Underground railway. There was no official directive about using the Underground: Londoners simply moved in. Eventually, the government yielded to

The frilly fashions of the 1930s had no place in war. Before long, fashion was reflecting the hostilities, with squared, 'military' shoulders on uniform-style jackets, 'pillbox' hats and straight skirts.

The Air-Raid Warden

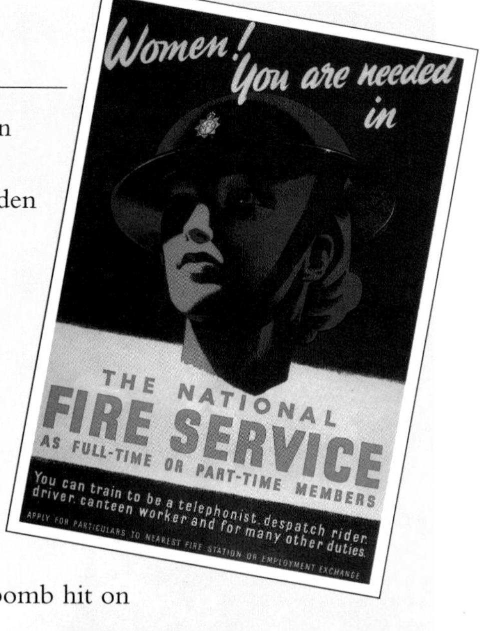

Incendiary bombs which started fires during air raids were a constant danger. Women in the fire service, top right, worked throughout the night as firewatchers and tackled flaming buildings with water pumps.

Despite its many grim aspects, wartime Britain had its lighter moments. Patricia Albert's mother Esther once alerted the local air-raid warden in Amersham to the possible presence of an unexploded bomb in her back garden. German aircraft had flown over the night before on their way to raid towns farther north, and Esther was worried that they might have jettisoned one of their bombs.

The air-raid warden, who was also the local fire chief and officious with it, got quite impatient with her.

'Madam! I'm a busy man,' he informed Esther. 'Don't bother me unless you get a direct bomb hit on your house!'

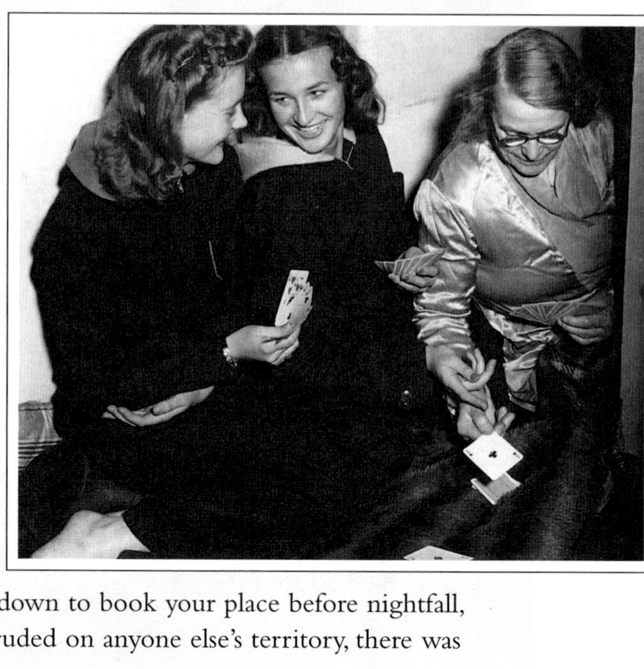

Nights in the air-raid shelter were not as much fun as the bottom right picture suggests. Many people were fearful and dispirited, not knowing what destruction they would find when they emerged.

Nights in the Underground

Lily Purvis and her two children spent nights in the Underground while the Luftwaffe was pounding the streets above in 1940 and 1941.

'It was safe, of course, but it was eerie,' she remembered later, 'and I don't think it was really healthy. The air in the Underground was stuffy and seemed to be full of grit. Before the bunks were put up, people took their bedding and laid it out on the platforms. You had to send someone down to book your place before nightfall, and if you intruded on anyone else's territory, there was hell to pay!

'There was all sorts of talk about it being immoral – young girls and young men sleeping close to each other and all that. But most of us could only think how cold and frightened we were, and whether or not our homes were being smashed to pieces while we slept. The children took it quite well. It was a game to them, I suppose. It was mothers like me who worried and wondered what the future held for them – for all of us.'

Despite the Underground and the public and private shelters at street level, some 60,000 Londoners had died in the Luftwaffe air raids by early 1942.

ARP (Air Raid Precaution) Wardens like the one below saw to it that everyone was carrying a gas mask and helped air-raid victims. Men were paid £3 ($4.35) a week full-time and women £2 ($2.90).

this *fait accompli* and made the Underground an 'official' shelter by building bunks on the platforms to improve sleeping arrangements.

'We can take it!' was a popular patriotic cry in Britain during the war, but in fact there was no other option.

NERVOUS STRAIN

It was often said that women bore the nervous strain of the war. The banshee wail of the air-raid sirens, the thunder of the bombing, the destruction and the blackout ranked among the main causes. The sky itself had become dangerous. Even in the countryside, less susceptible to the raids, the sight of an aircraft automatically prompted the anxious query: 'Is it theirs or ours?'

'Mostly the planes were "ours" – that is, British or American,' remembers Patricia Albert, who spent the wartime years in rural Buckinghamshire, close, but not too close, to London. 'But you never knew for sure – you could never be sure about anything you saw in the sky. I once heard an aircraft engine cut out and saw the plane twisting round and down in the sky. It looked as if it was going to crash, but it was only faking it, probably practising to fool some enemy pilot in a dogfight. If I saw that today, I'd think the pilot was just showing off or doing aerobatics, but during the war, you naturally thought of danger, including planes crashing.'

The British reaction to wartime pressures was outwardly defiant, whatever their private fears. 'We can take

This British family was taking refuge from an air raid in an Anderson shelter, which was made of corrugated iron: thousands of 'Andersons' were dug into Britain's back gardens during the war.

Queuing became a way of life for British women during the war (opposite). There were constant shortages and many people resorted to growing some of their own food in allotments.

it!' was a popular patriotic cry in Britain during the war, but in fact there was no other option. On the home front, the natural instinct of women – in both Britain and the United States – was to try to maintain 'life as usual' despite the war, but this soon proved impossible. Up until 1943, during a period termed 'The Happy Time' by German U-boat crews, the Atlantic Ocean was infested with surface raiders and submarines which preyed on the convoys carrying valuable food and supplies from America to Britain. Britain was dependent on this lifeline for its very survival, which is why Prime Minister Winston Churchill regarded the Battle of the Atlantic as the most important of the whole war.

RATIONING

The response to limited supplies was a fair but strict regime of rationing. British and American housewives were issued ration books containing their family's share of coupons for food and other household items like clothes. In Canada, gasoline, meat, coffee, tea, butter, beer, whisky and wine were severely rationed and the Wartime Prices and Trade Board saw to it that the sale of luxury items was very strictly controlled. As in Britain, automobiles, trucks and tractors virtually disappeared from civilian markets and did not return until the end of the war.

Canadian ration books, too, contained stamps that had to be torn off at the point of sale in the presence of the

Japanese families, too, were 'bombed-out' when Tokyo was raided in 1945. They built rough new homes from pieces of wood, bits of stone, straw and anything else they could find.

Women became careful with food and countered shortages by preserving as much fruit and other suitable produce as they could. The poster on the right advises bottling the summer's fresh vegetables for eating in the months ahead.

Early in the war, Britain's food supply was endangered by the Atlantic blockade. As the poster opposite makes clear, getting the food through was as much of a battle as direct confrontation with the enemy.

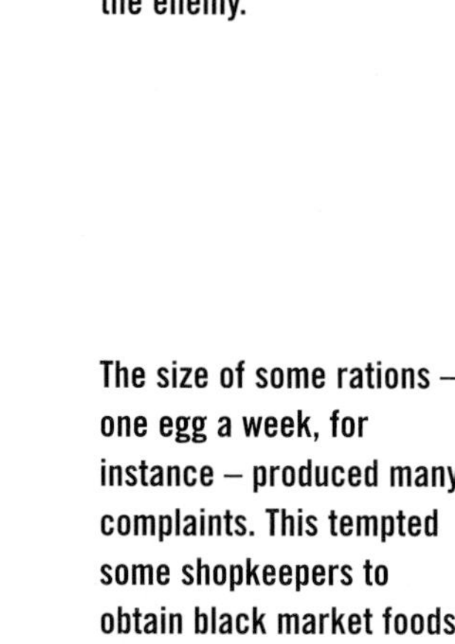

The size of some rations – one egg a week, for instance – produced many complaints. This tempted some shopkeepers to obtain black market foods, for which they risked going to jail.

shop assistant or clerk. The sugar rationing appears to have hit Canadians hardest and sugar became a 'hot commodity for some personal trade'. In some places, sugar was used as a wager in poker games. In Britain, even bath water was officially in short supply: the rule was a depth of 5 inches (13 centimetres), no more; even King George VI went around with a paintbrush marking lines around the palace baths.

Tea, jam, meat, fish, milk, cheese, butter, eggs and other items were strictly apportioned, and as the war went on and the shortages worsened, these rations were reduced. When supplies increased in the later war years, more coupons were allowed, although clothing allowances never reached earlier levels. In 1942, the clothing allotment was set at 60 coupons per person, reduced to 40 as shortages began to bite in 1943, then raised in 1944 to 48. A woollen dress required 11 points, a blouse five, and a woman's coat 15.

Luxuries like chocolate were also rationed, but were so scarce that it was possible to go for many months without seeing a single bar. Exotic fruit such as bananas and oranges were subject to intermittent supply, depending as they did on how many shipments from abroad managed to survive the Germans' Atlantic blockade. Treats like ice cream vanished completely and did not reappear until very late in the war.

Where our men are fighting
OUR FOOD IS FIGHTING
BUY WISELY – COOK CAREFULLY – STORE CAREFULLY – USE LEFTOVERS

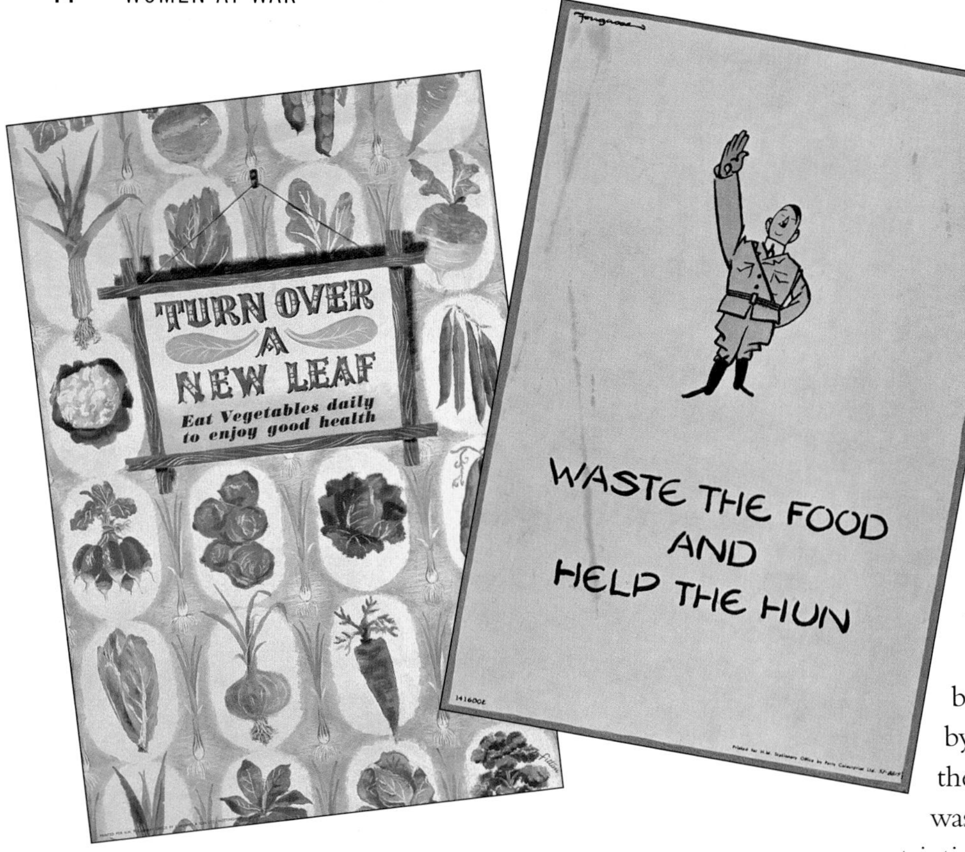

Pre-war, many poor British families lived on 'stodge': heavy carbohydrates like bread and potatoes. Encouraging them to eat vegetables was good health advice. Defying the Hun – the Germans – by preserving food supplies was an added incentive.

'I used to go and queue for oranges and bananas at six in the morning,' Patricia Albert recalls. 'Even that early in the morning, the queues were very long. Although I was only 10 or 11 at the time, I knew about the war and the destruction and the killing, and it made me feel guilty to cycle home with things that could have cost so many lives.'

Before long, queuing became a way of life. Queues formed for practically anything, leading to the wry wartime joke that, on seeing three or four people waiting in line, people would automatically join them without even knowing what they were queuing for.

SUBSTITUTES AND SPAM

It was certainly true that queuing outside shops became an everyday occurrence and also that women were confronted with some curious foods when at last they reached the service counter. Eggs were offered in a dried form which bore little resemblance to the original, except for their yellow colour. The butter ration was minute, but there was plenty of margarine, which tasted sour and salty and was detested by everyone, especially children. Jam tarts were made from vegetables, cakes made without fat. Meatless dishes and sugarless desserts were standard items on the wartime menu.

Newspaper articles and radio broadcasts addressed the situation by suggesting recipes that made the most of what food there was. It was an opportunity to show a bit of patriotism, and the dishes reflected that with names such as Victory Pie and Triumph Tart. A special publication, *Kitchen Parade,* appeared in 1941. Subtitled *Your Ration Problems Solved, Day to Day Menus for All,* it provided a range of recipes that made maximum use of available foods, though with a depressing emphasis on things like cabbage and beetroot soup.

Later on in the war, a tinned food called Spam came on the market. As the name implied, it consisted mainly of spiced ham, but there were other, more mysterious ingredients. It was widely suspected that Spam came from the same stable as wartime sausages, which contained too many breadcrumbs – or, as some rumour-mongers had it, sawdust.

One surprising result of wartime rationing was that more varied foods, however limited, had a beneficial effect on nutrition. Before the war, when the Depression caused high levels of unemployment and the dole money given to jobless workers and their families was too miserly to meet dietary needs, women had little to give their husbands and children except stodge – bread, potatoes and other foods full of carbohydrates, which staved off hunger but fell short on nourishment.

During the war, by contrast, the more balanced diet produced by rationing, with its emphasis on vegetables and proteins with minimal fats and sugar, vastly improved this situation. For the first time, cheap, healthy meals were made available at the Communal Feeding Centres, which were later given the more decorous name of British Restaurants. Mass feeding, which also went on in factory canteens, was another way of saving precious fuel.

MAKE DO AND MEND

Nevertheless, despite this more upbeat aspect of wartime Britain, rationing, shortages and other restrictions were all part of the 'make do and mend' ethos that prevailed at the time. Anything and everything had to be recycled, reused or given extended usefulness – from the mending or reusing of old sheets and towels, to the recutting of broken roof tiles. Clothes rationing meant that existing wardrobes were kept going by endless mending and patching. Patricia Albert remembers that for most of the war, her school socks were mended so often that they consisted more of darns than original sock.

But restrictions only inspired women to use maximum ingenuity in order to get around the rationing, or at least ameliorate it, and at times drove them to take advantage of the illegal black market. Patricia Albert was there when the police arrested an Amersham shopkeeper after one of his customers reported him for selling black market products.

Soap became something of a luxury in Britain during the war. In the absence of fine soaps like Lifebuoy, women resorted to rougher carbolic soap or bought unrationed shaving soap.

British housewives had to register with certain shops to receive their rations. The women shown in this picture just made it: they registered on the last possible day, November 23, 1939.

Wartime clothes rationing, as illustrated on the opposite page, meant existing wardrobes had to be kept going for years; 'make-do and mend', as seen on this poster, was one of the most important catchphrases of the war.

Celebrity recipes, shown right, were designed to encourage women to make the most of their family's rations and try out new cooking ideas as part of their personal war effort.

'The shopkeeper had been regarded as a hero,' she remembers. 'After he went to prison, that woman was ostracized!'

On the right side of the law, many women responded to the British government's campaign to 'Dig for Victory' by using their gardens or plot of land to grow their own food. Faced with a shortage of soap, women descended on barber shops to buy up quantities of shaving soap, which was unrationed. Women lay in wait for coal trucks to pass along their streets, then picked up any pieces that had fallen off. Carol Burton, who lived in Lincolnshire during the war, remembers her mother doing the same with sugar beet.

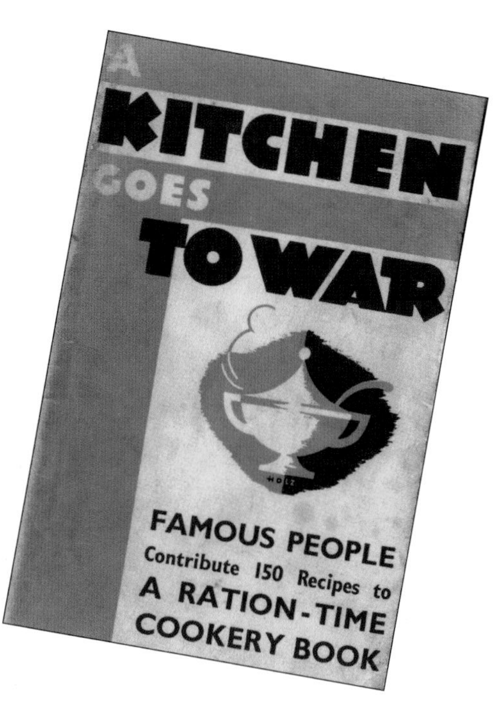

'[She] used to pick up any sugar beet that had been dropped from a cart and boil it for hours in a large saucepan over an open fire,' Burton recalls. 'The result was a syrup which could be used to sweeten cooked fruit. But the all-pervading smell was so unpleasant that food seemed less appealing, even in those days of acute shortage.'

The British government's wartime rationing scheme was so well thought out that from a nutritional viewpoint, many were much better fed then than they had been before. Here two American servicewomen check their weight at a London Underground station.

FORCE FOR CHANGE

Fortunately for Americans, they did not have to share the British experience of war on the home front. This did not mean, though, that there were no sacrifices to be made. American women soon learned how astute the author and journalist Max Lerner was when he wrote in 1943: 'When the classic work on the history of women is written, the biggest force for change in their lives will turn out to have been war.'

Indeed, the first force for change in American life came from the exigencies of World War II. The immediate imperative was the Battle of the Atlantic, which was fought on both sides of the ocean. German submarines (*Unterseeboots*), called U-boats, preyed on shipping along the East Coast of the Americas, and in 1942 their activities prompted Brazil's entry into the war.

Go through your wardrobe

Hitler's Vengeance Weapons

On June 13, 1944, a week after the Allied invasion of Normandy, Adolf Hitler unleashed his first 'Vengeance' or 'Reprisal' weapon on Britain – the V1 pilotless plane. The British were soon calling it the doodlebug, the buzz bomb or simply the flying bomb.

The V1 carried a 1 UK ton (1.015 metric) warhead and had an engine that would cut out at a preset time and then swoop down toward the ground. Even today, the deep, dull roar of the V1's engine sends shivers down the spines of those who heard it during the war. One of them was Sally Hamilton, then 15 years old. She was among several who saw what happened when the engine of a V1 cut out and the bomb fell out of the sky, exploding near St Paul's Cathedral in London's financial district.

'I was on my bicycle quite close to the cathedral,' Hamilton remembers. 'There was this big roar up above and suddenly it stopped. I heard a sort of rushing sound and then there was a mighty explosion about 20 yards (18 metres) from where I was.

'I can't remember whether I fell off my bike or dived off it, but I found myself down on the ground with bits of metal and earth and all sorts of things showering around me. When I looked up, there were bodies and blood everywhere. One woman was slumped against what remained of a wall, with her whole side torn away. I could see her ribs. I remember thinking – or maybe hoping – "She must be dead".'

Hamilton was one of the lucky ones. She wasn't hurt, just shocked. She managed to retrieve her bicycle, which was undamaged, and cycle home.

V1s and V2s

About 1,600 of the 8,000 V1s launched from sites near the northern coast of Europe succeeded in hitting their targets, yet they never demoralized the British public, as Hitler intended. Nor did an even more fearsome weapon, the V2, first launched three months after the V1. The V2 was a rocket that could fly at an altitude of up to 60 miles (95 kilometres) and explode without any warning. There was no defence against it. About 5,000 V2s were fired, not only against southern England but also the port of Antwerp in Belgium. Some 32,500 people were killed, 2,500 of them in England, before the 'Vengeance' campaign came to an end on March 27, 1945.

The German V1 flying bomb was small compared to a conventional bomber, but its effect could be devastating.

In the United States, scrap metal drives – essential for supplying the war industries – were given show business razzmatazz and glamour to encourage people to contribute everything from saucepans to spades.

Perceiving the danger to the whole continent, other Latin American countries followed suit.

American ships were among the many vessels from North and South America which suffered from German U-boat strikes. The shipping available for civilian uses was further reduced by the need for ships as troop carriers. The United States suffered, too, from the loss of rubber and silk imports when the Japanese followed up Pearl Harbor with conquests in Southeast Asia. It happened very quickly. Within six months, by June 1942, Americans were cut off from their pre-war markets when the Japanese swarmed over Pacific territories to form their so-called Co-Prosperity Sphere – in reality controlling an Asian empire with its resources, most importantly oil.

SCARCE METALS

Japanese supremacy was not to last long. They lost the initiative and never regained it after the American victory in the Battle of Midway early in June 1942.

Berlin 1945

Goering boasted that no Allied bomber could reach Berlin. He was wrong. Berlin and other German cities were battered by Allied air raids.

Early in 1945, the British and Americans were pounding Berlin and the Russian armies were closing in from the east. Ursula Grosser, a schoolgirl in Berlin in these last stages of the war, remembers what it was like.

'We all seemed to be in some kind of a daze...we listened to daily tirades of our propaganda minister Goebbels on the radio, telling us we could expect [terrible things] when the Red hordes reached the city. A couple of times I heard him tell the Berliners to fight with anything they could find.'

Under Russian Fire

Then the Russians started shelling Berlin.

'I saw people running in all directions.... I ducked into doorways of still-standing buildings whenever I heard the shelling coming close...whenever an artillery shell hit, I could see debris and dirt flying through the air and falling back down to the street....'

The results of Allied carpet bombing: buildings in cities like Hamburg or Dresden were ravaged by fire and reduced to piles of rubble.

Soon it became too dangerous to stay out of doors, and Ursula Grosser's parents decided they must head for the shelters and stay there.

'Inside,' Grosser recalls, 'I counted 32 people, mostly women, children and old men.... At first people were still going outside for a few minutes, just for some fresh air, although no one could call it that. A curtain of smoke hung low over our part of the city. The days turned into night, and time seemed to have no meaning.

'The noise of battle became louder with each passing hour.... We heard strange vibrating noises coming from the street. Tanks, someone said...a couple of times the shelter shook from a nearby rocket launcher.'

Terrible Sights

Eventually, the Grossers and everyone else had to evacuate the shelter. Once in the street, Ursula saw terrible things – dead soldiers, dead civilians, dead horses, overturned vehicles, a severed head still enclosed in a helmet.

At last, on May 2, 1945, Berlin surrendered. Six days later, the war in Europe was over.

'We...lost everything,' Grosser recalls, 'but we were alive. The guns were silent and...peace had come. It was as if the poet had addressed these words to us: "Here today begins a new epoch in world history and you can say that you have witnessed it".'

Nevertheless, the demands born of an all-out conflict that would last another three years inevitably put the home front in second place when it came to certain supplies. Metals were among the most important. Zinc, tin, nickel, steel were all diverted to the manufacture of armaments, tanks or ships, with little left for making bicycles, vending machines and many other common metal-based products. There was a shutdown in the production of toasters, waffle irons, batteries, zippers, vacuum cleaners, and some toys and games. Lunch boxes, once made of metal, were now constructed from fibreboard and stamped with the warning: 'Customary use of metal for your lunch kit has been forbidden…steel is needed for war materials. This Victory Kit is provided to take the place of your metal kit. Made of durable fibreboard, it is sturdily constructed to give you good service.… Because of the nature of the material, this kit should not be left or stored in damp or wet locations.'

'THERE'S A WAR ON!'

New bicycles were not seen on the streets of America for five years. Supplies of alcohol grew short since alcohol was needed for making explosives, and synthetic rubber proved an unsatisfactory substitute for the chicle which chewing gum had contained.

Now, Americans had to take on the equivalent of the British 'make do and mend' mentality. Posters went up all over the country, reading: 'Use it up, wear it out, make it do, or do without.' Cutting down on gasoline was particularly hard to bear, for Americans relied on their automobiles to a far greater extent than Britons, whose private car ownership was a fraction of their own.

Coffee was more important in America than in tea-drinking Britain. British wartime 'coffee' was barely drinkable and was often augmented with chicory or even acorns.

Americans began to discover uses for familiar products which they could never have imagined. A pound of waste fat, for example, from bacon, meat or cooking oil, could provide enough glycerine to make an equivalent amount of black

American women were enthusiastic buyers – and sellers – of war bonds, advertised above, which not only helped pay for the cost of the war, but gave them a personal stake in the victory.

Nazis were often depicted on posters as disgusting swastika-covered bugs – note the forked tail on the example opposite – to inspire loathing and produce money contributions to the war effort.

powder for bullets. Nylon and silk, used for women's stockings, were required for parachutes and towropes for military gliders. The iron in a shovel could make four hand grenades. Twelve thousand razor blades could make a 2,000-pound (907-kilogram) bomb.

Statistics like these – and stern messages like those on fibreboard lunch-boxes – were especially important in the United States, where the lack of any overt sign of war required a constant campaign of reminders. Rationing and shortages therefore served a dual function, not only preserving precious resources, but also emphasizing the fact that there was a war on. There was a risk, of course, that prices might rise rapidly as supplies grew short, and to stop that from happening, President Roosevelt set up the Office of Price Administration and Civilian Supply (OPA). The agency's brief was to set up a rationing system which also controlled some products sold in shops and stores. Twenty essential items were rationed, including butter, shoes and rubber. Sugar went on the list in May 1942, followed by gasoline in September and coffee two months later.

'We'd led such a free life,' one New Yorker, Lara Lafia, later recalled. 'Of course, the Depression meant that many people had no money to buy what they

American East Coast shipyard workers put ten percent of their pay into War Savings Bonds. These piles of Bonds, seen here being counted, represented a week's contributions from one shipyard.

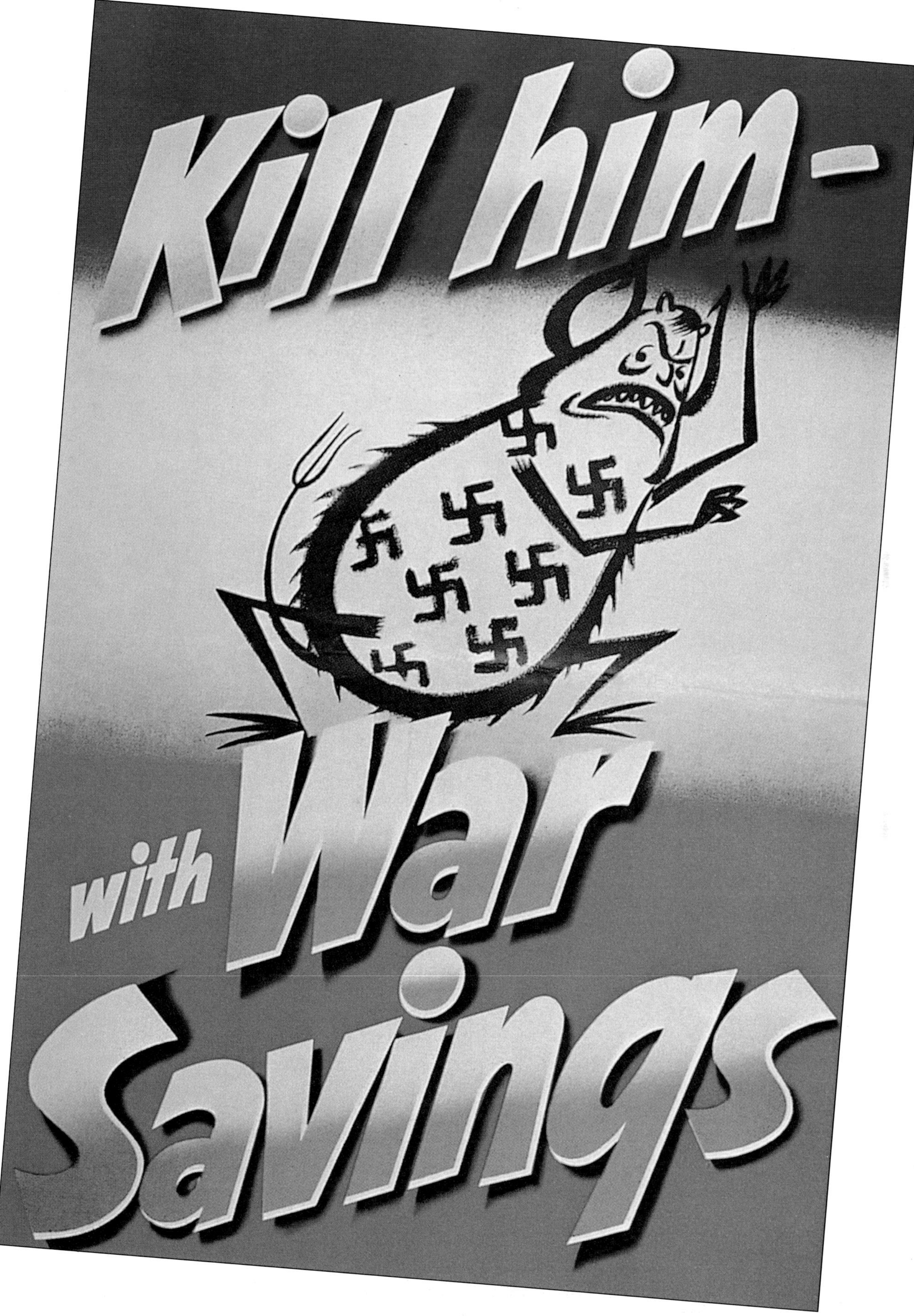
Kill him-
with War Savings

wanted, but those of us who had it, like me, were used to spending it. Being told we couldn't have this or that, and could buy only a certain amount of some foods, was an entirely new situation for us. It took some getting used to, but it certainly made us realize on a daily basis that there was a war on and that there were millions of people in Europe who were far worse off than us.'

Women formed home front aid groups which raised money for veterans' centres, wrote letters to men at the front and sold Victory Bonds.

METALS, JUNK AND VICTORY BONDS

Eventually, though, patriotism rose to the occasion. For American women at home like Lafia, the need to 'do their bit' for the war effort became a real driving force. They collected waste metals, newspapers, tin cans, rubber, nylons, silk stockings, even the tinfoil wrappers on chewing gum and cigarette packets, all in the cause of contributing to the various government 'drives' set up to collect as much useful waste as possible for the war effort. Women formed home front aid groups like the Spanish-American Mothers and Wives Association, which rolled bandages, raised money for veterans' centres, wrote letters to men at the front and sold Victory Bonds.

Americans bought Victory Bonds at $18.75 (£13) each, encouraged to do so by the women who held meetings or rallies, made speeches and generally publicized the war bond drive to make sure it remained at the front of people's minds. If the price per bond was beyond people's immediate means, they could save up the money by sticking 10-cent (7-pence) stamps in special little books.

Buying – and selling – war bonds was a top priority on the home front. The cost of the war was such that the bonds were an indispensable source of funds. For the buyer they promised an adequate, if not munificent, rate of interest: in ten years, each would have increased in value by one-third, or $6.25 (around £4).

Besides being pushed by private citizens, bonds were energetically promoted by film and stage stars, politicians and millions of advertisements

American GIs, stationed in Britain from early 1942, enjoying the fun at a party given by a London family who gave up some of their own rations to entertain them.

Coping Alone

Mary Gardner, mother of six, remembers the juggling that went on as she strove to make the most of the food rations Americans were allowed during the war.

'It was tight at times,' she recalls. 'You had to stop and think of what you were going to buy, and buy things that were going to stretch – maybe spaghetti, macaroni – and mix it up with something else.'

Mary's father was an enthusiastic fisherman, so there was a great deal of fish available, a convenience because meat was rationed. Some of her kids were put off fish for life because they ate so much during the war.

It was hard going, but Mary realized the importance of not worrying her absent husband with domestic problems.

'I took care of [everything] pretty well,' Mary recalls, 'but there were times when it should have been a man's job...It was just that [the boys] needed a firm hand to bring them back into line. But I never wrote to [my husband] and told him all the things that went on. I figured he had job enough.'

Bringing up children alone was one of the greatest stresses women had to cope with during the war. It was a complete reversal of their essentially dependent pre-war life.

Keeping Up Morale

The Department of Labor's publications were among hundreds giving guidance to women left on their own at home. Books, magazine articles and radio broadcasts specifically aimed at them contained every kind of advice, right down to the best way to write letters to absent husbands. Women were advised not to write of petty domestic troubles or problems with the children, nor to complain about the everyday difficulties of wartime life, but to present a cheerful picture in which they were coping well, had enough money and all was going smoothly.

Keeping up morale was probably the most vital civilian role women could play in World War II, and it was officially recognized by the government as a valid contribution to the war effort. This was an additional purpose of the government's patriotic poster campaigns, the Hollywood films that illustrated courageous sacrifice and the triumph of American arms, and the innumerable publications that cajoled women into keeping up a good appearance and looking after themselves.

In Britain, maintaining a good front was one reason why women were encouraged to go on wearing makeup and lipstick: it made them feel more attractive and, in any case, men liked it. In this context, a Canadian wartime magazine gave women beauty advice that was rooted in the female role as decoration:

'How fragile is the beauty of woman, yet it inspires the strength of man. Cheer the way to Victory by looking your loveliest...skin petal-soft and fresh, chin lifted, lips bright, hands caressingly smooth. Care for your beauty for the morale of your country ...your soldiers...yourself.'

For many women in war work, this must have seemed like a tall order after a day spent in a factory. Nevertheless, the message seems to have got through. For example, although many women workers cut their hair short in wartime, many others preferred to keep it long and rather more feminine. Among the latter, a practical style became fashionable: they would roll their long hair up and top it with a fetching curl. Inevitably, this style was called the Victory Roll.

During the Blitz on London in 1940, women still had to cope with the regular demands of motherhood. Babies often needed to be fed while the family was sheltering in the cramped conditions of an Anderson shelter.

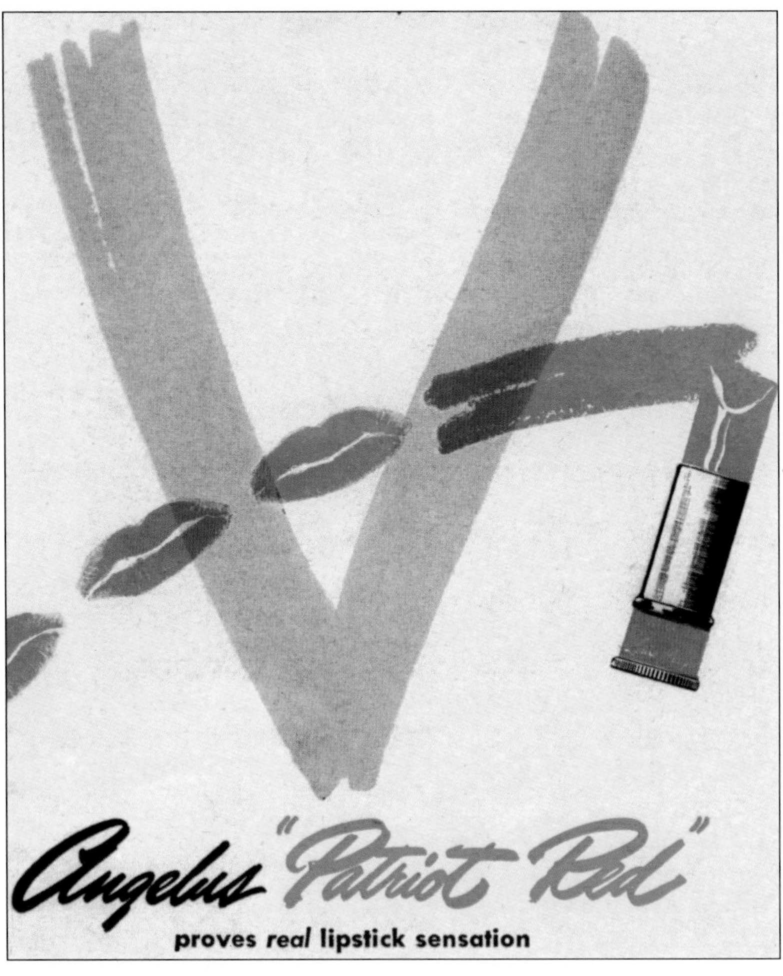
Angelus "Patriot Red"
proves *real* lipstick sensation

Lipstick and other makeup was considered vital to morale during the war. The message was underlined by naming the lipstick advertised above 'Patriot' and including a V for Victory.

pasted onto the sides of railroad cars or billboards. Even the clowns at Barnum and Bailey Circus pushed war bonds as part of their act. Booths selling the bonds were set up in the foyers of cinemas and in grocery stores and other shops. Before long, as was intended, buying bonds became a regular part of everyday life.

Dorothy Chastney, who lived in New Jersey during the war, remembers bringing ten or sometimes 25 cents to school each week for the purpose.

'[We'd] buy war-bond savings stamps and paste them in little booklets,' Chastney recalls. 'Practically every kid in my class did that.'

VICTORY GARDENS

The Chastney family also helped the American war effort by running a Victory Garden. Ultimately, there were more than 20 million of these gardens all over the United States, which between them produced 8 million tons (8.13 metric) of home grown food.

'We grew lettuce, soya beans, tomatoes and radishes,' says Chastney. 'My father did the digging. My job was to pull the Japanese beetles off the soya bean plants and put them in a bottle of kerosene.' Chastney's father used cow manure for fertilizer, apparently shocking his neighbours by having a great pile of it dumped in the driveway. 'My father loaded it in his wheelbarrow and shovelled it all around our Victory Garden. He insisted it was absolutely the best thing,' Chastney concluded, even though the smell was dreadful.

Shoe rationing – three pairs of leather shoes per year – began for Americans on February 7, 1942; clever designs like those shown opposite helped soften the blow.

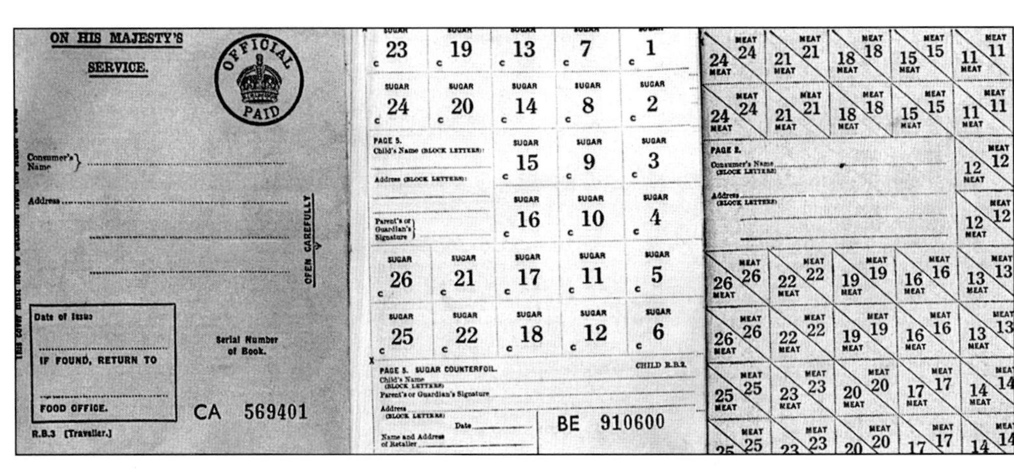
ON HIS MAJESTY'S SERVICE.

OFFICIAL PAID

Consumer's Name ....

Address ....

OPEN CAREFULLY

Date of Issue

IF FOUND, RETURN TO

FOOD OFFICE.

Serial Number of Book.

CA 569401

R.B.3 (Traveller.)

PAGE 5. Child's Name (BLOCK LETTERS):

Address (BLOCK LETTERS):

Parent's or Guardian's Signature

PAGE 5. SUGAR COUNTERFOIL. CHILD R.B.2.

Child's Name (BLOCK LETTERS)

Parent's or Guardian's Signature

Address (BLOCK LETTERS)

Date

Name and Address of Retailer

BE 910600

PAGE 2.

Consumer's Name (BLOCK LETTERS)

Address (BLOCK LETTERS)

When rations were purchased, the relevant coupons were cut out of ration books, shown here.

in the S
Natu
Stardust
Lulu
Liana
There's afternoon impo
rich suede with their so
dressmaker detail of br

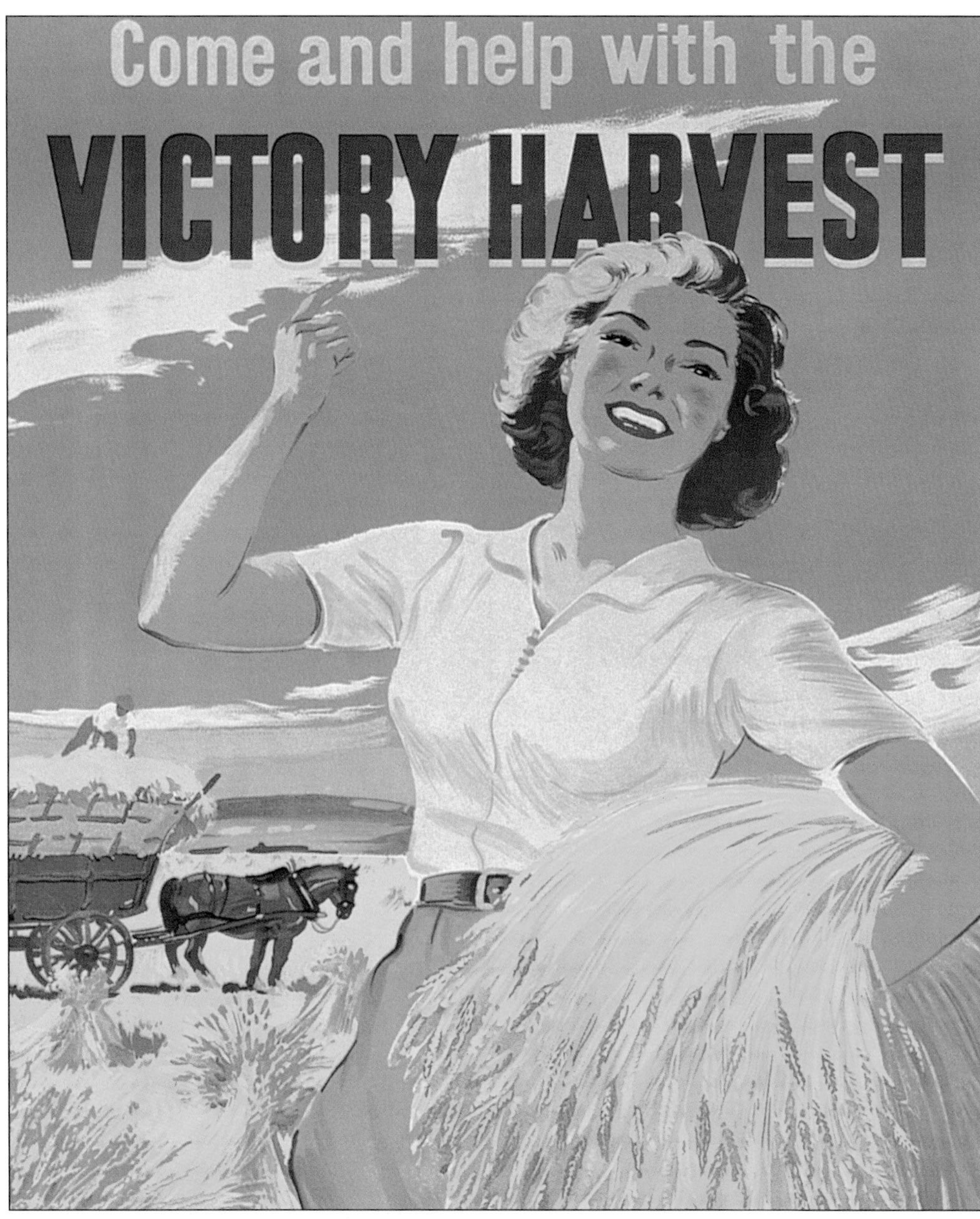

The British government encouraged volunteers to help gather the 'Victory Harvest' with these colourful and stylized posters.

In this, as in so many other ways, Americans were, in effect, being regimented. So were women who suddenly found themselves coping on their own with little or no experience of what that entailed. But government departments were there to tell them.

TRAVEL TIPS

The U.S. Department of Labor's Children's Bureau, for instance, considered the problem of travelling with babies and toddlers to be a matter requiring thought and preparation. For today's more independent women, the Bureau's advice would seem to state the obvious, but six decades ago it was clearly aimed at helping young wartime mothers who had never made such arrangements for themselves.

The Department of Labor issued several pamphlets and booklets giving women advice on how to book train reservations well in advance, the benefits of travelling light, planning a child's needs for food and clothing while en route, and how to keep young children entertained on a long, boring journey.

The design of utility clothing acknowledged the war by adopting a military look, emphasized by padded shoulders and boxy shapes.

FASHIONABLE UTILITY

Fashion played an important part in the drive to maintain the morale of women and, by extension, that of their men at war. The bleakness of wartime life, especially in Britain, could easily have seen women slump into dressing drably in line with the mood of the times. But a British government initiative, the Civilian Clothing Order of 1941, solved this problem in a particularly clever way by inviting members of the London Society of Fashion Designers to put out tenders for new 'Utility' fashions, which were to be quality- and price-controlled. The label, soon termed 'CC41', consisted of two round 'cheese' shapes with wedges cut out on the right-hand side and the number 41.

The CC41 designs had three basic attractions. First, the new styles were intended to keep within the wartime clothing allowance and cut out unnecessary frills – or, as the fashion magazine *Vogue* put it, 'simply pare away superfluities'. Jackets, for example, were to have no more than three buttons and there was to be no bias cutting, which used up too much material. Second, while retaining a certain femininity, CC41 acknowledged the war by adopting a military look, which was emphasized by padded shoulders and boxy shapes: wearing the designs therefore became a sign of patriotism. Third, the Utility clothes were the work of famous designers such as Hardy Amies, Norman Hartnell (who designed clothes for King George VI's consort, Queen Elizabeth, now the Queen Mother), Bianca Mosca, Worth, Victor Stiebel and Digby Morton. The involvement of these well-known names, some of whom had worked for Paris fashion houses until the invasion of France in 1940, gave a fashionable cachet to clothes. This helped to obscure the rather makeshift, inferior image conjured up by the name 'Utility'. Above all, it elevated fashion above the rather depressing but nevertheless important business of 'make do and mend', and showed that even if women had to 'take it' and endure the conditions of wartime, they could at least do so in style.

Austrian and German women, too, knew how to look smart in wartime. Even so, the herringbone jacket and plain trousers were businesslike and in tune with the war mood.

American GIs in Britain

On January 26, 1942, the first 4,000 of an eventual 1.5 million GIs arrived in Britain to prepare for the invasion of Europe that took place on D-Day, June 6, 1944. Their arrival proved a culture shock to the British, who had never before seen a large body of young men so breezy, chatty, friendly, generous, kind-hearted, self-confident – and girl-crazy.

British girls were mightily impressed by the GIs, though parents of young girls became convinced that the first casualty of war was not truth, but virginity. Not all girls were as innocent as they were supposed to be, but the GIs' compulsive pursuit of female company hardly dampened parental trepidation. The subsequent statistics seemed to bear out British fears: illegitimacy rates in Britain rose three times over after the GIs arrived, as they fathered an estimated 22,000 children.

Free-and-easy enjoyment in off-duty hours was not always typical of U.S. military female postings abroad: they were often carefully guarded or confined to camp to preserve their reputations.

Hunting Women

The vigour with which the GIs pursued women was both alarming and extraordinary in British eyes. It was not unknown for GIs to lay siege to a house or hostel where a goodly supply of women was known to be inside. American military police often had to be called in to disperse the would-be Lotharios. They were not discouraged, of course. They simply made other arrangements.

A young British taxi driver later recalled driving off-duty GIs around villages in the Cotswold hills of Gloucestershire and overhearing their talk about 'camp followers in cottage attics' or 'illicit trysts with local ladies'. He was very young and very British. Shocked when the GIs made crude comments about the female anatomy passing by on the sidewalks, he fled after they offered him a piece of the action.

Glamorous but Dangerous

There were, of course, dangers in a situation where women, left at home by boyfriends and husbands serving overseas, became involved with the glamorous Americans. Some British soldiers became depressed by it, some accepted it, some even encouraged it, but inevitably, these triangular arrangements had their darker side. One British Tommy who came home unannounced found his wife in bed with a GI. He seized his rival and threw him out of the window. The GI was killed. How the wife fared is not known.

Girls on the Hunt

However, the quest for the opposite sex was not all one-sided. British girls also went hunting in packs. They invaded U.S. Army bases, stalked off-duty GIs in the streets and flirted shamelessly whenever an American uniform came in sight. It took little time for British girls to discover that GIs were paid vastly more than their British counterparts – $3,000 (£2,080) a year as opposed to $400 (£277) – and that, through the PX and American clubs in London like Rainbow Corner, they had access to undreamed-of luxuries like nylons and scented soaps.

GI generosity soon became legendary, but a bulging billfold was not the only reason for the allure they held for British women. Their greatest asset was their courtly approach. In total contrast to 'Mr Frigidaire', as one girl called the average British male, the Americans knew how to make women feel good. Their opening gambit – 'Hello, Duchess!' or 'Hiya, beautiful!' – sounded 'fresh' at first, but the troubadour treatment that followed dazzled women unused to such attentiveness and warmth.

British girls were thrilled by the glamorous American GIs who showered them with gifts, much to the chagrin of the less well-paid and less sophisticated British soldiers.

GI Brides

There were, of course, many genuine romances, and some 70,000 British women later went to the United States as GI brides. Many other love affairs ended more tragically when the men were killed fighting on the Continent.

Although cynically described as 'overpaid, overfed and over here', the GIs in Britain had been more fun than trouble, and the sparkle they brought to the drabness of wartime left with them when they embarked for the D-Day landings in France in June 1944. More significant, though, was what the GIs left behind. Through them, the British had glimpsed another world beyond their own island confines – a world that seemed much more exciting, energetic and liberated than their own.

CHAPTER 3

War Work

Hard going: women in war factories faced up to the heat, dust, noise and other discomforts that had always been endemic in industrial work. They coped well, despite male prejudice.

Women learned new skills as they replaced men in war work, using expertise and physical strength many never realized they possessed. This did not always go down well with men still working in the wartime factories.

Women had been working in factories for almost two centuries by the time of World War II, but this wide-ranging and destructive conflict presented them with new challenges. The rigid social divisions in which everyone knew their place and kept to it were becoming obscured. The war was a great social leveller, making lowly typists and professional women into companions at the factory workbench.

In addition, the war upended a common concept about the functions of men and women in society. Although a proportion of women had always gone out to work, particularly working-class women with low-paid husbands, the typical family pattern was the male breadwinner at work and the woman at home. There was a also a distinctly patronizing attitude towards women in the context of the war or anything else that was serious man's business. As one Canadian wife put it:

'My husband enlisted right away in the Air Force. This was something that wasn't discussed. The fact that it was going to change my life completely somehow wasn't pertinent. I wasn't to worry my little head.... '

However, war had quite different and much more urgent imperatives. No

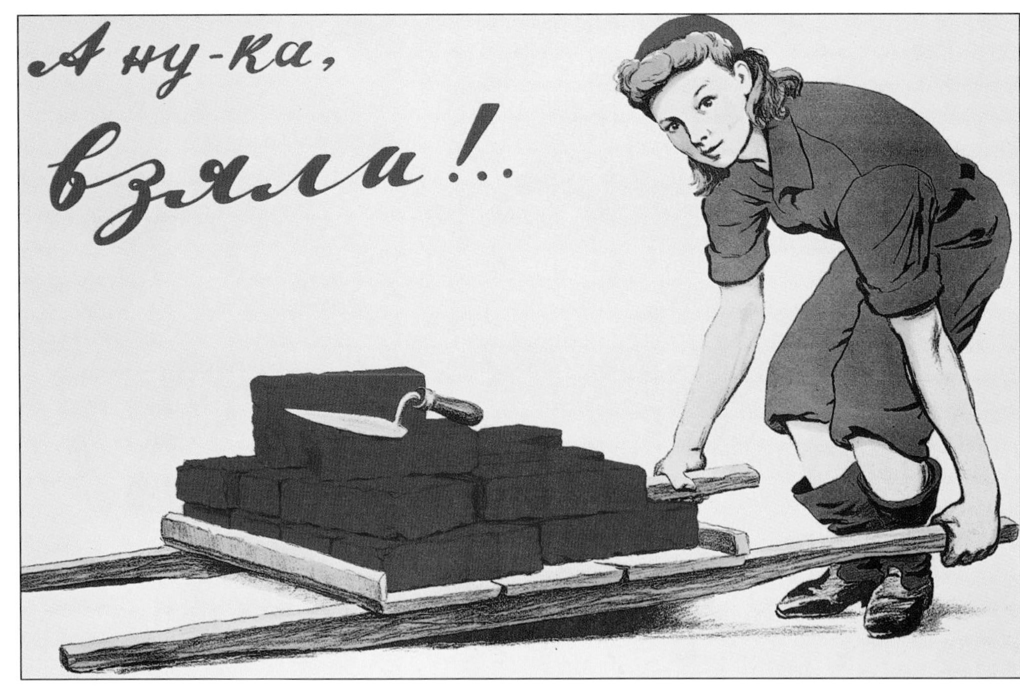

The Russians were neither sentimental nor restrictive about women and women's roles. Despite individual prejudice, women were expected to pull their full weight in the war, just like the men.

Men supervising women at work in factories was a common arrangement before increasing numbers of troops were required for the fighting. After that, female supervisors took over more and more.

government with a war to win could afford to let women remain dependent and economically inactive once their men went off to fight. The men's jobs still had to be done, and war factories went into overdrive compared to peacetime production as hostilities absorbed vast quantities of munitions. In Canada, as in the United States, it was soon realized that the departure for war of so many men left gaps that only the women could fill. Women who were not supposed to worry their little heads went into war production in a big way, working as welders, riveters, shipyard workers or at lathes making gun barrels and other jobs in heavy industry previously thought to be beyond their capabilities. The same applied to other manufacturing work and the service sector.

These women's success was soon apparent. As the Imperial Munitions Board of Canada put it: '[before the war] no thought of woman labour was in the mind of any manufacturer. Experience has now proved that there is no operation on shellwork that a woman cannot do; and as a matter of fact, is doing, even the heavy operations that require great physical strength.'

MAJOR SOCIAL CHANGE

Nevertheless, behind this accolade, major social change was something many found hard to accept. Traditional ideas about the roles of men and women came under assault. One of these concerned wages. Before the war, women were routinely paid less than men, in keeping with the role of men as breadwinners. This was not usually a problem since men's and women's jobs rarely overlapped. However, the war brought about a situation in which men's and women's jobs became interchangeable, with women taking up tasks in shipbuilding, heavy engineering

A Night with an Air-Raid Warden

Doreen Ellis worked as an air-raid warden, in addition to her daytime job, in the Maida Vale district of northwest London. Maida Vale was a 'dormitory' area a few miles from the centre of London and featured numerous blocks of flats. With greatly increased population density, when such an area was bombed, the casualties could reach many hundreds.

The German Luftwaffe bombed Maida Vale intensively on the night of May 10, 1942, during the infamous Blitz that was designed to terrorize London's population – an aim it never achieved. Nevertheless, there was plenty of work that night for Doreen Ellis and her fellow air-raid wardens.

'It was a very noisy night,' Ellis recalled. 'We had several incidents and people coming in for shelter and first aid. About 1:00 AM, a doctor called in to help. I had difficulty bandaging a knee and calf. I also put a tourniquet on a girl's wrist while out on patrol. She had passed out and I left her propped up sitting against a wall for an ambulance to pick her up. She had a note on her good wrist saying who she was.

'During this time, several bombs had dropped. One sheared off a whole front of a block of flats, and we had a steady stream of people coming in for shelter and first aid. A friend of mine was caught in the blast from a nearby bomb and was taken to hospital with shrapnel wounds. The all clear went about 6:00 AM and we were able to go home to bed, very weary. I got up at 8:00 AM and went to work.'

Female air-raid wardens faced the danger of collapsing walls and the horrors of digging victims out of bombed-out buildings.

and factory work. But although the jobs were the same, the pay was not. In Australia, for example, women doing men's jobs in the wartime factories were paid between 25 and 30 percent of the standard male rate. Canadian women were slightly better off, but their pay rate still lagged behind, even though learning welding or riveting skills could put around $25 (£17.60) a week on female pay packets.

There was strong male resistance to the idea of women in war work, and this centred mainly around an inability to accept them as wage labourers.

INEQUALITIES THE NORM

In the United States, the War Labor Board officially adopted the principle of equal pay for equal work in 1942. Redstone Ordnance and Huntsville Chemical plants in Alabama promptly adjusted pay levels to the new rules, abandoning the previous policy which had paid men producing mustard gas at Huntsville $5.76 (£3.90) a day compared to $4.40 (£3) for women. The Alabama plants were not typical, however. Despite the War Labor Board, average pay for men working in American factories during World War II stood at $54.65 (£38) a week, whereas the women averaged $31.21 (£26).

pecial Permission of Carnegie-Illinois Steel Corp.

Photo by Korth

...industrial center of the world...maker of steel...miller of flour...weaver of cloth . . . vast producer of the comforts of life. This is <u>your</u> America.

...Keep it Free!

Lithographed in U. S. A. Form No. 25

American industrial might was crucial to Allied success in World War II – and, as extolled in the powerful propaganda poster opposite, its achievements represented one of the freedoms Americans enjoyed.

Checking components on a production line at an aircraft factory, shown left, could be a repetitive and mind-numbing job, but it was essential for the U.S. war effort.

And this was only one instance of inequality. Government initiatives, by the Labor Board or any other department, had an uphill struggle against ingrained concepts about women's work, which took for granted that it differed from men's. There was strong male resistance to the idea of women in war work, and this centred mainly around an inability to accept them as wage labourers. The women, it was said, were getting 'out of hand', which in effect meant 'out of the house'. This led to dire predictions about the breakdown of family life, even though married women – one in four by 1945 – worked at traditional child care, cleaning, mending, shopping and cooking tasks while holding factory jobs at the same time.

GOVERNMENT INITIATIVES

It was as much a psychological problem as a practical one – and a problem that had to be solved if industrial production was going to be sufficient for war needs. Governments at war had far greater powers than in peacetime, and could deal with inequality through new regulations. The War Labor Board thus decreed that pay should be equalized. In Britain, the conscription of women had a similar effect by requiring women aged 18 to 60 to register for war work. However, rule by decree sat uncomfortably with democratic principles, even in war, and the U.S. government generally preferred to persuade rather than demand.

Its powers of persuasion were extremely effective, using Rosie the Riveter and other posters, magazine articles and radio talks. Much was made of a woman's duty to stand by her man and match his exertions on the battlefield in her own way.

AT REDSTONE ARSENAL

The positive response this drew from women was exemplified by Eugenia

Women such as those on the right undertook all sorts of war work in the factories – tooling, mechanics, drilling, riveting, munitions work or wiring bomb fuses. None of it had ever been considered 'women's work' before.

The American propaganda poster opposite was designed to break down male prejudice in the war industries and, by inference, apologize for the prevalent idea that women were unable to do the job.

Hundreds of thousands of aircraft were built in the United States during the war. These included 12,726 'Flying Fortresses', over 18,000 'Liberators' and over 9,800 'Mitchell' bombers. The woman pictured below is fixing rivets into the wing of a bomber.

Holman, a WOW (Woman Defense Worker) at the Redstone Arsenal. 'I remember when I came to work here.... I wanted to win the war, naturally.

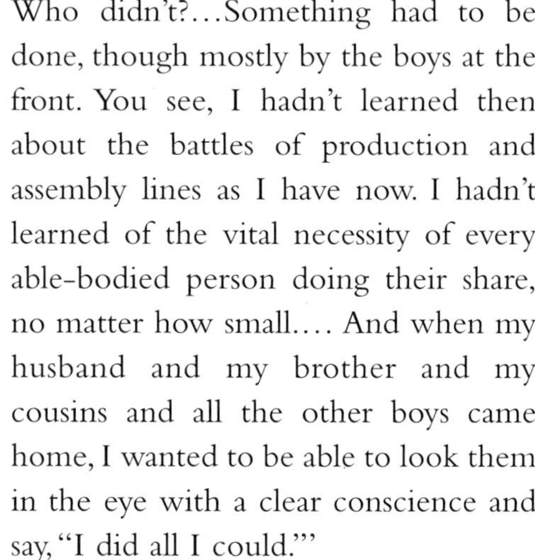

Who didn't?...Something had to be done, though mostly by the boys at the front. You see, I hadn't learned then about the battles of production and assembly lines as I have now. I hadn't learned of the vital necessity of every able-bodied person doing their share, no matter how small.... And when my husband and my brother and my cousins and all the other boys came home, I wanted to be able to look them in the eye with a clear conscience and say, "I did all I could."'

The authorities realized, however, that a feisty approach like Holman's could not be taken for granted, and the Office of War Information made no bones about promulgating the female war effort in publications like its *Basic Program Plan for Womanpower:*

"GOOD WORK, SISTER
WE NEVER FIGURED
YOU COULD DO A
MAN-SIZE JOB!"
PACKER
AMERICA'S WOMEN
HAVE MET THE TEST!

War work was dirty work. Dust got into the hair and caked the skin, oil smeared arms and hands, iron filings and other bits of metal seemed to be everywhere.

'Jobs will have to be glorified as a patriotic war service if American women are to be persuaded to take them and stick to them. Their importance to a nation engaged in total war must be convincingly presented.'

PATRIOTISM AND PAY

In the end, patriotism proved to be the most powerfully persuasive factor in drawing women into war work, but another obvious lure was financial. The Great Depression of the 1930s had thrown millions of American men and women out of work. Although the labour needs of the war helped remedy this situation, unemployment, especially among women, was still a problem. Wartime job opportunities were the light at the end of a long, dark tunnel – not only for those who had been out of work, but for the low-paid as well. In the defence industries, in particular, the money was good.

Working fast, working accurately and, where possible, beating previous production records became the quest for many women in war work who were spurred on by a keen sense of patriotism.

Margarita Salazar left her low-paid job in a beauty shop to work in an aircraft factory.

'Sure, the money was in defence,' she commented. 'You worked more hours, and the more hours you worked, the more money you made. And it was exciting,' Salazar added. 'You figured you were doing something for your country – and at the same time making money!'

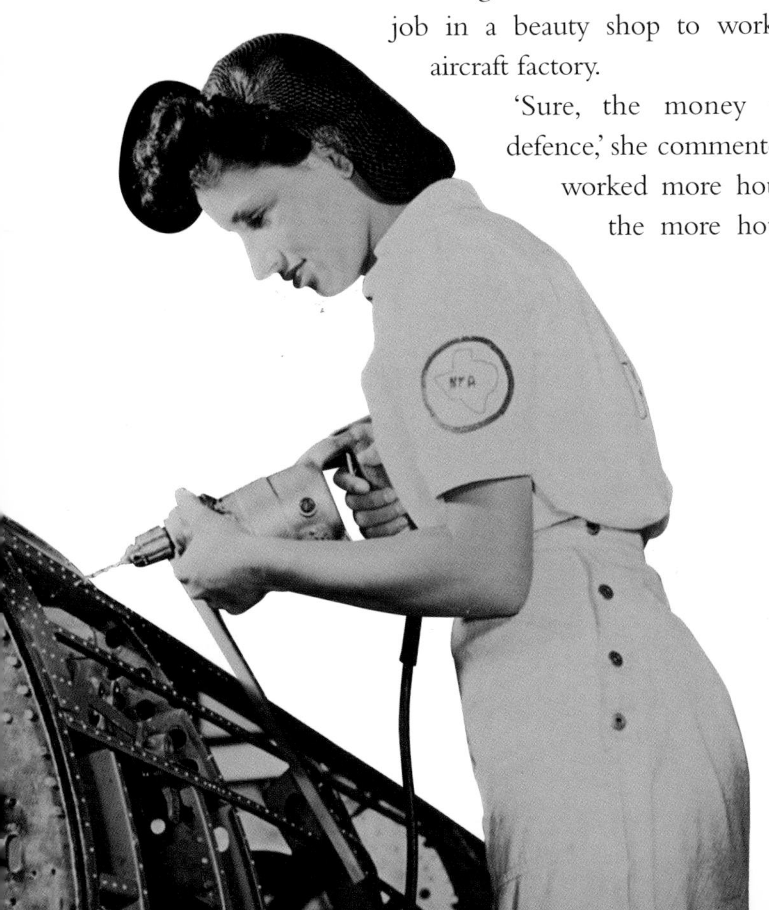

Differences in pay were substantial. In Mobile, Alabama, for example, a waitress was paid $14 (£9.70) a week and a sales clerk $21 (£14.50). By contrast, a wartime shipyard worker earned $37 (£25.60). In Vancouver, Washington, a woman teacher increased her weekly pay by two-thirds, from the school's rate of 75 cents (52p) an hour to $1.25 (88p) in the shipyards.

War work also made new opportunities for a neglected sector of the employment market – older women. Pre-war, these women had great difficulty finding jobs, and even the early years of the war saw little improvement. One woman's situation was fairly typical.

'The spectre of age reared its ugly head whenever I struck out in the direction of an employment office.... A little later, though, it became evident that the supply of acceptable young workers would soon become exhausted.... Sure enough, before long...the age limit rose

Britain's War Factories

By 1943, 1.5 million women were working in Britain's essential industries – engineering, gas, water, electricity, shipbuilding, aircraft and munitions production, and chemicals. The drive to recruit women for factory jobs was as intensive as it was in the United States. Parades were organized to persuade them to sign up, fleets of trucks driving slowly through the streets with women factory workers in the back. Wearing coloured overalls, they stood around parts of Spitfires and other aircraft which were inscribed with the message 'We Made These'.

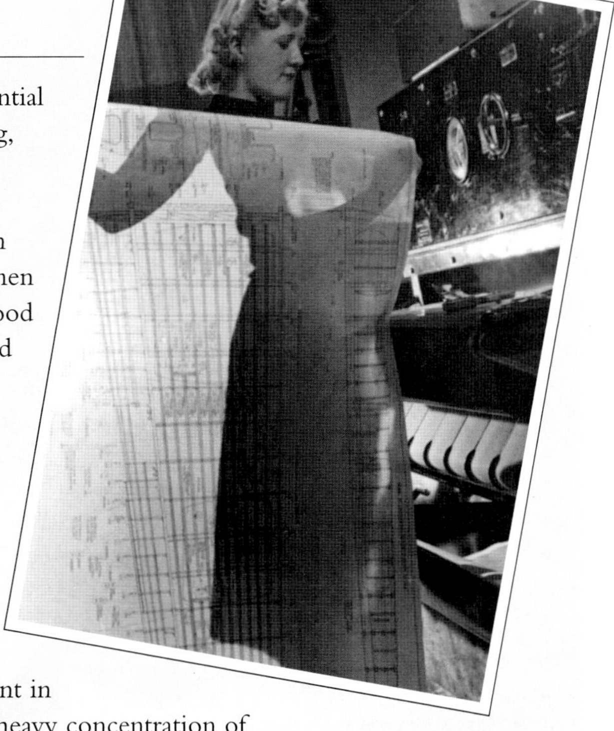

Delicate work, 1942: putting a technical drawing through the blueprinting machine for the production of the British Avro Lancaster bomber.

Luftwaffe Target

British factories, needless to say, were prime targets for German air raids. Some were built underground to protect workers while ensuring that production was minimally disrupted. This was not possible everywhere, though, and women had to take their chances during the night shifts.

Gladys Reeves worked at the Armstrong Siddeley aircraft plant in Coventry, a city subject to almost constant raids because of its heavy concentration of war factories. Often, Reeves had just reached the plant to start work when the sirens sounded. Production stopped and everyone had to go down into the shelter. Reeves found this arrangement rather ironic, because the shelter was built inside the factory – 'and if the factory was bombed, the...shelter would have gone, too.

'We expected bombers to come every night, but we soon got used to it,' Reeves recalled. 'When the attack was not too bad, we just donned our tin hats and hoped for the best. But as time passed, the raids became heavier. They even started shooting down the barrage balloons [protecting the factory] so that they could get through to us.... One night we lost the factory roof when a bomb hit the graveyard next to it. The next thing we knew, bodies, skeletons and coffins were flying everywhere, like a scene from a horror film.'

Women workers in a General Electric factory during the war. Women had plenty of patience for repetitive work and nimble fingers ideal for handling delicate wiring and small components.

Women
in the war
WE CAN'T WIN
WITHOUT THEM

from 40 to 45, 45 to 50…and then, in the more congested factory districts, it disappeared altogether.'

INSIDE MALE DOMAINS

Once women, young and old, had secured war jobs, there was another hurdle: winning acceptance from the men whose enclaves they were invading – in unprecedented numbers. By 1943, women accounted for 34 percent of workers in the ammunition factories alone, and the first of them were forced to serve as 'shock troops', fighting a lone battle for acceptance.

Only after her male colleagues learned about Sanna Benton's Harvard scholarship did they go 'out of their way to be nice'.

One was Inka Sanna Benton. Coming to live in the United States in 1940 after two years under German occupation at home in Poland, she found herself the only woman in a male workforce about a dozen strong. Benton was a qualified architect waiting for a Harvard scholarship to pursue her master's degree, but realized what she was up against after she went to work at Steuben Glass in New York. One sexist remark she received was kindly meant, but very patronizing.

'One day,' Benton recalled later, 'the inspector…came in…to check on the work. He said to me, "Hello, young lady, what do you think you are doing?" and I said, "I'm making a copy of this hospital design on linen." He said, "You are doing very nicely, but

The U.S. government pulled out all stops to persuade women – and men – that women's contribution to the war effort was vital. The propaganda poster opposite had overtones of strength and power.

Early on in the war the British press made much of women's inferior physical strength. Women exploded this uncomplimentary theory by succeeding at a variety of strenuous factory jobs, as shown below.

Women workers in the British Royal Ordnance Factory needed special creams to prevent their skins from absorbing the potentially toxic explosive that hung about in the air while they were working.

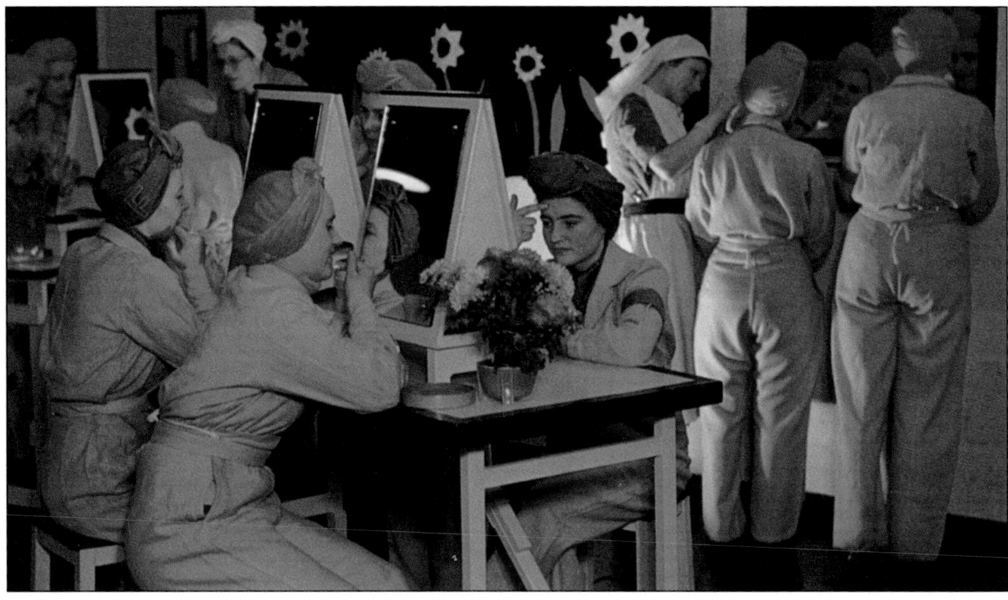

I will give you some advice. It would be much better, I think, if you stuck to kitchens and gardens. Much easier for you, young lady.'"

Benton's reception by the male workers at Steuben Glass was not as blatantly condescending as this. However, she was not initially taken seriously. It was only after the men learned about her Harvard scholarship that they 'went out of their way to be nice'.

The intrusion of women into heavy industrial work, like sheet metal working, was a culture shock for their male colleagues. Some reacted resentfully, but most learned to accept women working alongside them.

GAUNTLET OF HOSTILITY

By contrast, Alison Ely Campbell of Portland, Oregon, had to run the gauntlet of male hostility in the Progress Department of Kaiser Shipyard. Campbell encountered outright harassment after leaving her field office job for another in the assembly bays, tracking the welding. Her department manager kept her confined for two months at typing work before releasing her to the assembly bays. When she finally got there, Campbell found another woman already there with the all-male crews.

'They met us with stony stares,' Campbell recalled. The foreman showed the two women what to do and they were each given a 'territory', but it was soon evident that the men intended to ignore them.

'The guys obviously made a pact not to talk to us...to freeze us out,' Campbell remembered. But the women responded with a surprisingly effective attitude of their own – patient perseverance. 'We were friendly, doing the job, and after a couple of weeks they not only thawed out but actually enjoyed us – and we enjoyed them.'

Benton and Campbell discovered that breaking into a man's world meant treading in tricky territory. Another, geologist Dorothy Henderson Smith, was actively prevented from doing her job at the Magnolia Oil Company in Oklahoma City by men who 'sat on the well' to stop her taking samples of cuttings.

'We were friendly, doing the job, and after a couple of weeks they not only thawed out but actually enjoyed us – and we enjoyed them.'

GLOW OF ACCOMPLISHMENT

Pioneers in any field have the hardest time, but fortunately the early phase that saw suspicion and resistance, even outright sabotage of the kind encountered by Dorothy Henderson Smith, began to fade in time. Confidence grew as more and more women came into the factories in response to powerful government persuasion, and self-assurance blossomed as they proved they could succeed. Some even set records, like Rose Bonavita and Jennie Florito, who fixed 3,345 rivets into the wing of a torpedo bomber during a six-hour evening shift on June 8, 1943.

Before long, women were spurred on by the glow of accomplishment that came from doing well at a hard job once thought beyond their scope. It was a new experience, and most women enjoyed it for the first time in their lives.

However, this stage was not reached without growing pains, as 18-year-old JoAnn Hudlicky discovered when she became a shipyard welder. On her first day at the shipyard, Hudlicky put on her protective hood, picked up her welding tool and got to work.

'I started to run a weld up this bulkhead,' Hudlicky remembers. 'It looked terrible. I didn't know what to do.... I sat there and cried. I said, "I'm

(continued on page 78)

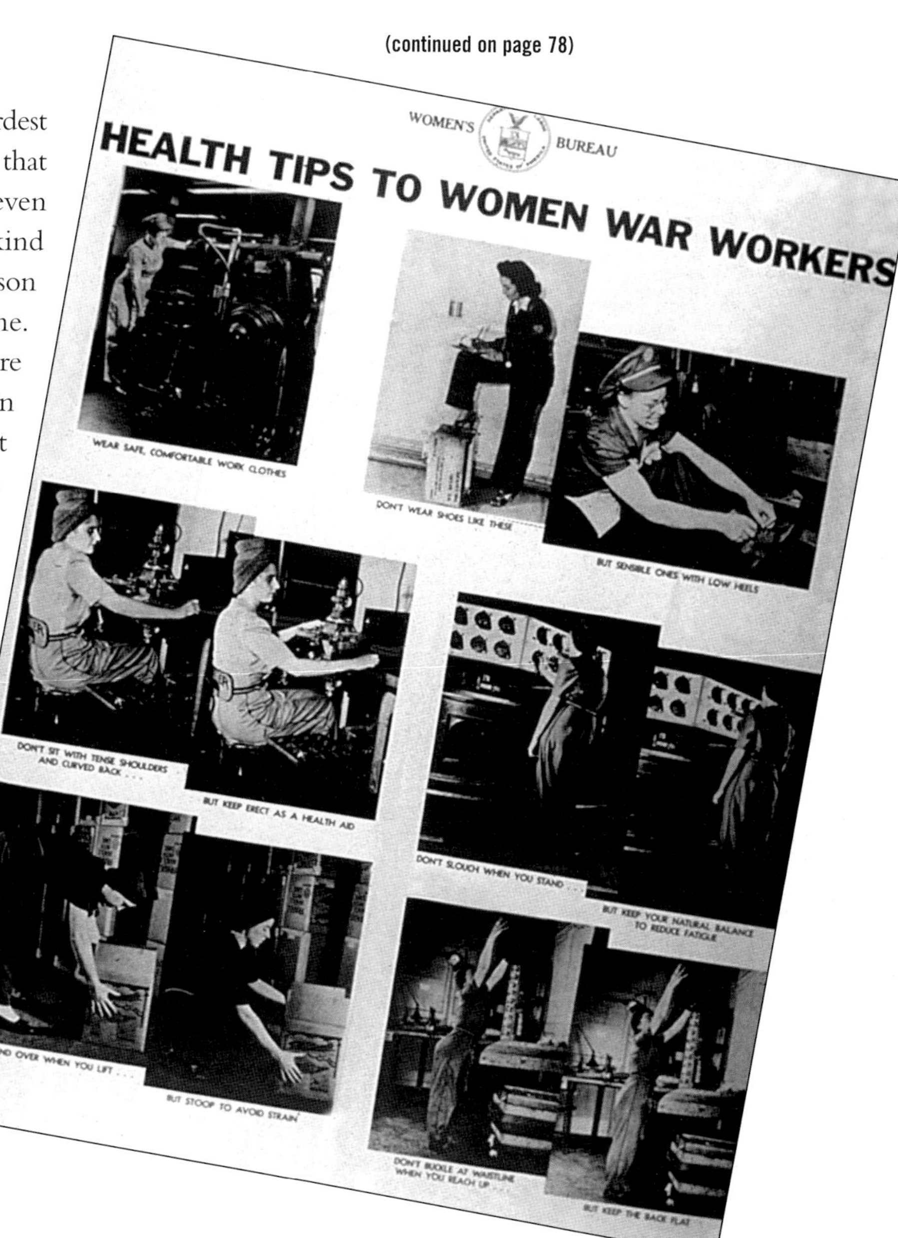

Do's and Don'ts: Women war workers received safety advice on wearing proper shoes to work, how not to slouch when sitting and the do's and don'ts of lifting heavy objects.

Women in Agriculture

In Britain, the Women's Land Army of World War II took up where the Land Girls of 1917 had left off. Because of these First World War predecessors and the fact that women had always had work to do on the farm, gaining acceptance in local communities was not as problematic, even though rural society could be very insular.

One of the Land Army recruitment posters promised a warm welcome in the countryside, picturing a smiling farmer saying to a girl, 'We could do with thousands more like you...' A closer look, however, revealed a hint that the Land Girls were not going to be confined to the traditionally female farm jobs, such as feeding chickens or milking cows: the poster girl held the reins of a large dray horse fitted with a sturdy collar for ploughing, which was normally a male job, requiring strength and stamina.

Nevertheless, during the war the women of the Land Army worked a 50-hour week in summer (48 in winter), ploughing fields, driving tractors and making hay, and undertook the full rigours of harvesting, thatching and threshing. They also reclaimed land, herded livestock, worked in orchards and market gardens and, though they had to steel themselves to do it, caught rats.

Agricultural labour was not as idyllic as its advocates made it appear: there was back-breaking work to be done, even though workers at least enjoyed the benefits of fresh air.

Varied Tasks

The nature of farm work meant that the next job could never be predicted. 'None of us knew what job was coming up,' recalled Pat Vaughan, who joined the WLA in 1941. 'Sometimes tractor work, sometimes ploughing or field work such as potato or root-crop planting or harvesting.

'Haymaking was always a popular task. Fruit-picking was, well, all right. But harvesting of grain crops, especially barley and white clover, was not only hard work, but also a dusty, filthy job.'

Pat Vaughan got married near the end of the war, in 1944, and remembers how amused – or was it amazed? – the minister was by her war work, so much so that he insisted on recording Pat's occupation on her marriage certificate.

The Women's Land Army of America (1943–1947) employed over a million women to drive tractors, tend crops or shear sheep for unskilled pay of 25 to 40 cents (17 to 28 pence) an hour.

Heavy Work, by Anyone's Standards

Britain's Timber Corps, formed as part of the Women's Land Army in 1942, took women into that quintessentially male activity – lumberjacking. Inevitably, the women were called 'lumberjills'.

Rosalind Elder joined up as one of the early recruits, even though by her own admission she had no idea what the work was going to entail. She soon learned, though, that she was in for the hardest physical work she 'had ever dreamed possible'.

The day after arriving in Glasgow, Scotland, Elder and other girls began training at Brechin in Angus. Clambering into an open truck, they were driven to the woods to encounter the first of many surprises.

'It was something of a shock,' she recounted, 'when handed a four-and-a-half pound [2kg] axe and shown how to "lay-in" a tree.' After a short demonstration on the use of it, felling, snedding (cutting off branches) and the loading of tractors and trucks followed.

Russian wartime propaganda promoted the strength and capability of women, particularly their fitness to take over men's jobs in agriculture. This unglamorous female tractor driver had impressively mighty arm muscles.

Toughening Up

At the end of the day, the lumberjills had more blisters in more places than they had ever known before. However, the sheer exertions of the job gradually toughened them up, and within a month they were 'tossing and cross-cutting logs, felling trees and loading vehicles'.

Their training completed, the lumberjills were dispersed throughout Britain. Rosalind Elder went to the Scottish Highlands and the small Morayshire village of Advie. The camp was sited in the middle of a field. The accommodation, for 40 girls, comprised two long wooden huts. It was December and the cold was intense.

Elder became a horsewoman, guiding her animal through the forest to a nearby clearing. There the trees were cut into mill logs, pit props, telegraph poles and pulpwood. Elder's quota was 330 trees during a five-and-a-half-day week, in addition to looking after the horse.

'Early morning found me up at dawn, shovelling out the stables, feeding, watering and grooming the horse before starting work. [It was] no fun in winter, but in summer I was very happy being outdoors all day long, tanned and healthy.... I have very fond memories of my women's Timber Corps days, and when I reminisce I think of sunshine, laughter, the scent of freshly cut wood and the voices of the lumberjills calling.... Timmm—berrr!'

These Soviet women from Kirghizia, Central Asia, undaunted by the size of the machines they had to drive, replaced their men at farm work once they went to war.

too young. I'm too little to do this job." So I sat there about 15 or 20 minutes and said, "Well, I'm going to try it anyway." So I worked my way up to the top and, lo and behold, it got better and better all along!'

Hudlicky's sort of experience was repeated over and over again among the six million women who replaced men in American factories at welding, machining, riveting, aircraft construction or weapons manufacture. Like her, they became more adept with experience, even better than men at certain tasks. Domestic skills such as needlework and knitting required nimble hands and fingers, which were a distinct advantage in much of their war work, especially wiring bomb fuses and filling metal casings with gunpowder.

At first, older American women were largely excluded from war work. Eventually, the U.S. war effort could not afford this waste, and older women, including grey-haired grandmother types, were recruited.

FACTORY ACCIDENTS

Overall, though, war work in the factories was anything but a soft option, despite many safety precautions. It was a gruelling environment, with a daily regime of noise, extremes of temperature, vibration, tension and peril. One small

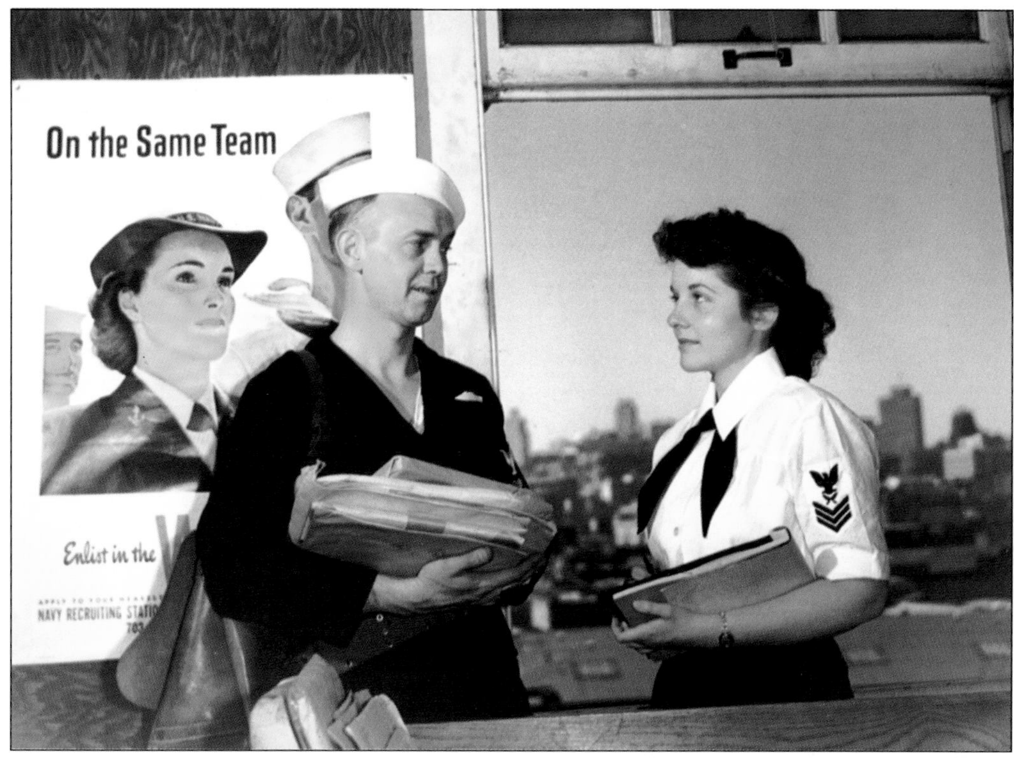

For secretaries, typists and other office workers, roles were unchanged by the war. Sorting and delivering the post, however, were new roles, as women replaced mailmen called up to fight.

lapse could mean an accident, and accidents could mean injury or death.

In the United States in wartime, more than 210,000 women were permanently disabled in factory accidents. Some 37,000 died. The Redstone and Huntsville arsenals saw five killed. The first was Easter Posey, who lost her life at Redstone Arsenal on April 21, 1942. More than 50 years later, on May 10, 1994, the U.S. Army Missile Command renamed a military recreation area in Posey's honour and unveiled a plaque reading: 'Dedicated to the Women Workers of Redstone and Huntsville Arsenals who gave their lives in service to their country.' Thousands of other less severely injured women refused to be deterred and returned to work after their injuries healed.

Domestic skills such as needlework and knitting required nimble hands and fingers, which were were a distinct advantage in women's war work, especially when it came to wiring bomb fuses.

Despite such dangers, the female workforce expanded so rapidly that, by war's end, it had grown to more than 50 percent above peacetime levels. In the first two years following Pearl Harbor, most female factory workers in the United States were single women, some as young as 14 or 15, but there were not enough to meet the demand, so married women were recruited in large numbers after 1943. By 1945, three-quarters of women workers were married, most without young children at home.

THE FIRST LADY

Women's dual roles inevitably entailed problems, as pinpointed by President

The more WOMEN at work the sooner we WIN!

WOMEN ARE NEEDED ALSO AS:

FARM WORKERS	WAITRESSES	TIMEKEEPERS	LAUNDRESSES
TYPISTS	BUS DRIVERS	ELEVATOR OPERATORS	TEACHERS
SALESPEOPLE	TAXI DRIVERS	MESSENGERS	CONDUCTORS

—and in hundreds of other war jobs!

SEE YOUR LOCAL U.S. EMPLOYMENT SERVICE

Roosevelt's wife, Eleanor, in her numerous articles and speeches boosting the war effort. The First Lady, an inspirational figure during the war, understood very well the difficulties of women caught between the demands of factory and home.

'Some of the married women workers are not doing their best because we haven't taken into consideration their personal problems,' the First Lady wrote in *Reader's Digest* in 1944. 'Their homes must still go on. Their children must be cared for. Day nurseries are now being established, but they are not always properly organized. Sometimes they are not located conveniently for mothers – I was told of one nursery which was five blocks from a bus stop and meant that a woman had to walk 20 blocks every day. To a tired woman carrying a child, those blocks seem very long.'

RELOCATION AND ITS PROBLEMS

The difficulties involved in war work were all the more onerous for female war workers who had to relocate in order to take up their jobs, often much farther from their home territory than they had ever ventured. Women's domestic difficulties were thus amplified by the need to adjust to a new and strange environment: setting up a new house, coping with a different climate, finding new schools for the children, and settling down among strangers whose customs and culture might be very different from their own.

Many women in the factories would never have met but for the war. For instance, the workforce at the Ford bomber production plant at Willow Run, near Ypsilanti, Michigan, included teachers, waitresses, homemakers, an advertising copywriter and a pilot, as well as a budding actress, Nancy Schaefer, a graduate of the University of Michigan who gave up her stage career for war work. Another was Paula Lind, the first female instructor for the Link Trainer, which taught pilots how to fly by instruments – more commonly known as blind flying.

In joining the production line at Willow Run as riveters, light assembly workers, inspectors or trainers, these women were, in the words of Edsel Ford,

As usual, the Russian poster above made no concessions to glamour, but, once more as usual, emphasized keen-eyed strength of purpose.

The U.S. wartime poster opposite advertised a whole raft of jobs for which women were invited to apply. The glamourized illustration emphasized the value of delicate fingers in aircraft production.

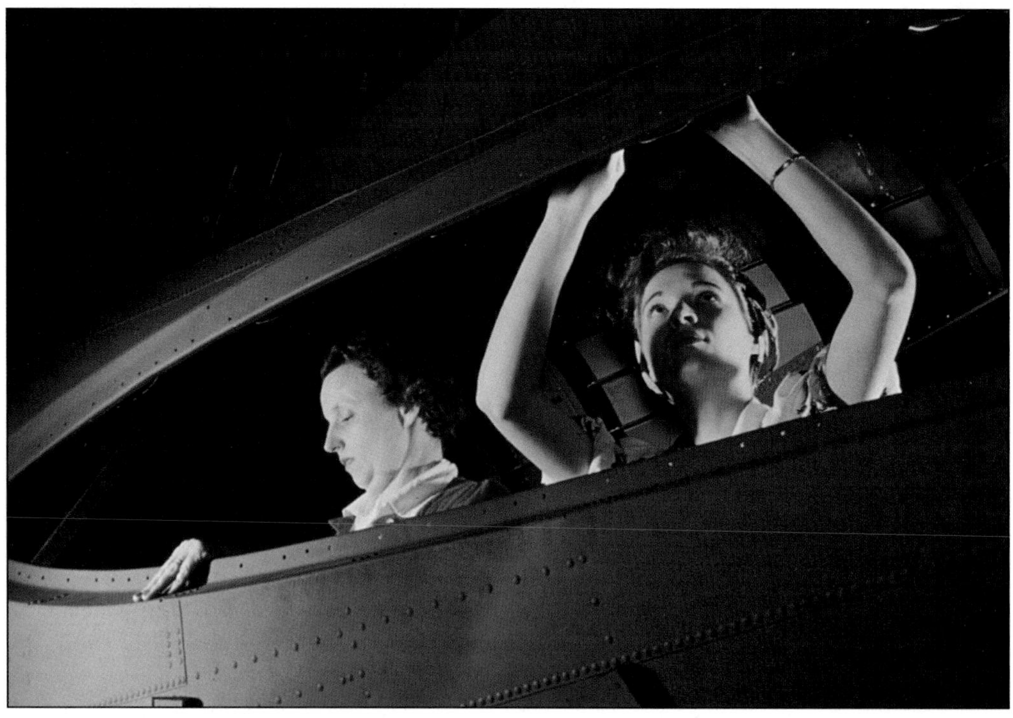

Two women aircraft production workers put the finishing touches to the interior of a fuselage; airmen's lives depended on the care and accuracy of women like these.

son of Henry, showing a high degree of 'intelligence, will and determination' in 'work that [was] entirely foreign to them'.

This unprecedented mixing of women from different backgrounds was a common occurrence in wartime Arizona, which saw a vast rise in population because of the upsurge in defence efforts after Pearl Harbor. Tucson, for example, had been a quiet community, mainly occupied in ranching, where the warm, arid climate drew people relocating for health reasons, those who wanted a pleasant place to spend their retirement, and tourists attracted by the local beauty spots.

A service industry had grown up to cater to such folk, but the facilities it offered were inadequate to deal with the influx of war workers who arrived after the building of military camps and defence plants. There was a training camp for military personnel at Fort Huachuca, about 100 miles (160 kilometres) from Tucson, the Davis–Monthan Air Force Base in Tucson itself, and the Consolidated Vultee Aircraft Company plant, opened on the south side of the city.

The difficulties involved in war work were all the more onerous for female war workers who had to relocate in order to take up their jobs.

ALABAMA'S ARSENALS

Alabama was another state that saw fundamental change as workers, male and female, flocked to the new Redstone and Huntsville arsenals in the second half of 1941. Although the December 7 attack on Pearl Harbor was to come as a shock, the U.S. government had seen war coming long before this, and was already making preparations.

The United States was also actively

In the poster opposite, a fresh-faced GI advertises his pride in his girl's achievements in war work – a subtle psychological touch designed to validate women's roles in former male preserves.

ADOLPH TREIDLER
"My girl's a WOW"
WOMAN ORDNANCE WORKER

aiding the British war effort while still officially neutral. So, on July 3, 1941, five months before Pearl Harbor, the local *Huntsville Times* put out a special 'Extra' edition announcing that a new $40 million (£28 million) war plant was planned in the south-west of the town.

This was to be Huntsville Arsenal. Its speciality would be the manufacture of coloured-smoke munitions, though it was also a major producer of gel-type incendiaries, toxic agents such as phosgene, lewisite, white phosphorus, mustard gas and tear gas. Huntsville was meant to complement Edgewood Arsenal in Maryland, the Army's only other chemical manufacturing plant.

According to the Arsenal's records, the absence of black workers at the start was due to a lack of 'toilet facilities to take care of race distinctions peculiar to the South'.

It was to transform what had previously been a quiet northern Alabama farming town with a comparatively laid-back way of life.

The proximity of dangerous war materials to their town was shock enough for the people of Huntsville, but the arsenal was not to be the only newcomer. Before long, the U.S. Ordnance Corps realized the value of having its own shell-loading and assembly plant close to a factory that manufactured chemical munitions. Within two months, on October 25, 1941, the first shovelful of earth was officially turned at the site of what was to become Redstone Arsenal. Redstone's specialities were burster charges, chemical artillery ammunition, demolition blocks, rifle grenades and a variety of bombs.

Women in war work became adept at handling unfamiliar industrial equipment like this hand drill, being used at North American Aviation to assemble a section of an aircraft's leading edge.

THE EMPLOYMENT OFFICE

If social change, especially for women, could come as if a bolt from the blue, it happened at Huntsville – even though, at first, women were slow to show their hand. Among the workers who initially registered for work at the arsenal, men outnumbered women by more than six to one: 1,200 men staged what was called 'the storming of the employment office' on July 7, 1941, just a few days

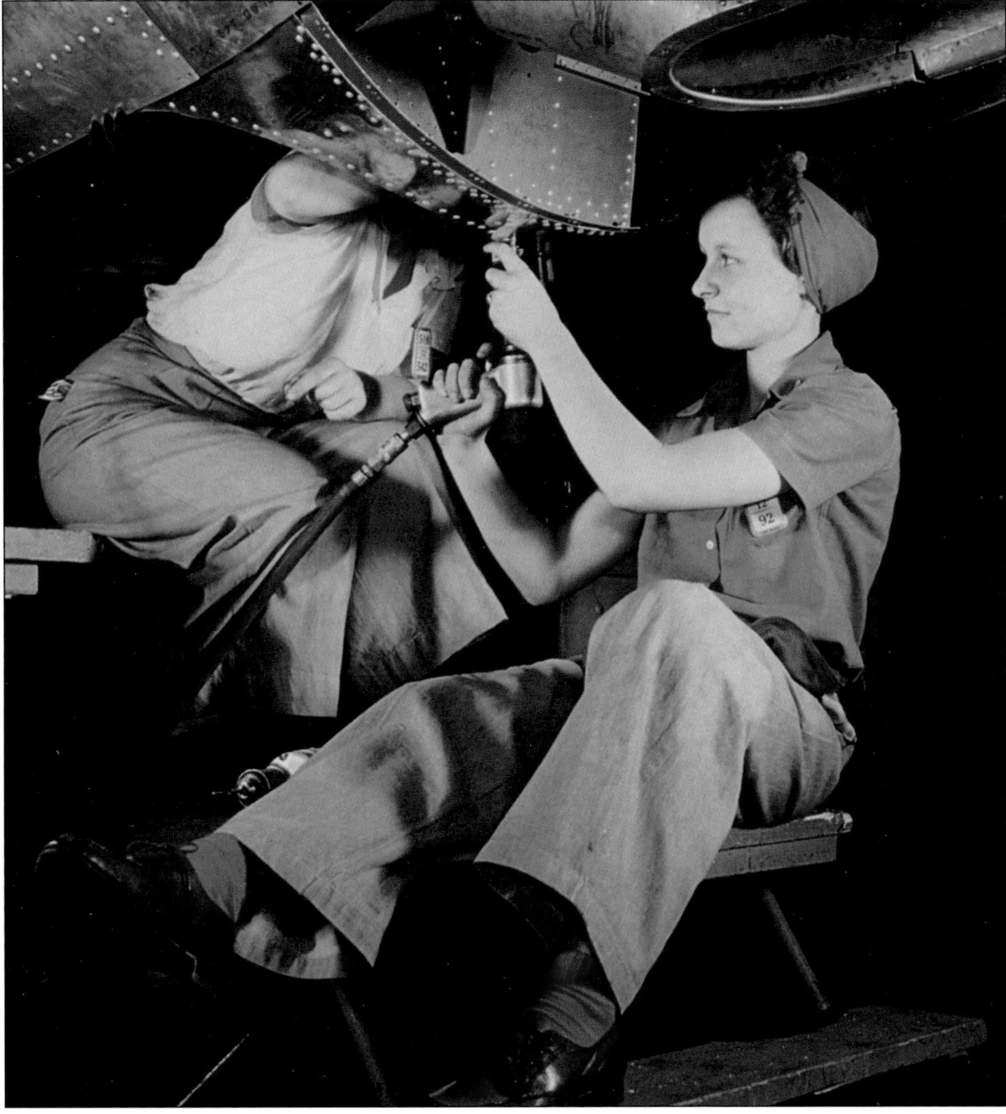

At work helping to construct a bomber at the Douglas Aircraft Company in Long Beach, California, in October 1942. The women performed this work far better than at first expected.

after the announcement of plans to build the arsenal. At this early stage, 200 of the women on file were black, but other black women had to wait their turn at Huntsville until the local supply of white female labour had been used up. According to records, the absence of black workers at the start was due to the lack of 'toilet facilities to take care of race distinctions peculiar to the South'.

Huntsville, however, could not afford to exclude black women for this or any other reason. Although the numbers of black women employed never equalled those for whites, both eventually made significant contributions to the arsenal's production records. By May 1944, when the workforce at Huntsville had risen to 6,707, women accounted for 37 percent of employees – 26 percent white and 11 percent black.

FEMINIZING HUNTSVILLE

Until 1943, men, black and white, did the heavy work at Huntsville Arsenal, with white women being placed on the production lines. However, as more and more men went to war, the workforce at Huntsville became more 'feminized'.

The problem with all workers had

Doing heavy railroad jobs, wielding heavy equipment: one of the more overt signs of the female takeover of men's jobs. Both British and American women performed this demanding war work.

been their general lack of qualifications for the specialized tasks they had to carry out, so in 1941 both men and women were given free 12-week defence-training courses, including elements of structural design, mechanical and electrical maintenance, chemical engineering and other subjects relevant to the war effort. The last of these courses took place – not a moment too soon – in 1943. By then, America's war effort was escalating into the final massive push for victory on both the European and Pacific fronts – already, preparations for the invasion of France in 1944 were gathering pace in Britain.

In 1941, both men and women were given free 12-week defence-training courses in relevant scientific and engineering subjects.

Even before the end of the defence courses, run by the University of Alabama and Auburn University, it was anticipated that women would take over male jobs in increasing numbers. Incentives for local women to take up technical training opportunities included earning good money while performing a patriotic service at the same time.

STIMSON'S DETERMINATION

Huntsville and Redstone were fairly typical of the metamorphosis that

Women in Transport

Women reported for jobs on Britain's transport system soon after conscription was introduced in 1941. For some, like telephone switchboard operators, their work was little different from peacetime. Others, like so many women during the war, found themselves in far less familiar territory. They became tanker drivers, mechanics, railway guards, bus conductors or railway signallers. Some women, like Zelma Katin, found their jobs strange and not a little mystifying.

'I was troubled with uncertainty,' Katin wrote in her book *Clippie: The Autobiography of a Wartime Conductress.* 'Was it I who was going to dress up in a conductor's uniform, run down to the tram depot in the blackout, shout "Fares please!" [and] punch tickets...Was this woman in navy blue myself?'

Operating signals on Britain's railways: women proved they could do responsible jobs like this during the war, disproving the prevalent view that women were not technically competent.

Mutual Bemusement

Bus passengers were just as bemused at first, especially when they found that both driver and conductor were women. This was understandable. Unlike factory workers, the Land Girls or female military personnel, whose war work was not much in the public eye, women who worked on the transport system provided visible, everyday evidence of the vast changes the war had wrought in the labour market.

Nevertheless, everyone soon became accustomed to the presence of females where men had been before. After a while, it was no longer a strange sight to see women cleaning cars, connecting hoses between railroad carriages, using powerful pumps to douse fires after air raids, or repairing motorcycles and other vehicles.

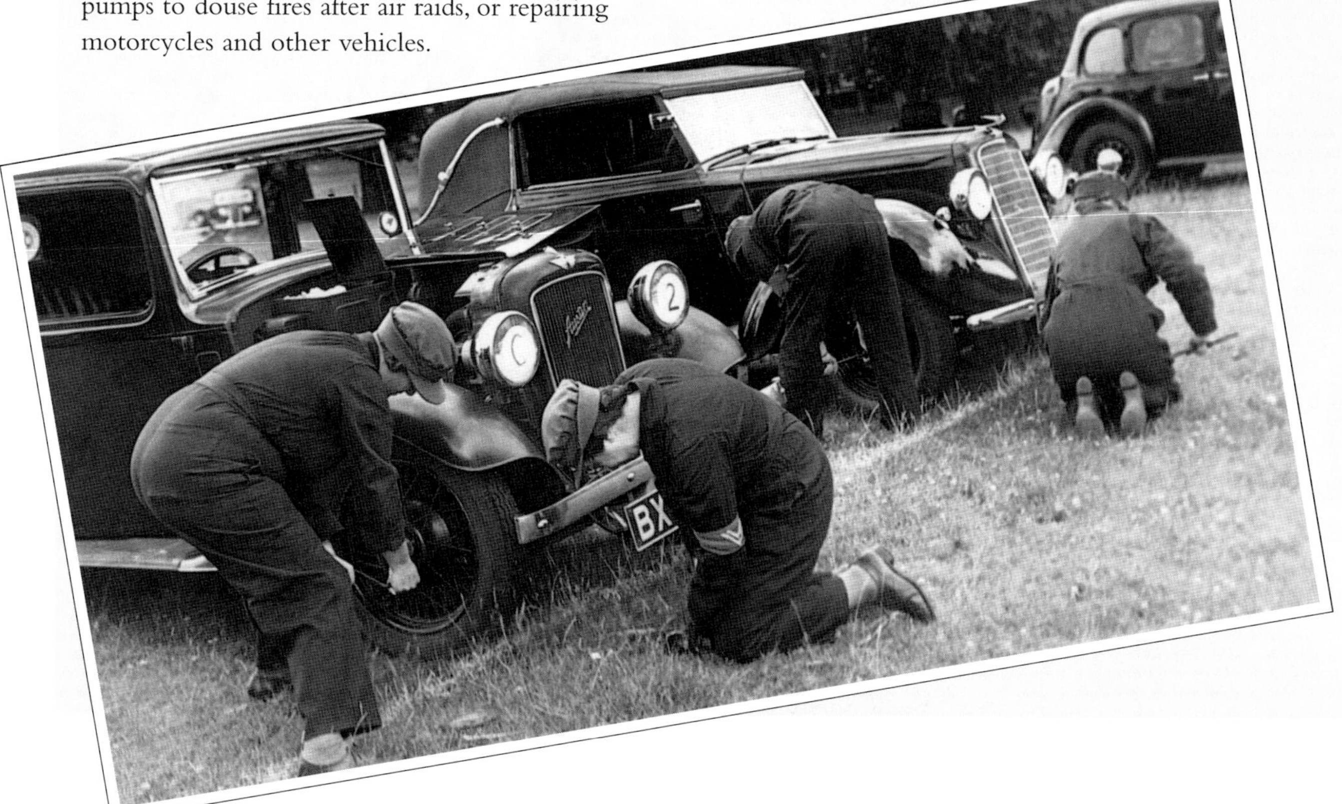

The ATS were trained in vehicle maintenance: this role received royal sanction when Queen Elizabeth II, then Princess, was recruited for this work in 1945.

Prejudice against recruiting black women for war work was hard to break down, especially when they would be working alongside whites on an equal basis for the very first time.

occurred in American industry before and after the United States entered World War II.

At Willow Run, Edsel Ford was ordered by the War Office to recruit 12,000 women for the bomber production plant there, and similar instructions were sent to other factories. In just over a year, there were 140,000 women working in the defence industries. Willow Run hired 117 of them in a single week.

The management at Redstone Arsenal in Alabama preempted Stimson and Ford. In February 1942, Redstone announced that women would take over men's jobs wherever possible. The Redstone management was as good as its word. On February 28, the first two women 'production soldiers' joined the workforce; by the end of the year, 40 percent of those employed in manufacturing ordnance on Redstone's four production lines were female. Later, in 1944, women accounted for 54 percent of all workers at Redstone arsenal, a figure that had risen to 62 percent by the time the war with Japan came to an end in August 1945.

At first, Redstone officials had been apprehensive about the results women could achieve, but before long their aptitude was beyond doubt.

BLACK WOMEN STUDENTS

At first, Redstone officials had been apprehensive about the results women could achieve, but before long their aptitude as tool-crib and fork-lift operators, inspectors, guards, truck drivers and press operators was beyond doubt. But both Redstone and Huntsville held back somewhat over the employment of black women, regarding their efficiency or otherwise as an 'unknown quantity'. Nevertheless, 100 black women students recruited by Huntsville as production-line workers did so well that the authorities – probably quite relieved – declared themselves much gratified. Redstone Arsenal went even further after the first black female production crews went into action in April 1944. 'From all appearances,' said the plant's newspaper, the *Redstone Eagle,* 'their work and attendance [set] an example any of us would do well to follow.'

All-female work crews at Redstone were supervised by men at first, but by 1943 several supervisors were women and they were very proud of 'their girls'. One of them, in charge of 15 women working at smoke-pot assembly, reported that her crew was 'one of the most efficient…at the arsenal. They…[were] usually ahead on production requirements and…[were] never known to fall behind.'

THE RIGHT STUFF

Subsequently, a local newspaper report, published in August 1945, shattered a number of commonly held misconceptions about women working in the U.S. defence industries.

'These girls are all handling a man's job. Every one of them believes she has a personal stake in this war. Their morale is about the highest at the arsenal. They are expert press operators, ball table operators and they handled these 124- to 150-pound [56–68 kilogram] pallets with the ease and efficiency of old timers…Each one of them is capable of substituting for the other in case of need…. This spirit of knowing their assigned job well, and the job of the girl working next to them, has made every one of them valuable operators.'

The competence of black women was doubted: this woman, working at the Pratt and Whitney aircraft engine factory, was one of relatively few to be accepted for such complex work.

For information
go to your local hospital or write
U. S. CADET NURSE CORPS
Box 88, New York 8, N.Y.

A Lifetime Education *FREE*

FOR HIGH SCHOOL GRADUATES WHO QUALIFY

CHAPTER 4

The Role of Nursing Staff

In World War II, nurses tending the wounded in makeshift hospitals near the front line lived in constant danger as they worked to preserve life while everything happening around them was designed to destroy it.

The nursing profession as we know it today was born in war. When England's redoubtable Florence Nightingale made it a respectable task for women, the horrific truths she had learned in the Crimean War of 1853–1856 taught her what needed to be done by those tending wounded men close to the battlefield. In subsequent conflicts, including World War II, nursing the wounded was the nearest that women came to combat status. In that discipline their traditional caring and nurturing roles confronted the brute force that sought to destroy all they were striving to preserve.

SHOULDER TO SHOULDER

In this context, America's war began in an unusual way: at Pearl Harbor, men and women entered the conflict together. On December 7, 1941, while pilots scrambled to get airborne in those planes that had managed to escape the Japanese bombing, and crews rushed to man the anti-aircraft guns, the nurses headed for the hospitals.

Lieutenant Ruth Erickson of the U.S. Navy Nursing Corps had to run through a shower of shrapnel in an atmosphere already thick with smoke rising from Battleship Row. Once inside the orthopaedic dressing room,

Many wartime jobs for women lasted only as long as the war lasted. Nursing offered women jobs for life in a caring, nurturing role for which they were naturally suited.

Demand for nurses burgeoned as the war intensified. This recruitment poster was meant to appeal to the sense of dedication and vocation which nurses needed to do this demanding work.

The shock of Pearl Harbor was highlighted in the poster opposite, without revealing too much about the horrific nature of war injuries – burns, bullet and explosion wounds or blown-off limbs.

she quickly got to work.

'We drew water into every container we could find and set up the instrument boiler,' she recalled. 'Fortunately, we still had electricity and water. The first patient came into our dressing room at 8:25 AM with a large opening in his abdomen which was bleeding profusely. We started an intravenous drip and transfusion.... Everyone was terrified. The patient died within the hour.

'Then the burns patients started to stream in...the tropical dress at the time was white T-shirts and shorts. The burns began where the pants ended. Bared arms and faces were plentiful. Personnel retrieved a supply of flit guns from stock. We filled these with tannic acid to spray burned bodies. Then we gave these gravely injured patients sedatives for their intense pain.'

RED CROSS
VOLUNTEER NURSE'S AIDE
ENROLL TODAY AS A RED CROSS VOLUNTEER NURSE'S AIDE
YOUR HELP CAN SAVE MANY LIVES ... FIND THE TIME ... GIVE IT NOW
Call Your Red Cross Chapter or Local Civilian Defense Volunteer Office

UNPREPARED

Being thrust into the war, as Ruth Erickson and her colleagues were at Pearl Harbor, was not, of course, a common occurrence – fortunately so, in those circumstances. Units that already existed were seriously undermanned. Even before the United States entered the war, the U.S. Army Nurse Corps, colloquially known as 'GI Nightingales', had a complement of only 942 nurses in

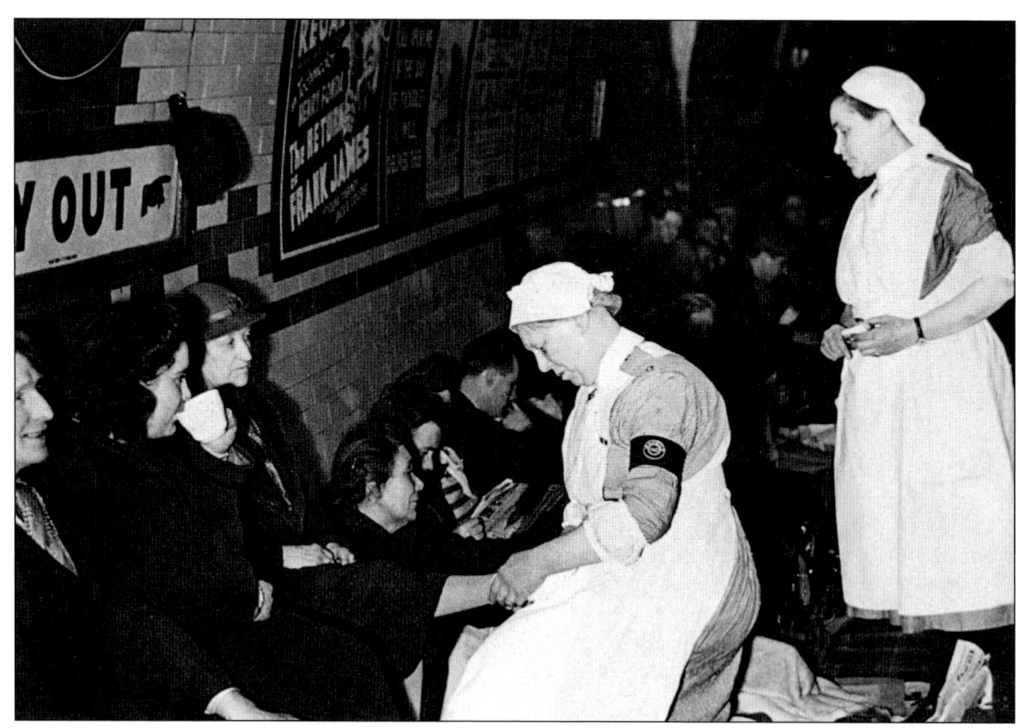

Londoners crowded into underground stations like Piccadilly Circus to escape the bombing during the Blitz. St. John Ambulance nurses were on hand to give first aid in emergencies.

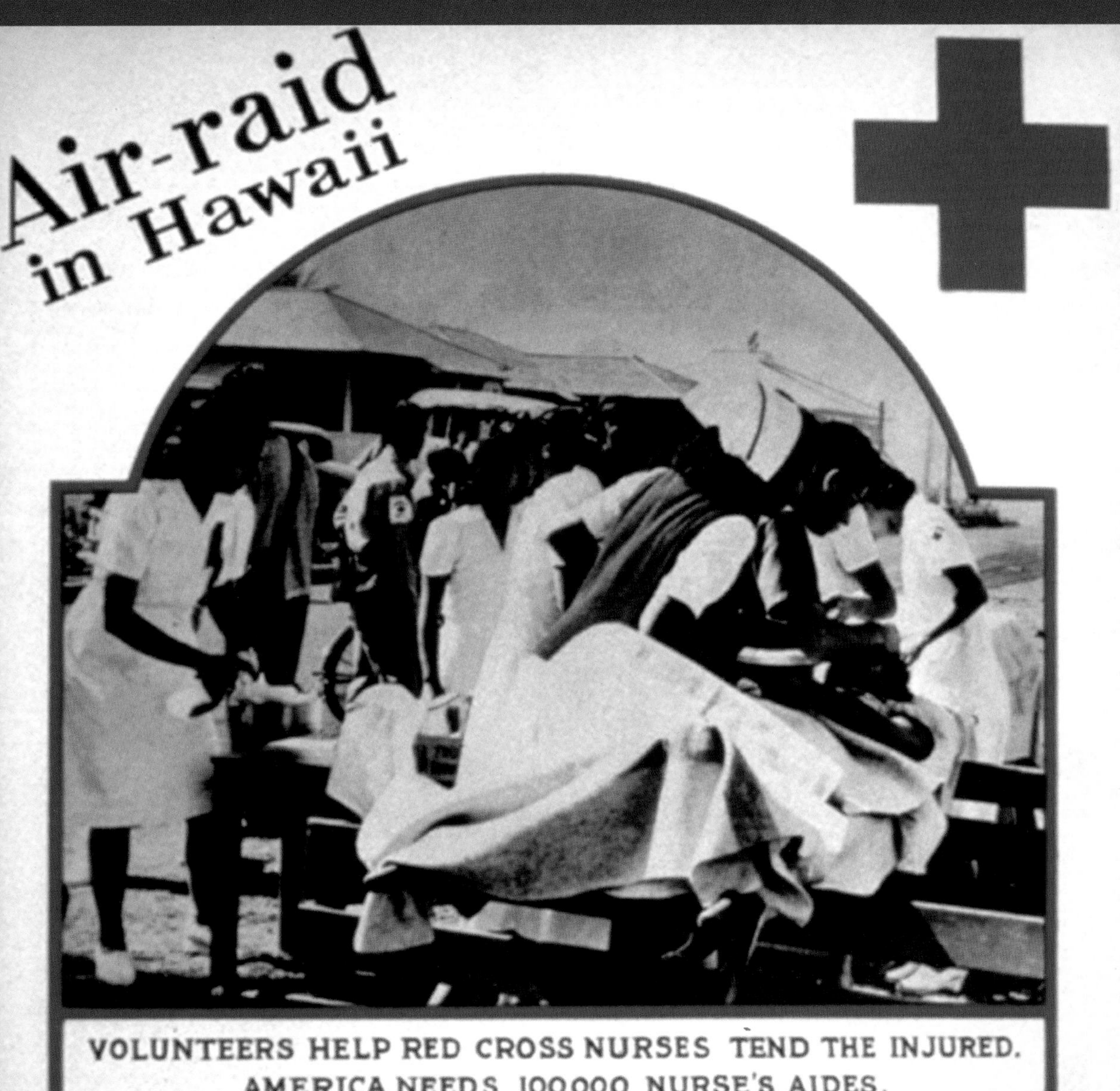

VOLUNTEERS HELP RED CROSS NURSES TEND THE INJURED.
AMERICA NEEDS 100,000 NURSE'S AIDES.

Serve your Country
as a
Red Cross Volunteer
NURSE'S AIDE

APPLY TODAY FOR TRAINING INFORMATION

Stationed Abroad

As the forces of Nazi Germany swept across Belgium, the Netherlands and France in the early summer of 1940, the British Expeditionary Force, originally sent to France in September 1939, looked as if it was going to be trapped in the onrush of conquest. To escape this fate, the British were ordered to head for Dunkirk on the northern French coast, where an eventual total of 338,226 men, including French and Belgian soldiers, were taken across the Channel to Britain by the Royal Navy and a fleet of small private boats.

While the rescue was going on, the soldiers could do little but wait on the Dunkirk beaches, where they were prey to Luftwaffe strafing and bombing runs. On landing back in Britain, one wounded man paid a heartfelt tribute to the British nurses who had tended them:

'I cannot describe what we felt about those girls. Out on that dreadful beach, with the sun pouring down on them, with German planes continually overhead and shells bursting all the time, they worked without stopping for days.

Nurses near the front lines were in ever-present danger from enemy shelling or air raids. They were expected to remain calm for the sake of their patients, reassuring and comforting them.

'Attacked by German planes and even by tanks, with machine-gun bullets whistling all around, I have seen them crawling into the open and dragging wounded men to shelter beneath the sand dunes. I saw one party of [nurses] dressing the wounded who were lying out in the open. A plane began bombing. They just lay down by their patients and continued bandaging. They fetched water and food, helped the wounded to reach the rescue boats, even waded in the water to assist the men.

'Angels is the only word you can use to describe them. I have seen some of them killed as they went about their work. We asked them to go back in the rescue ships, but they refused. Each one said, "We shall go when we have finished this job – there's plenty of time, so don't worry about us!"'

Nurses at a British base hospital in France, 1940. Keeping injured soldiers cheerful and upbeat was an important part of the nursing job and a vital factor in their survival chances.

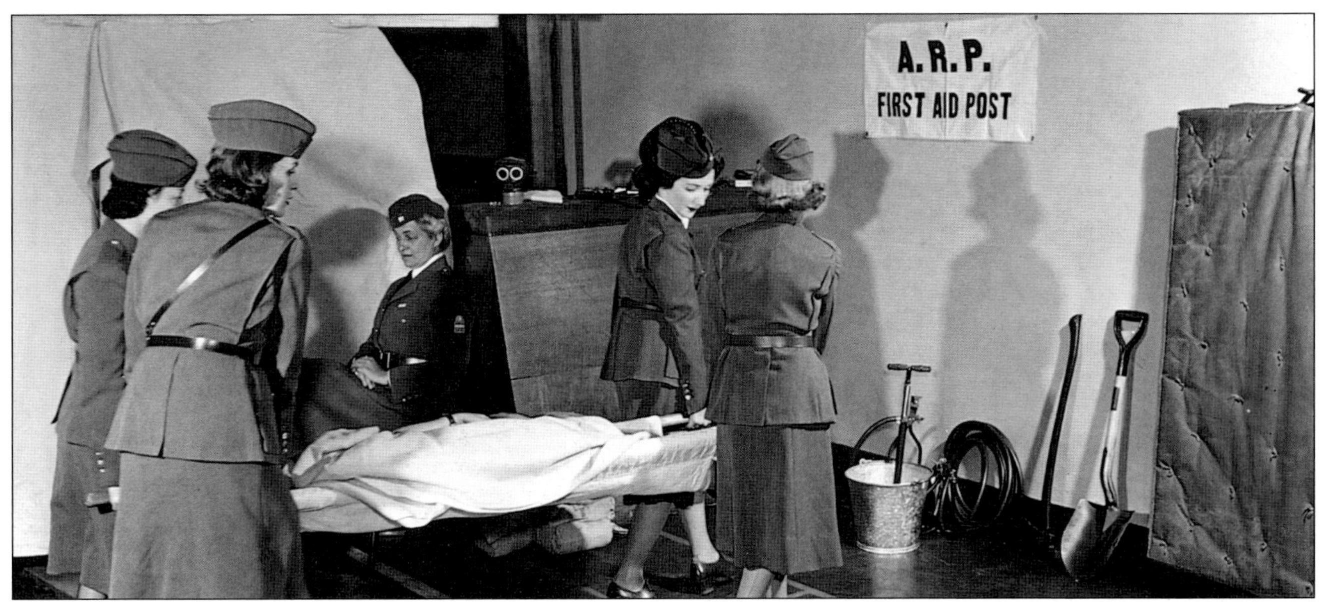

June 1940, so the Nursing Council for National Defense set in motion an urgent scheme to train more. The first of the new recruits, Agnes Rosele, a Red Cross nurse, was transferred from the reserve into the ANC on October 8, 1940, and by the end of the war in 1945 another 4,018 had been drafted.

Europe, of course, had already been at war for two years. Poland was the first Nazi conquest at the end of September 1939, when the Emergency Medical Service of Britain's Ministry of Health enrolled a total of 15,000 trained nurses from various sources: the British Red Cross, the Order of St. John of Jerusalem, the First Aid Nursing Yeomanry (FANY), originally formed in 1901, and the Voluntary Aid Detachments (VAD), formed in 1910. There were also 20,000 trained auxiliaries and another 76,000 women due for training. Retired nurses and those who had left when they got married – a common experience for women workers in pre-war Britain – were called back to duty.

Like the FANY nurses, those who enlisted in the VAD already had a history of war service behind them: 48,000 VADs had been ready for action at the start of the First World War in 1914. A total of 126,000 served during that four-year conflict, of whom 129 were killed. The VADs were a special section among the nurses: formed specifically to fill the inevitable gaps that occurred in war, they were classed as civilians.

Although the U.S. mainland was never attacked, members of the American Women's Voluntary Service were trained to administer first aid in the event of an air raid.

Military-style discipline and obedience to orders were vital in nursing. Sisters in charge of nurses acquired reputations as 'dragons', but it was all in the cause of saving lives.

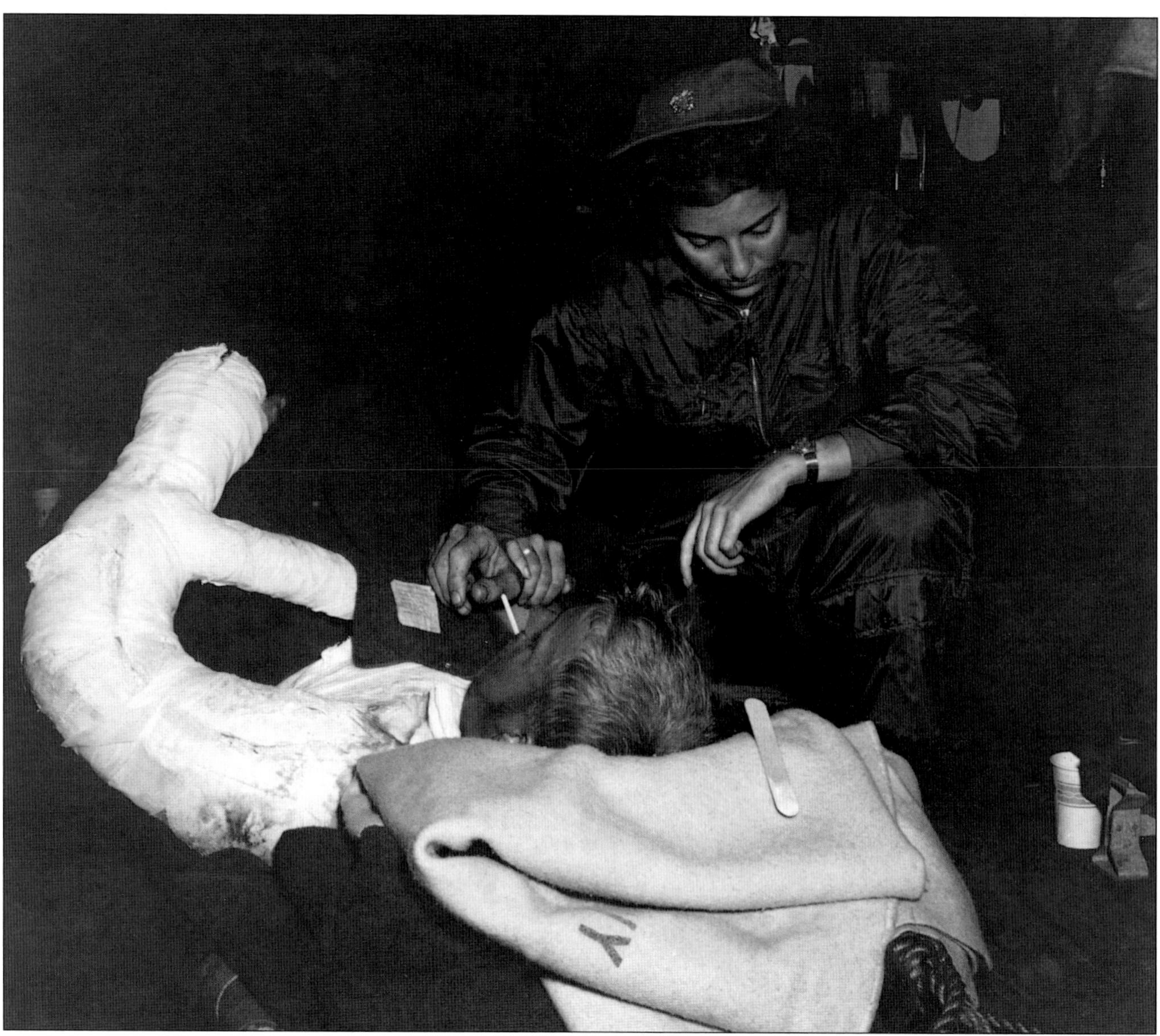

Okinawa, 1945 – one of the bloodiest and most costly battles fought by the Americans in the Pacific. This nurse is tending one of the wounded on board an evacuation aircraft.

NEW CHALLENGES

Like all women involved in World War II, nurses were confronted with challenges that had never existed before. One new task came with the introduction of 'air evac' units into the U.S. Army Nurse Corps: this enabled casualties to be airlifted to safety from the front lines so that they could benefit from advanced medical facilities not immediately available close to the battlefields. Air evac saved many lives that would otherwise have been lost and prevented permanent injury among the wounded. However, it required additional expertise, and on November 30, 1945, the U.S. Army appealed for volunteers aged 21 to 35 with experience as commercial airline hostesses and with nursing qualifications. The benefits of air evac became apparent at once. Out of every 100,000 wounded evacuated in this manner, only five died during the flights.

Air evac illustrated the radical change in the handling of war situations that had developed by the 1940s. This was only part of the story, however.

Fundamental assumptions about the way in which wars were fought underwent a great shift: World War II, unlike the First, proved to be less a matter of static fronts, more a conflict that involved rapid movement from one theatre to the next. In these circumstances, nurses and troops alike had to be prepared to follow the action wherever it led. The experience of Canadian nurses was typical. Aged from 24 to 26 and all commissioned officers, they were the first to go overseas when they followed Canadian Army units to Britain in 1940.

Air evac saved many lives that would otherwise have been lost and prevented permanent injury among the wounded.

THE DIEPPE RAID

The nurses spent the next three years in Britain, a stay not without incident. On August 19, 1942, 5,100 Canadian and 1,000 British commandos staged a raid on Dieppe, a port in northern France. It was meant to be a rehearsal for the full-scale Allied landings which came two years later, but it was a disaster. The Canadians, fighting in seven battalions, suffered appalling losses, with three-quarters of their men killed, wounded or taken prisoner. Half of those who managed to make it back across the Channel to England were wounded, and the Canadian Hospital at Basingstoke, in Hampshire, received an influx of 600 men, many of them requiring surgery. Nurses and doctors worked almost non-stop, performing 98 operations in just under 20 hours.

TO SICILY AND ITALY

About a year later, after the defeat of the German Afrika Korps in North Africa in June 1943, the Allied armies took the war into what Prime Minister Winston Churchill called the 'soft underbelly of Europe', and the nurses went with them. This first Allied intrusion into German-occupied territory occurred in Sicily, which was invaded in July 1943. The first women to venture there were nurses of the

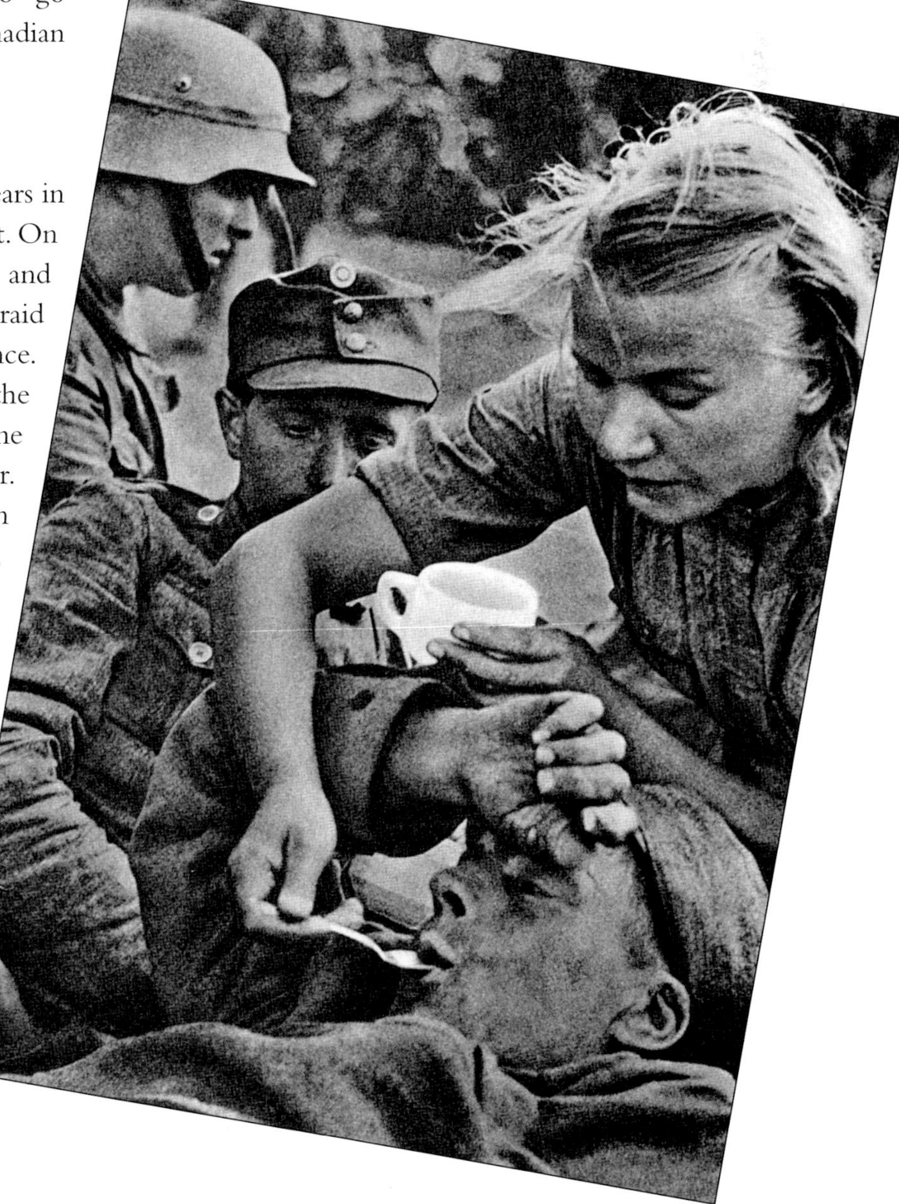

The nurse looking after this wounded German soldier was a volunteer from Finland, which joined in the German invasion of Russia to retrieve territory lost to the Russians in 1940.

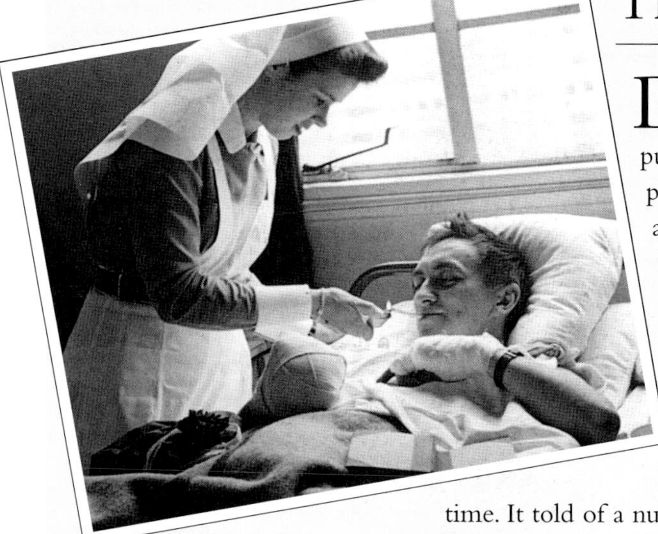

During the war, smoking was considered a form of relaxation, good for the nerves and helpful during convalescence. The men valued their cigarette ration as relief from the stress of battle.

The Public Image of Nursing

Detailed accounts of the work done by nurses during World War II were not all that frequent in British publications. *The War Illustrated,* a contemporary account published in weekly parts, largely confined itself to pictures and the limited wordage of the captions to get across what the nurses were accomplishing. This lack of information was partly due to the attitude of British nurses themselves: they refused to dramatize their work, just got on with the job. As a result, much of what is known today about the work of wartime nurses comes from more recently published reminiscence.

One story, however, became well known in Britain at the time. It told of a nurse, Catherine Selby, who belonged to Queen Alexandra's Imperial Military Nursing Service. Selby spent 12 days in a lifeboat with other survivors after their ship was torpedoed. Every day, Selby held a 'sick parade' and comforted her companions when hysteria threatened to take over. She operated on boils with a safety pin dipped in iodine, and began a routine of daily saltwater bucket baths to allay thirst. It was all done, according to the witnesses, with the competence and quiet assurance of a ward sister in a civilian hospital in peacetime.

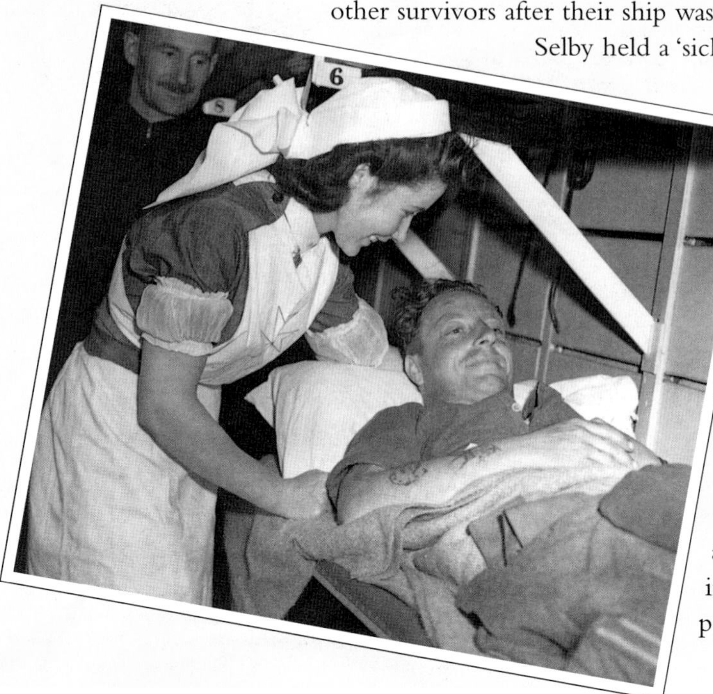

Nurses had to do their job in all sorts of makeshift environments; this nurse cheerfully tends a soldier on board a train heading for a hospital in England in 1944.

No. 1 Canadian General Hospital Corps. Their stay was brief. Sicily fell within a month and the war moved on to mainland Italy, where the Allied invasion troops landed on September 3. One Canadian nursing unit had to run the gauntlet of German dive-bombers when their ship was attacked on the way: although forced to take to the lifeboats, they were fortunately without casualties.

Over the next year, the Allies inched their way up the long leg of Italy. Nurses and medical units followed, setting up casualty clearing stations as they went. Almost all of these stations were makeshift affairs, built under canvas. It was extremely perilous work. Italy is set out in a series of mountains and valleys: it was terrain full of vantage points for defenders to exploit, and the German

Racial segregation made it unacceptable for black nurses to tend white patients. Consequently, only 479 black nurses served in the Army Nurse Corps out of a total of 50,000. This group were the first black nurses to arrive in England in 1944.

defence was extremely skilful.

This meant that Canadian nurses and other medical staff were frequently within range of the German guns, and the facilities they set up to receive and treat the wounded were always at risk. Where the fighting was particularly fierce, the nurses were caring for hundreds of patients at a time. This is what happened in the Ortona salient south of Rome towards the end of 1943. There the No. 4 Casualty Clearing Station received over 2,000 patients, 760 of them requiring surgery.

ANZIO 1944

The U.S. Army Nurse Corps, also present with the Allied armies in Italy, had to handle an even more appalling casualty rate in the Anzio campaign of 1944. The landings by British and American troops at this small port 30 miles (48 kilometres) south of Rome on January 22 were intended to relieve the pressure on the forces attempting to capture Montecassino about 60 miles (100 kilometres) to the east. The landings also posed a threat to Rome, which was still in German hands at the time.

Easier said than done. The assault force at Anzio was small, it was cut off from other Allied troops, and the actual landing beach proved to be an easy target for the German defenders. Nevertheless, the Allies managed to hold Anzio for four months, during which time 23,850 American and 9,203 British wounded had to be evacuated.

The task of caring for the sick and wounded at Anzio was immense: the nurses handled 33,128 patients, including 10,809 battle casualties. Some became casualties themselves. Three American nurses – Lieutenant Blanche Saiman, First Lieutenant Carrie Sheetz and Lieutenant Marjorie

During the D-Day invasion of 1944, some British citizens were injured on home soil by German coastal gunfire. This nurse is shown to a driver at a Ministry of Health emergency hospital in England.

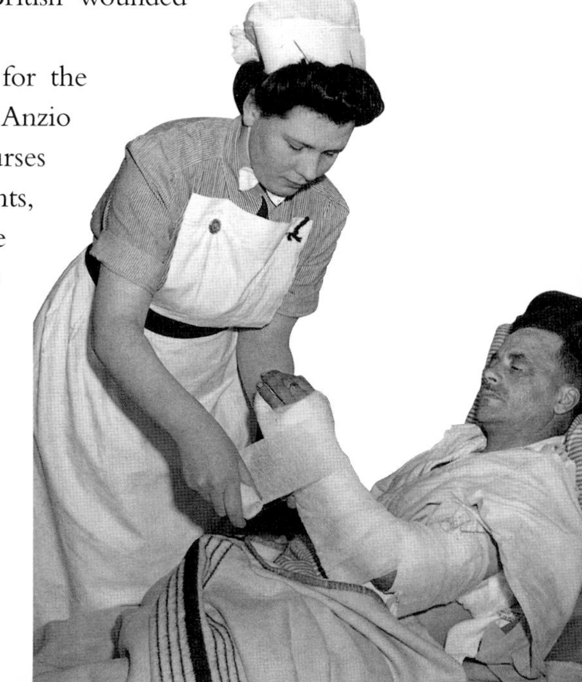

There were few more arduous battlefields than Burma. These nurses had to put in hard training – including 8 mile (13km) hikes through jungle country carrying heaving packs – before taking up their assignments.

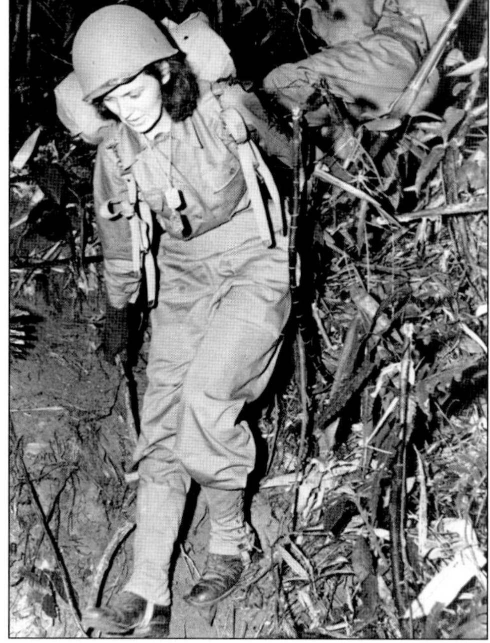

Morrow – were killed on February 7, 1944 in the bombing of Evac Hospital. Two more nurses died shortly afterwards: Lieutenant Gertrude Spelbourg and Lieutenant La Verne Farquah died when the Germans shelled the 33rd Field Hospital. They were among 201 U.S. Army nurses killed during the war.

Some 200 U.S. Army nurses served in the Anzio campaign, and two of them became the first women to receive the Silver Star for meritorious duty. They were among 1,600 Army nurses awarded Distinguished Service Medals, Silver Stars, Distinguished Flying Crosses, Soldier's Medals, Bronze Stars, Air Medals, Legions of Merit, Commendation Medals and Purple Hearts during World War II.

The task of caring for the sick and the wounded at Anzio was immense: the nurses handled 33,128 patients, including 10,809 battle casualties.

THE LONGEST SLOG

The campaign in Italy was arguably the longest and most testing slog in the whole of World War II: the Allied forces had to bludgeon their way forward at virtually every step. Their task was made even more difficult by the demands of the D-Day landings of 1944.

Allied nurses were among the mass of personnel transferred to northern France in order to bolster the invasion and the push towards Germany that followed. Within a few days of the landings, the first nurses arrived in Normandy, followed on June 19 by the first two Canadian nurses, who were serving with No. 2 Royal Canadian Air Force Mobile Field Hospital. Four casualty clearing stations were set up in the area around Caen, which saw fighting so savage and costly that it called to mind the trench warfare of 1914–1918. From Caen, the nurses followed the fighting into Belgium and the Netherlands, and in four weeks had to deal with nearly 4,000 casualties. The medical facilities around Antwerp held special perils: this Belgian port, vital to Allied supply lines, was being

These nurses were no strangers to the discomforts of military life; seen here in France, they had three years' service behind them, including experience of the harsh deserts of Egypt.

Nursing the Wounded in China

When Agnes Smedley, an American nurse, found herself in China in 1941, she was a comparative newcomer to the business of war. For the Chinese, however, the war had begun on July 7, 1937, when the Japanese, advancing out of Manchuria, which they had annexed six years earlier, attacked the capital, Beijing. From then on, Chinese nurses were an integral part of their country's war effort. Some of them belonged to the American Baptist Surgical Unit in China. Others were members of the 'New Life' organization, which supplied nurses to the fighting areas.

China was a somewhat forgotten battlefield: this American poster elicited desperately needed funds to improve medical services that were primitive or sometimes even non-existent.

Primitive Conditions

Arriving on horseback at the Chinese defence line in North Hupeh province in central China, Smedley discovered that nurses and all other medical staff had to work under very primitive conditions.

'We halted at a mud hut in a narrow valley which one of the armies was using as its first dressing station to care for the wounded,' Smedley told a British newspaper, *The Manchester Guardian*. 'There was but one door to the hut. Inside, on the earthen floor, lay a number of wounded men in a row: in the fading light their dark forms were like a part of the mud walls and the earth floor beneath them. On a rude table near the door stood a half dozen half-filled bottles, a pair of black native scissors, a few rolled bandages and some small squares of gauze.

'From a dusty rafter hung a big wad of unwashed cotton. An army dresser sometimes reached up, took a bit of the cotton, dipped it in a small bowl of liquid and washed the wound of one of the men lying on the floor. Then, he took a bit of gauze and a bandage and bound the wound. He did not wash off the blood that had caked on the man's neck and face.'

From Another World

The Chinese treated Smedley as if she were a creature from another world – which, in a way, she was. When a troop of soldiers arrived to rest briefly at the hut, their commander ordered the men to salute her, and told them, 'This is a foreign friend. She works for our wounded.'

Perhaps overawed by their 'foreign friend', the troops saluted Smedley again when ordered, then filed out of the hut on their way back to the battlefield.

'[They] marched past me, each one turning his face to me,' Smedley recounted. 'They were like shadows as they passed and I reached out to touch them. Then, they were all gone, and I stood until their figures blended with the darkness. Somewhere in the hills a shell burst and machine guns hammered.'

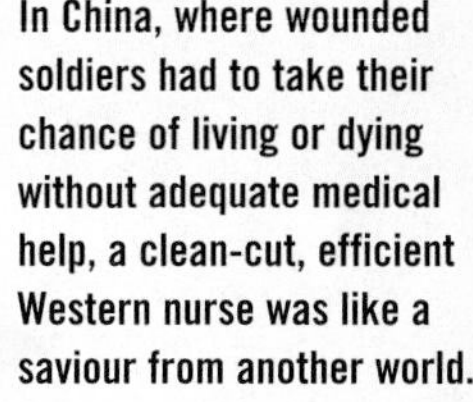
In China, where wounded soldiers had to take their chance of living or dying without adequate medical help, a clean-cut, efficient Western nurse was like a saviour from another world.

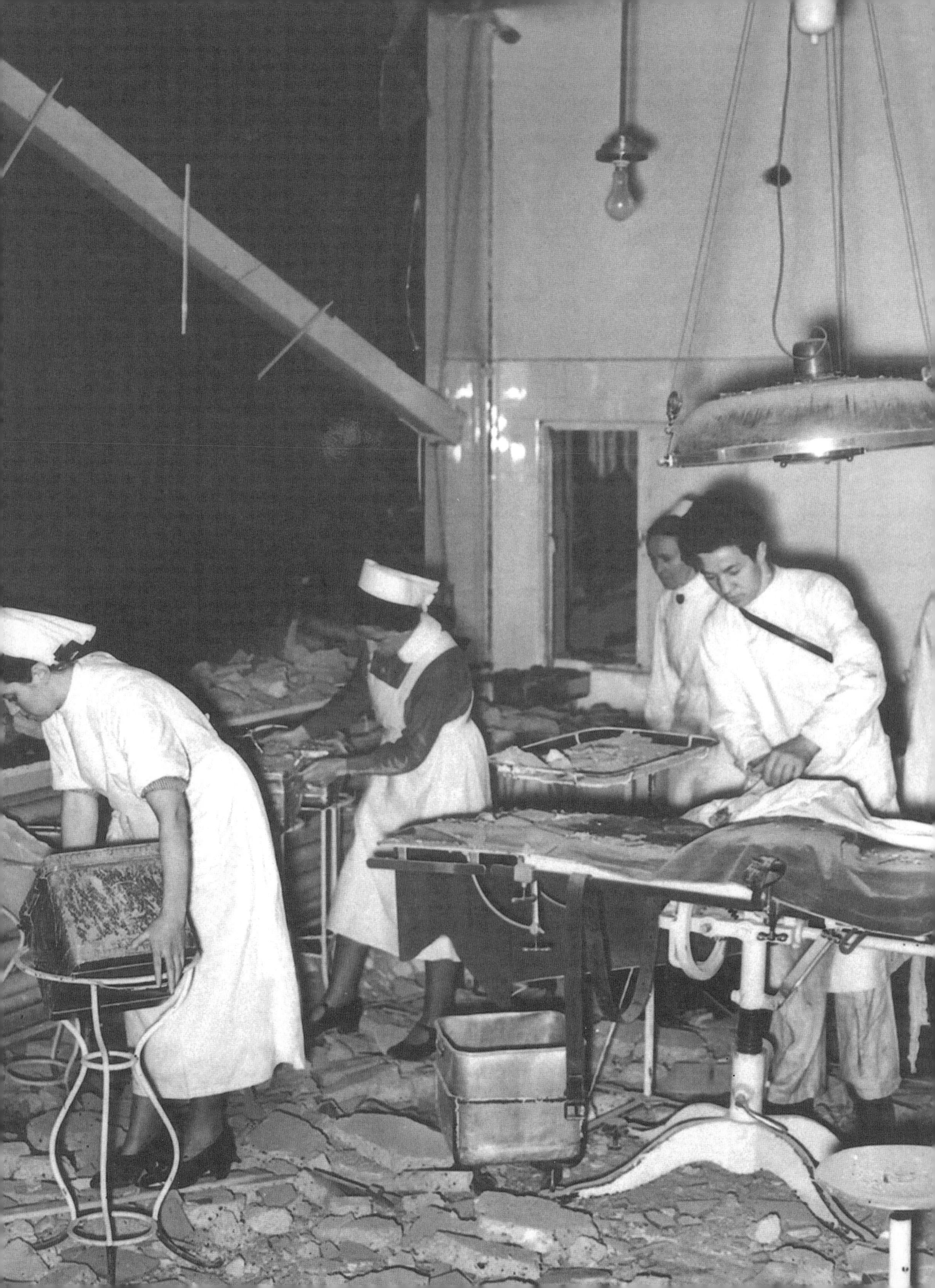

hammered by German V2 rockets which fell out of the sky without warning.

Britain itself was also a prime target for the V2s and their predecessors, the V1 flying bombs. But, although the threat from these terrifying weapons was a new experience, the results were an old story for the British nurses stationed at hospitals in the target areas of southeast England.

Emergency shelters were set up, staffed by nurses who often had to walk through the streets in the blackout while the raids were still going on.

BRITAIN UNDER FIRE

The Blitz of 1940 and 1941, which saw intensive raids on British cities like London, Birmingham, Liverpool and Coventry, had already killed and injured 94,000 men, women and children. For the survivors, emergency shelters were set up, staffed by nurses who often had to walk through streets in the blackout while the raids were still going on. Moira MacLeod, a British Red Cross nurse, was showered by bits of falling metal as she made her way through the streets of London. About two years later, in early 1944, she was on duty as a State Registered Nurse at the capital's North Middlesex Hospital when it was hit by a stick (cluster) of bombs from a German dive-bomber.

'I was on night duty as a theatre nurse and was on my meal break at the time. I heard a plane dive and threw myself and a junior nurse to the floor. There was an almighty bang.... All the lights were out, but the ward was on fire.... I ran outside, trying to get back to the theatre, and tripped and fell heavily because of the debris on the path.'

McLeod encountered a disorientated male patient wandering about in a daze.

The picture opposite shows the Robert Koch Hospital in Berlin after it was hit by an RAF incendiary bomb on October 8, 1940, causing critical damage to its operating theatre.

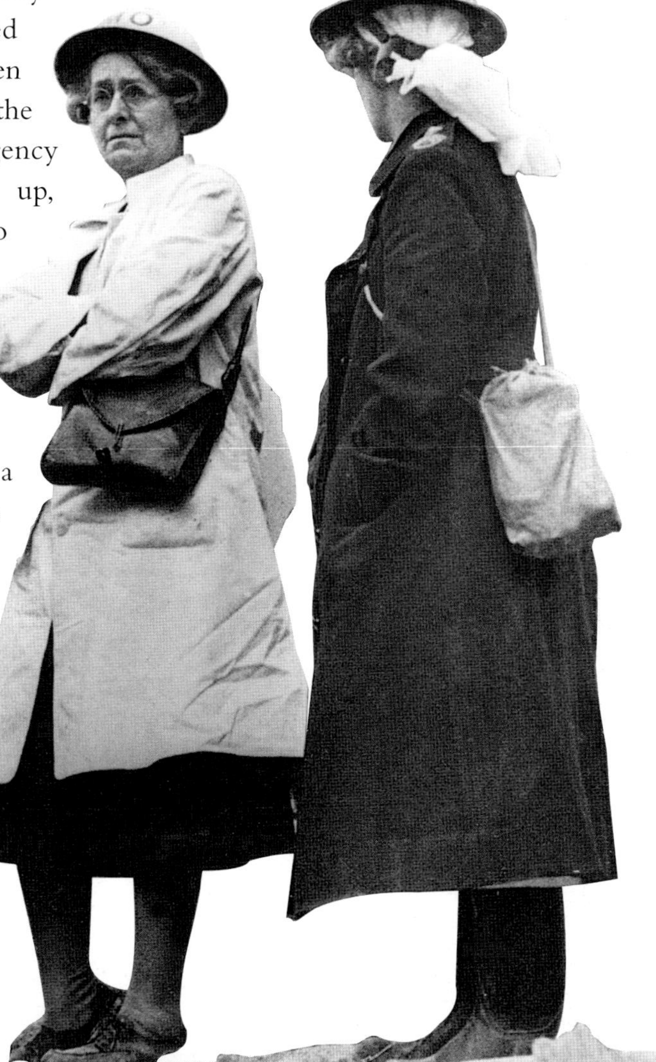

These wardens are pictured surveying air-raid devastation, an all-too common sight in London during the Blitz in 1941.

A Terrible Secret

The German nursing service kept a terrible secret during World War II: more than 100,000 patients with incurable physical or mental disabilities were killed by lethal injection or starvation under the Nazi Euthanasia Programme run by the Nazi SS and designed to dispose of 'useless eaters'. Some of the nurses involved cooperated willingly, others with reluctance: the few who refused risked official retribution. In 1946–1947, 23 SS physicians who were chiefly responsible for the Programme, among other medical perversions, were put on trial; seven were sentenced to death and hanged.

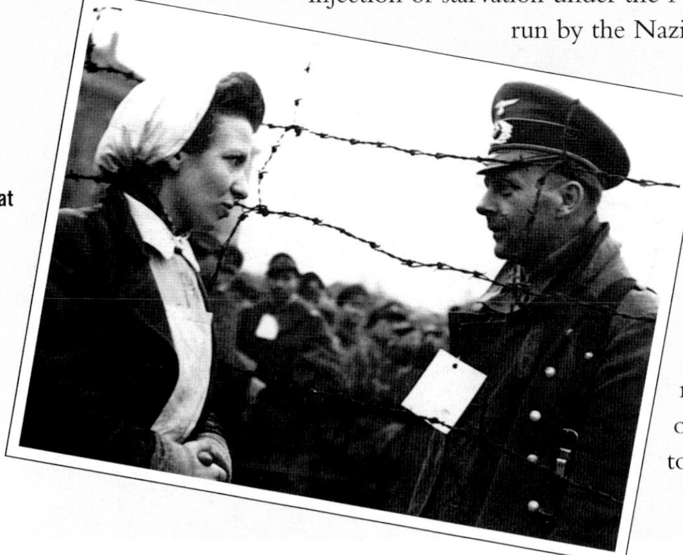

This German officer and his wife, a nurse, both of them prisoners of war, were pictured talking across the barbed-wire fence that separated their enclosures at a holding camp.

'He had come from the top floor ward and together we went up the stairs, scrambling over debris to find a part of the top ward sheared off, the roof gone and all the windows blown out.'

McLeod was a curious sight – bleeding from superficial scratches, blackened by debris and dust, her uniform torn, her nurse's cap nowhere to be seen. At least she was unhurt, unlike one student nurse who was very badly injured.

'Our staff stood ready as she was briefly examined to see if she needed surgery,' MacLeod recalled, 'but before she could be helped, she died. That was a terrible moment. We clung to each other and wept.... '

British nurses were required to demonstrate gas mask drill to children. There were fears, fortunately unfounded, that the Germans would use gas in World War II, as they had in 1914–18.

These black U.S. Nurse Corps members were pictured waiting to disembark at Greenock, Scotland. In June 1944, 63 black nurses went to the 168th Station Hospital in England to tend German prisoners of war.

WOMEN ARE NOT PERSONS

In the crisis that had faced Britain four years earlier, all qualified nurses – and many who had not yet reached that stage – were eagerly enlisted into the war effort. Moira MacLeod had been only 18, too young to assume full nursing duties, when she was 'blooded' in the Blitz of 1940 and 1941. By age 22 in 1944, she had become a seasoned campaigner in the business of rescuing and tending casualties and confronting the physical dangers of war. In the United States, by contrast, nurses were not so easily or speedily accepted for war duties. Acceptance was never total, even for the highest-ranked nurse in U.S. Army service, Major Julia Flikke. Flikke was Superintendent of the Army Nurse Corps when, in 1942, she was given a temporary rank as a colonel. Flikke's assistant, Florence Blanchfield, received another temporary rank, as a lieutenant-colonel. Although both of them were entitled to wear insignia indicating their rank, they did not receive the pay and benefits that went with it. This situation was justified by the Comptroller General, who judged that 'women [were] not persons' under the laws that governed pay in the military.

This statement came despite the fact that Flikke and Blanchfield belonged to a long tradition of nursing service with the armies of the United States. American nurses had already proven themselves as far back as the Revolutionary War of 1775–1783, and

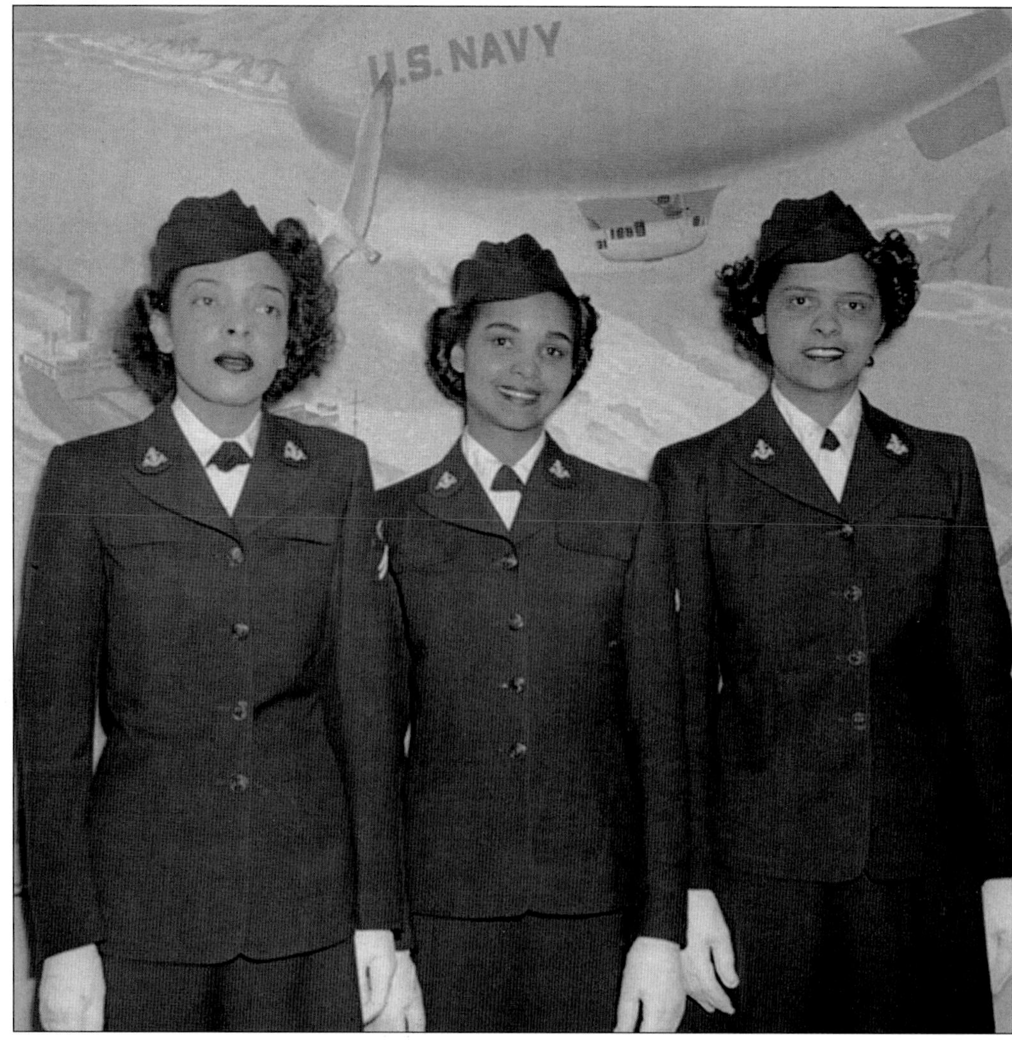

These three hospital apprentices (Second Class) were the first black WAVES to be admitted for training at the Hospital Corps School at the National Naval Medical Center in Bethesda, Maryland.

later served in the Spanish–American War of 1898 and the First World War. Clara Barton, founder of the American Red Cross, was a Civil War heroine. Nevertheless, despite these historical precedents, the recruitment of nurses in World War II had to surmount a reluctance to allow women to participate in war at all.

BREAKING FREE OF LIMITS

Other problems included the Nurse Corps' own reluctance to accept married women and women over the age of 45, as well as limitations on the number of blacks allowed into the nursing service. In January 1941, when the U.S. Army Nurse Corps was officially opened to black women, the limit was set at 56. Once the United States entered the war, this miserly quota became untenable, but even so, another two years went by before Congress passed a Nurse Training Bill barring racial discrimination. Subsequently, 2,000 black women enrolled in the Cadet Nurse Corps.

The black quota was finally abolished by the U.S. Army in July 1944, but the Navy failed to follow suit until January 1945. The first black commissioned U.S. Navy nurse, Phyllis Daley, received official sanction on March 9, by which time Nazi Germany was well on its way

Women As Doctors in the War

Equality in the medical profession was non-existent in World War II; resistance to the recruitment of women as doctors was intense despite the increasingly urgent need for medical staff.

Nurses' struggle for acceptance in World War II was difficult enough, but the women who sought to serve as doctors faced even greater obstacles. Prejudice against them was so ingrained that even the desperate and growing need of the military for their services could not entirely break it down.

Eventually, women doctors received credentials for much the same reason as the nurses: there was a shortage of male doctors, so women were called in to fill the gap. It was April 16, 1943 before President Roosevelt signed a bill allowing women to practise as doctors in the military, and it was long overdue. A great deal of time had been wasted on deciding whether or not women doctors were a practical proposition in war, and many of those who might have qualified lost patience and committed themselves to other war work. Ultimately, fewer than 100 women doctors enlisted.

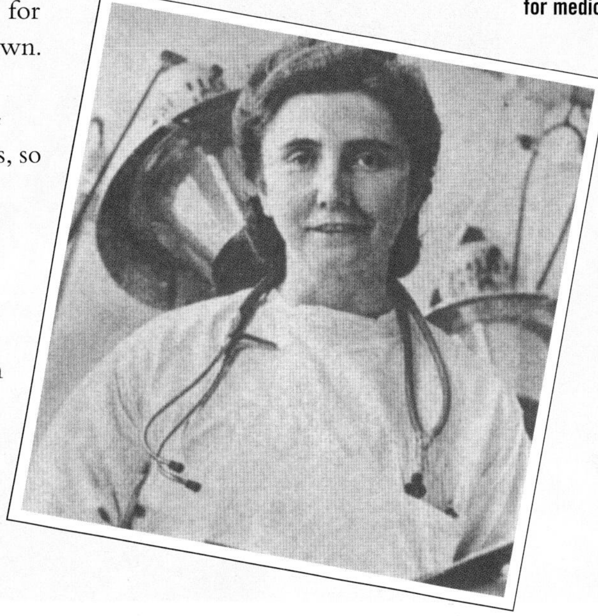

to defeat in Europe and victory over Japan was only five months away. Despite these successes in promoting black women, only about 500 of them saw service during the war, either at home or overseas.

The existence of quotas and bias, racial or otherwise, ran counter to the escalating needs of the war: the military was all but overwhelmed by the demand for nurses. Men were never encouraged to enlist as nurses at any time during the hostilities, which left women as the only feasible pool of recruits. But their future in the fighting forces of the United States, although settled by default, had become a future nonetheless.

The recruitment of nurses in World War II had to surmount several obstacles. One of these, inevitably, was reluctance to allow women to participate in the war at all.

TOUGHEST OF THE TOUGH

Even after the principle of sending nurses to the fighting fronts had been established, only the toughest of the tough were allowed to qualify, and they needed to survive one of the most arduous training courses ever inflicted on potential recruits. The course lasted four weeks – and it was four weeks of unmitigated effort which took the women to the very edge of endurance. To survive, they had to absorb a vast amount of new knowledge. They had to become familiar with the techniques of camouflage. They had to learn how to chlorinate water and how to identify poison gas and toxic chemicals.

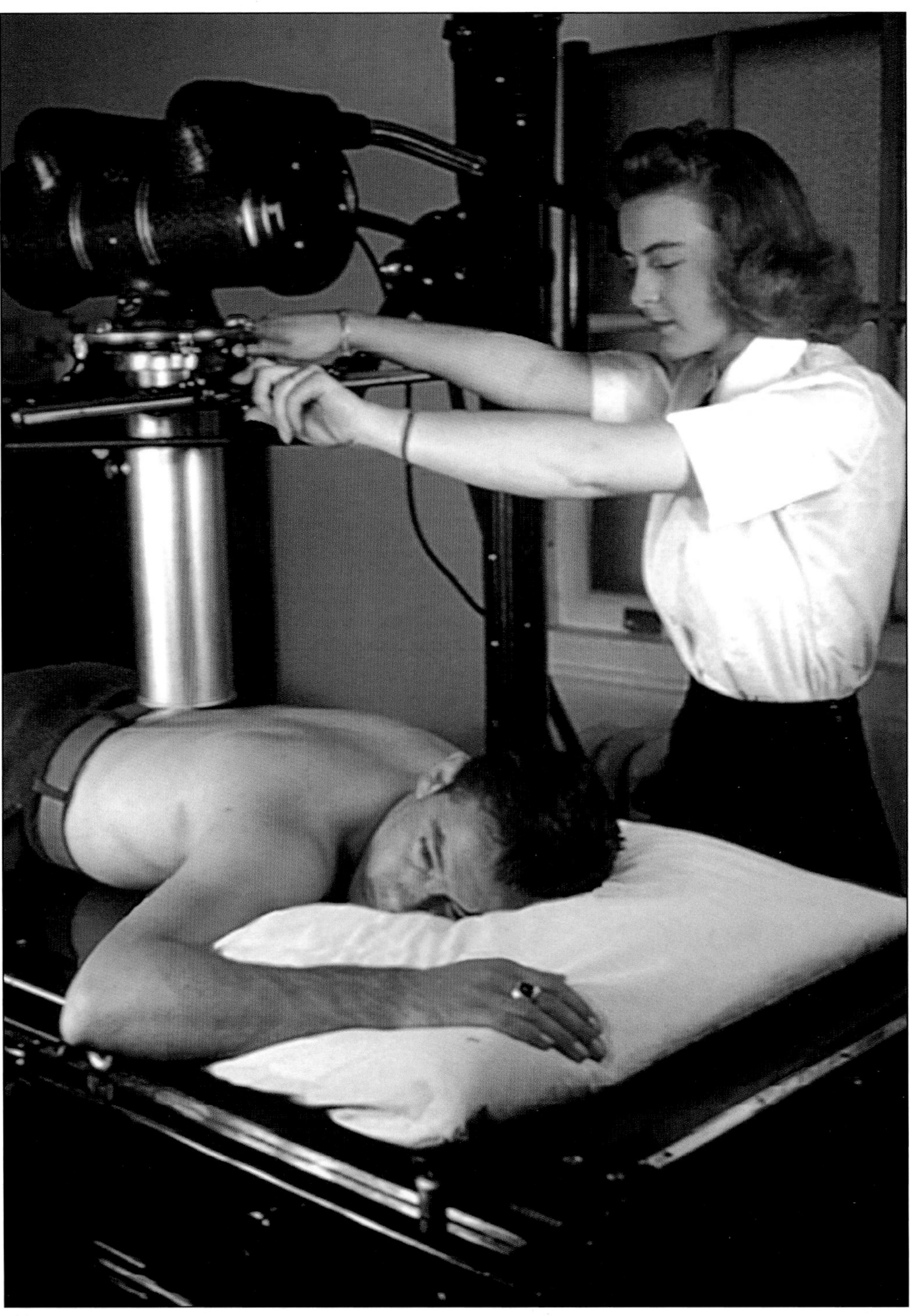

The war saw tremendous advances in medicine, with the development of penicillin for treating wounds, the mass collection of blood for transfusions, and the use of radiography and other machines.

World War II encompassed almost every type of climate and terrain the earth had to offer, including scorching deserts where daytime temperatures rose to 120°F (49°C). To accustom them to this exhausting environment, nurses were sent out to hike 20 miles (32 kilometres) through the desert, wearing a four-pound (1.8-kilogram) steel helmet and combat boots and carrying a 30-pound (13.6-kilogram) mess kit and gas mask on their backs. The nurses pitched tents, dug foxholes, put out fires caused by incendiaries. They had to go through a tear gas chamber and crawl flat on their bellies for 75 yards (69 metres) across land gouged with trenches and spiked with barbed wire while charges of dynamite were exploded around them and machine-gun bullets were fired over their heads.

Yet even these punishing experiences could not begin to replicate the conditions the U.S. Army Nurse Corps would encounter when, at last, the élite among them came face to face with real action. In battle areas where medical supplies were limited, nurses had to wash bandages and use them again. Where there were no stretchers, they had to rig up pairs of trousers to carry the wounded. When blood supplies for transfusions ran low, they had to give their own to make up the shortfall.

When blood supplies for transfusions ran low, nurses had to give their own to make up the shortfall.

GUAM AND THE PHILIPPINES 1941

The island of Guam in the western Pacific was raided by Japanese bombers only three hours after Pearl Harbor, and this attack was the first of a series. After three days' pounding, the American garrison was forced to surrender. Five Navy nurses were among the prisoners. Despite their capture, they continued their work at the U.S. Naval Hospital until they were moved to Japan and held for three months in Zentsuji Prison on Shikoku Island. After such misadventures, these nurses got lucky: they were released into the care of the diplomatic corps in the neutral territory

(continued on page 112)

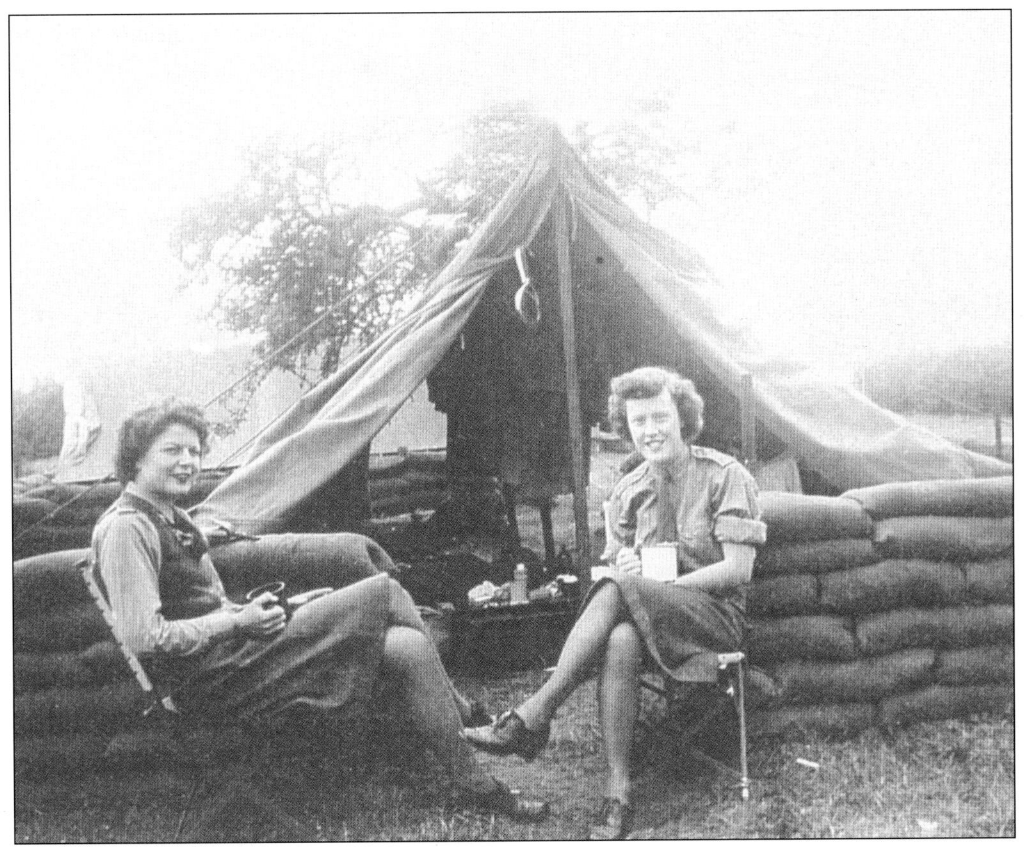

The accommodation provided for nurses close to the front line was far from luxurious, despite the smiles of these Canadian nurses who were camped near Caen in northern France in 1944.

Massacre on Banka Island

Vivian Bullwinkel was among 140 Australian nurses who were in Singapore when the proximity of the Japanese, advancing through the jungles to the north, made quick evacuation necessary. The nurses were taken off in three vessels, and Bullwinkel was among the 65 who boarded the SS *Vyner Brooke*. It was the start of the most dramatic adventure of their lives, an episode that would leave Bullwinkel the only survivor of a brutal massacre.

Crammed with 265 civilians in a vessel designed for only 12 passengers, and short of food and water, the *Vyner Brooke* sailed off into the darkness on February 12, 1942 as fires burned behind them along the entire front of Singapore. The *Vyner Brooke's* captain, disorientated, sailed straight into a minefield, where he was forced to halt until daybreak.

Eluding the Enemy

Although Singapore would not surrender for another three days, the Japanese were uncomfortably close, and once clear of the minefield, the captain decided to hide his vessel among the small outlying islands. After nightfall on February 13, the *Vyner Brooke* made a dash for freedom, at last reaching the Banka Strait near the southeast coast of Sumatra in the Dutch East Indies.

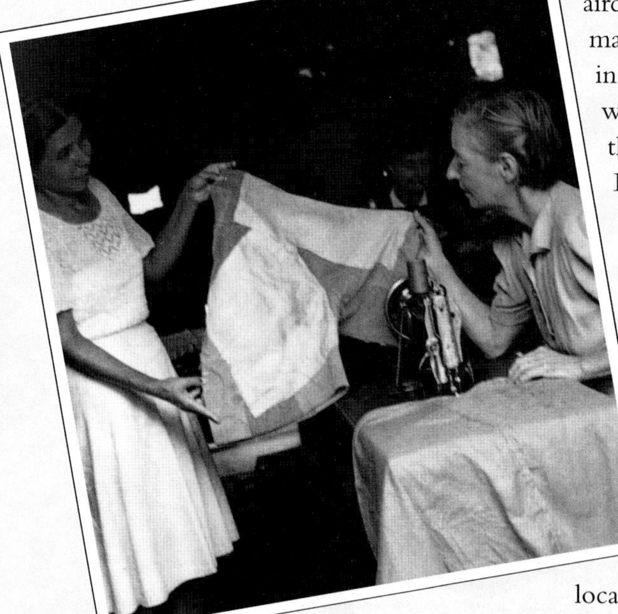

Prisoners in Singapore were segregated, but the men were allowed to send their ripped and worn clothes to the women's camp to be patched.

Almost at once, the vessel was spotted by Japanese aircraft, which bombed and strafed the ship with machine-gun fire, scoring three direct hits. The ship sank in only 15 minutes. The Japanese returned to strafe men, women, children – and nurses – as they floundered in the water. Some of them managed to get ashore on Banka, including Bullwinkel, who made the journey clinging to the side of a lifeboat.

By the time the survivors of the *Vyner Brooke* were gathered on Radji Beach, they numbered fewer than 66 civilians and 22 Australian nurses. The other nurses were nowhere to be seen.

On the Beach

Before long, British soldiers adrift in a lifeboat from another sunken ship came ashore on the beach, swelling the numbers to almost 100.

Hungry, thirsty and desperate, and spurned by local villagers too terrified of the Japanese to help them, some decided to give themselves up. They walked up off the beach and went in search of soldiers to whom they could surrender.

The rest remained where they were until the Japanese arrived. The Japanese took the men away out of sight to a nearby headland and killed them, then returned to the beach to clean the blood off their rifles and bayonets. There were 23 women on the beach – the nurses plus an elderly woman who had wanted to remain with her husband. The Japanese began pushing the women toward the edge of the sea. Opening fire, they shot them in the back.

'They just swept up and down the line and the girls fell one after the other,'

Bullwinkel later revealed. Bullwinkel herself was hit by a bullet above her left hip, and the force of it threw her into the surf. She floated, half-conscious, until the current carried her close to the shore and she managed to struggle onto the beach. She was alone. 'I looked around and there was no sign of anybody…there was nothing. Just me,' she said.

Hiding in the Jungle

After a while Bullwinkel managed to reach the jungle behind the beach, and from there she saw the Japanese returning. Bullwinkel hid among the trees until they had gone. There she noticed a spring of fresh water nearby and was making for it when she heard an English voice asking, 'Where have you been, nurse?' Private Patrick Kingsley, a British soldier, had somehow managed to escape the massacre on the headland.

Together, Kingsley and Bullwinkel hid in the jungle for 12 days. Both were injured, and although Bullwinkel looked after the soldier as best she could and managed to persuade local villagers to give her food, their situation was clearly hopeless. Once again, the only prospect was for them to surrender to the Japanese. They gave themselves up on February 28 and were taken to a makeshift prisoner-of-war camp. There, Bullwinkel was reunited with 31 other Australian nurses who had managed to survive the sinking of the *Vyner Brooke*. Sadly, soon after her arrival, she learned that Kingsley had died of his wounds.

The Survivors

After three and a half years in Japanese captivity, Vivian Bullwinkel returned home to Australia, one of only 24 nurses from the *Vyner Brooke* to survive to the end of the war. Apart from the 21 slaughtered in the Banka massacre, 12 were believed drowned when the *Vyner Brooke* sank and eight died in POW camps.

In 1992, Vivian Bullwinkel returned to Banka Island with some of the other survivors. Standing on Radji Beach, they unveiled a shrine dedicated to the 41 nurses from the *Vyner Brooke* who never returned home.

Soldiers captured by the Japanese were aware of events like the massacre on Banka Island. They could expect brutal treatment as prisoners of war.

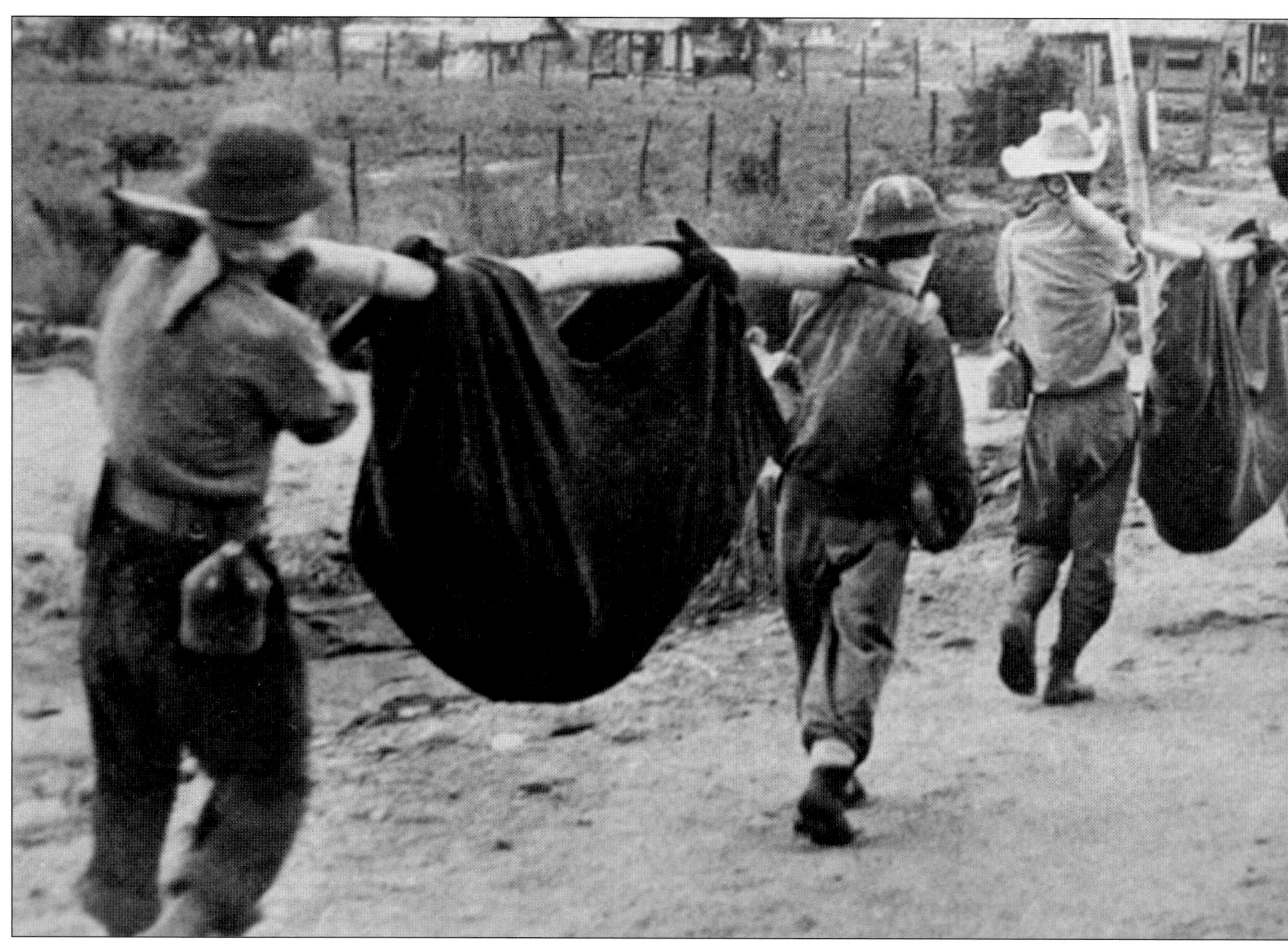

of Mozambique, Portuguese East Africa, in August 1942.

Their counterparts in the Philippine Islands were not so fortunate. Nurses and their patients in the island capital, Manila, soon learned what it meant to be under Japanese attack as, despite the circumstances, they celebrated Christmas in 1941. General Douglas MacArthur, Supreme Commander, Southwest Pacific Area, wanted to declare Manila an open city to save it from destruction, but the Japanese had other ideas.

'The Filipinos have named this day well – Black Christmas,' commented one nurse, Tressa Cates. 'Apparently, the Japanese were not guided by international law and ethics. "Open city" meant nothing to them. They raided the city four times [on Christmas Eve] and six times [on Christmas Day]. The patients in my ward ate their Christmas dinner under their beds when the bombs started to drop all around us.'

ORDER TO RETREAT

Already, on Christmas Eve, General MacArthur had given the order for his forces to withdraw to Bataan, a peninsula on the west side of Manila Bay. Conditions there were appalling. The sick and wounded had to be nursed in

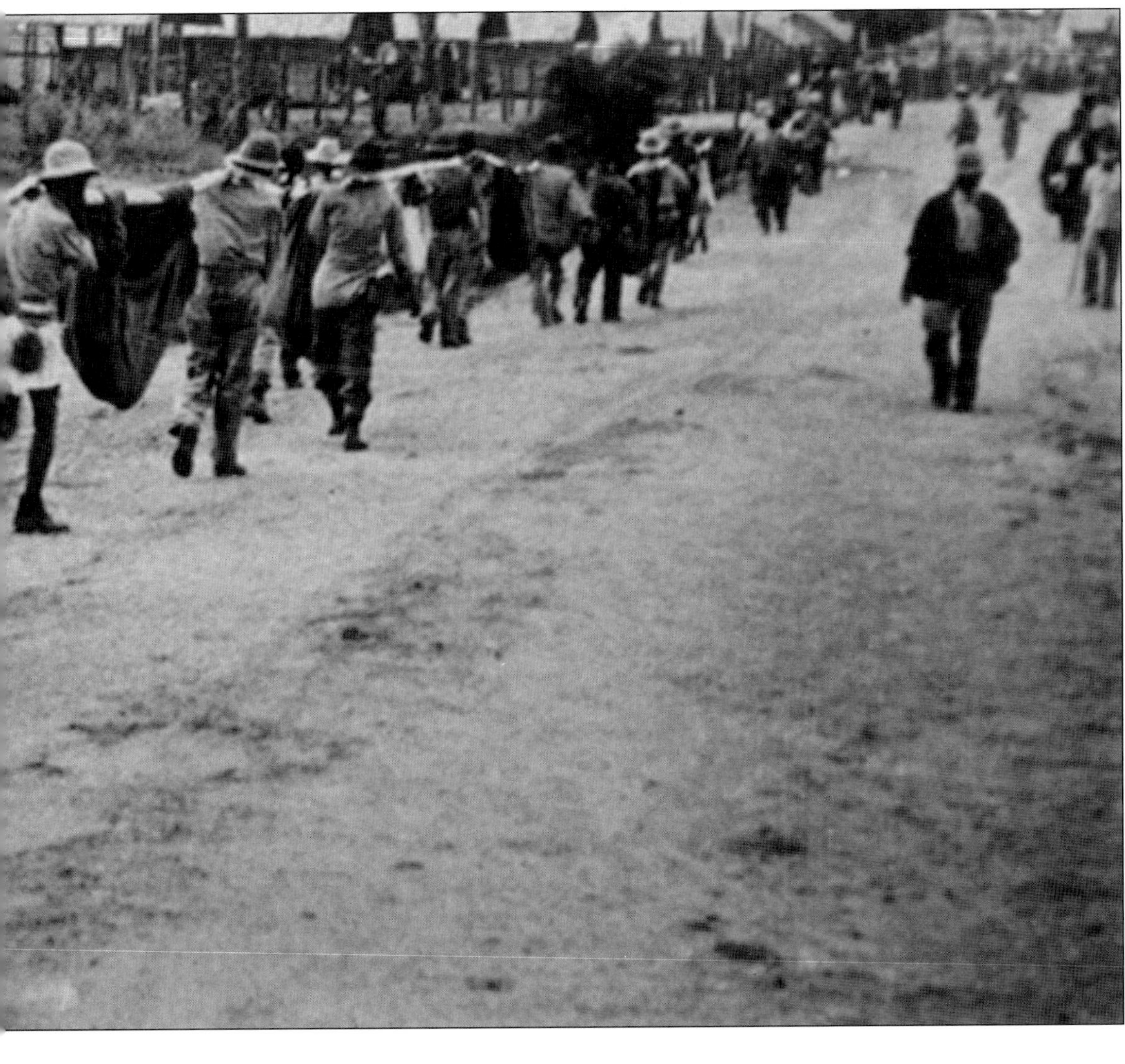

This Japanese photograph of American prisoners in the Philippines carrying exhausted comrades shows the primitive conditions nurses and doctors had to face when treating patients on the Asian fighting fronts.

makeshift canvas tents in the jungle. There were upwards of 9,000 patients to be tended, 2,000 in Hospital 1 and another 7,000 in Hospital 2. Before long, medicine, food and water ran low. Dysentery was rife. So was malnutrition, as both patients and medical staff tried to subsist on a diet reduced from 2,000 calories a day in February 1942 to 1,000 in March.

'The days and nights were an endless nightmare until it seemed we couldn't stand it any longer,' wrote one nurse, Enid Hatchitt. 'Patients came in by the hundreds and the doctors and nurses worked continuously under tents amid flies and heat and dust.'

'The days and nights were an endless nightmare until it seemed we couldn't stand it any longer. Patients came in by the hundreds and the doctors and nurses worked continuously amid flies and heat and dust.'

ABANDONING BATAAN

General MacArthur had hoped to hold out in Bataan until May, but the hope proved futile. On April 8, 1942, he was obliged to issue

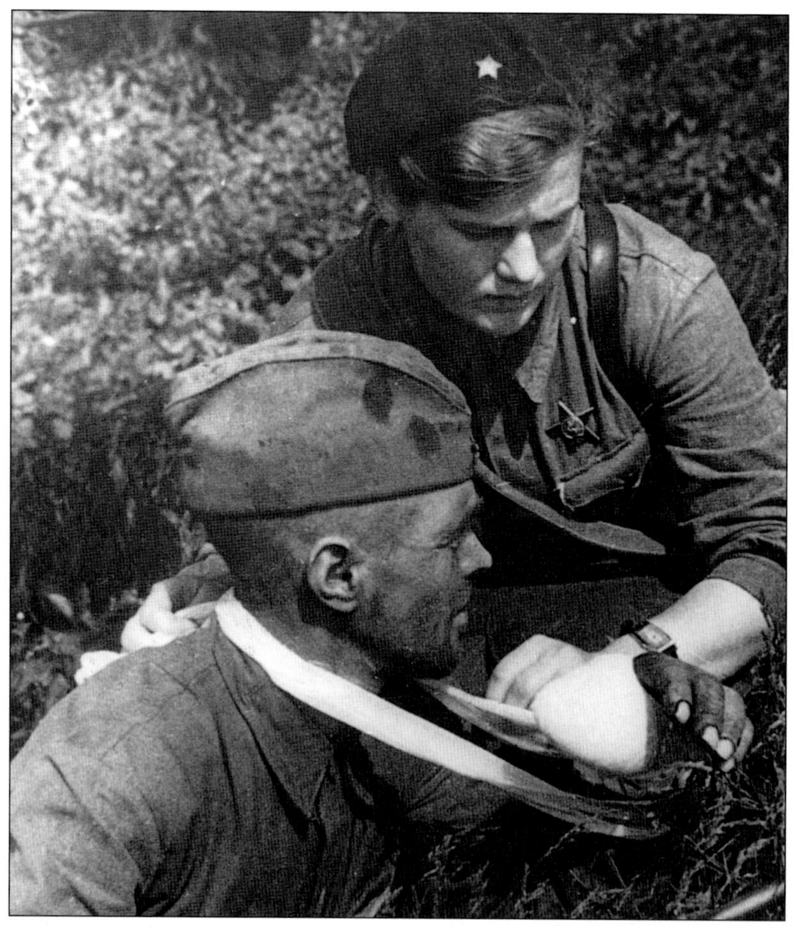

Military Surgeon's Assistant Raisa Troyan, seen here tending an injured soldier behind the firing line, won the Order of the Red Star for saving 135 men from a burning house.

another order to withdraw, this time to Corregidor, the fortified island at the entrance to Manila Bay. Bataan surrendered on April 9. Only about 2,300 managed to escape, including nurses from the two hospitals. Patients too ill to move had to be left behind in the care of Navy nurses. But escaping was no easy matter. The roads on Bataan were jam-packed with refugees and were constantly strafed and bombed by Japanese aircraft.

Second Lieutenant Dorothea Daley of the U.S. Army Nurse Corps escaped in a truck, only to find the route blocked.

'I wish I could forget those endless, harrowing hours. Hours of giving injections, anaesthetizing, ripping off clothes, stitching gaping wounds, amputations... covering the wounded we could not save.'

'We ran into a convoy of soldiers about 10 miles [16 kilometres] long, all on their way to the wharf at Marivales,' Daley later remembered. 'The firing kept getting closer and closer. There was shellfire in it, going over our heads. The road was full of civilians and crying children who had got lost.... we were stopped at one place for an hour.... '

After finally struggling through to Marivales port, the fugitives found it in flames. The harbour was empty. All the available ships had already gone. But Corregidor lay only 8 miles (13 kilometres) away, and one group of nurses managed to make the crossing in rowboats. That night, however, the beach on Corregidor where they were sheltering came under constant Japanese shelling. At dawn, fortunately, an ancient steamer arrived to take them off.

HOSPITAL IN A TUNNEL

Nurses and doctors set up an underground hospital in a 1,400-foot (427-metre) tunnel hewn out of Malinta Hill. Considering its location, it was quite sophisticated and included wards, a good supply of dressings and sulfa drugs, a laboratory and quarters for the medical staff. Nevertheless, though comparatively safe, it was a stressful environment. The pounding of Japanese shelling from Bataan echoed and re-echoed through the rock, and venturing outside the tunnel was dangerous.

On April 24, 1942, for example, a large group of men was standing out in the open close by the tunnel's western gate when a 240-millimetre shell exploded among them. The resulting carnage was described by one of the nurses, Juanita Redmond.

'I wish I could forget those endless, harrowing hours. Hours of giving injections, anaesthetizing, ripping off clothes, stitching gaping wounds, of amputations, sterilizing instruments ...covering the wounded we could not save. I had still not grown accustomed,' Redmond concluded, 'to seeing people torn and bleeding and dying in numbers like these.'

Inevitably, the persistent shelling affected the working of the hospital itself. The dynamos ceased providing electricity, cloaking the tunnel in utter blackness. The air grew hot, damp and deathly still. Water supplies, which were running low, were cut off altogether for hours at a time.

SURRENDER OF CORREGIDOR

In less than four weeks the military situation had become hopeless, and on May 6, 1942 Corregidor surrendered. Some of the nurses managed to elude the Japanese and were evacuated in anything that would float, including two seaplanes and a submarine, the USS *Spearfish,* which took off the last 13 women on the night of May 3. Eleven U.S. Army and Navy nurses eventually reached Australia, but 106 were left behind on Corregidor. They became prisoners and remained so until the end of the war.

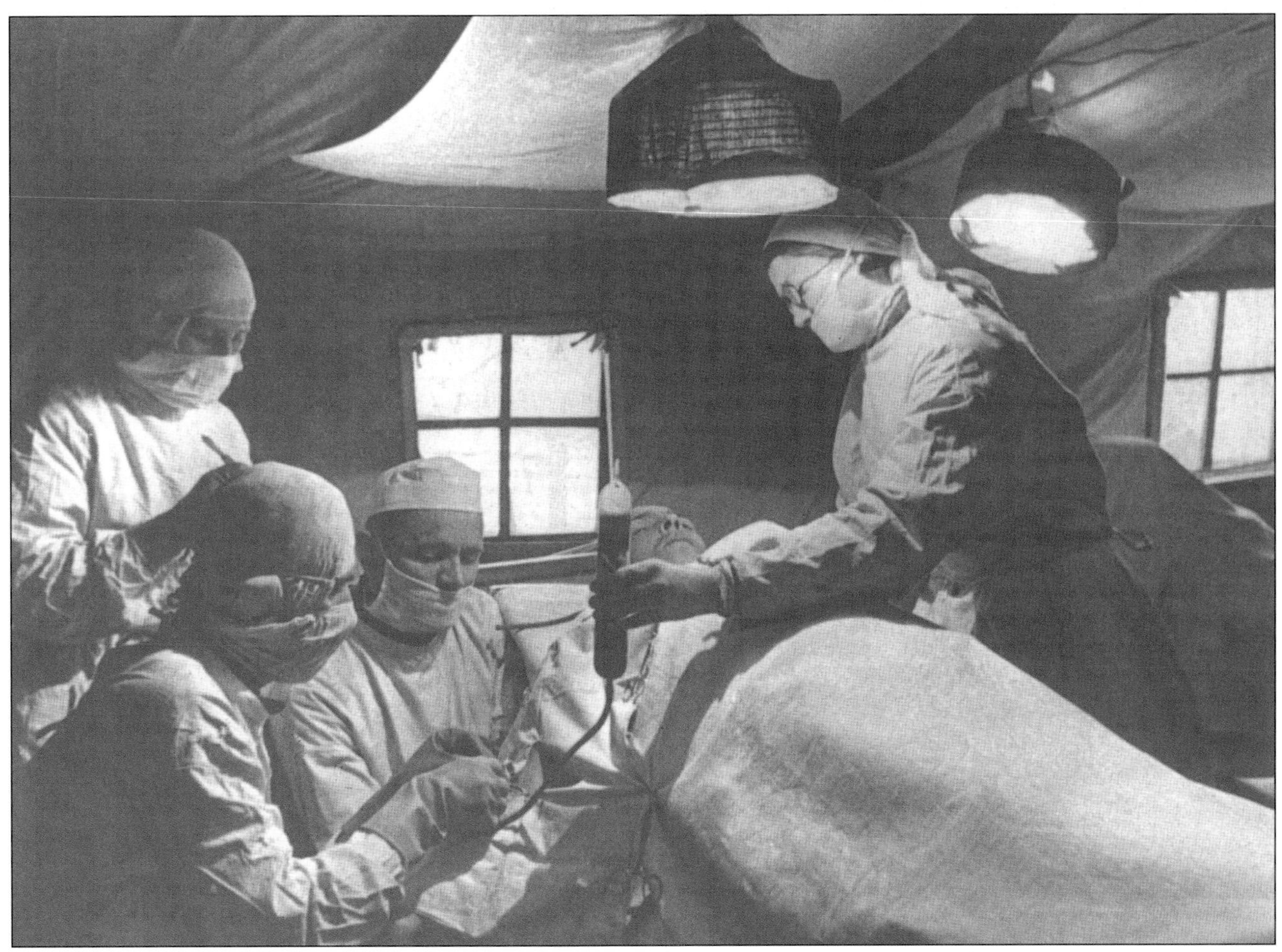

These Russian nurses and doctors were pictured working in a tent at a field hospital, giving a blood transfusion to an injured soldier, in October 1942.

Share the Deeds of Victory

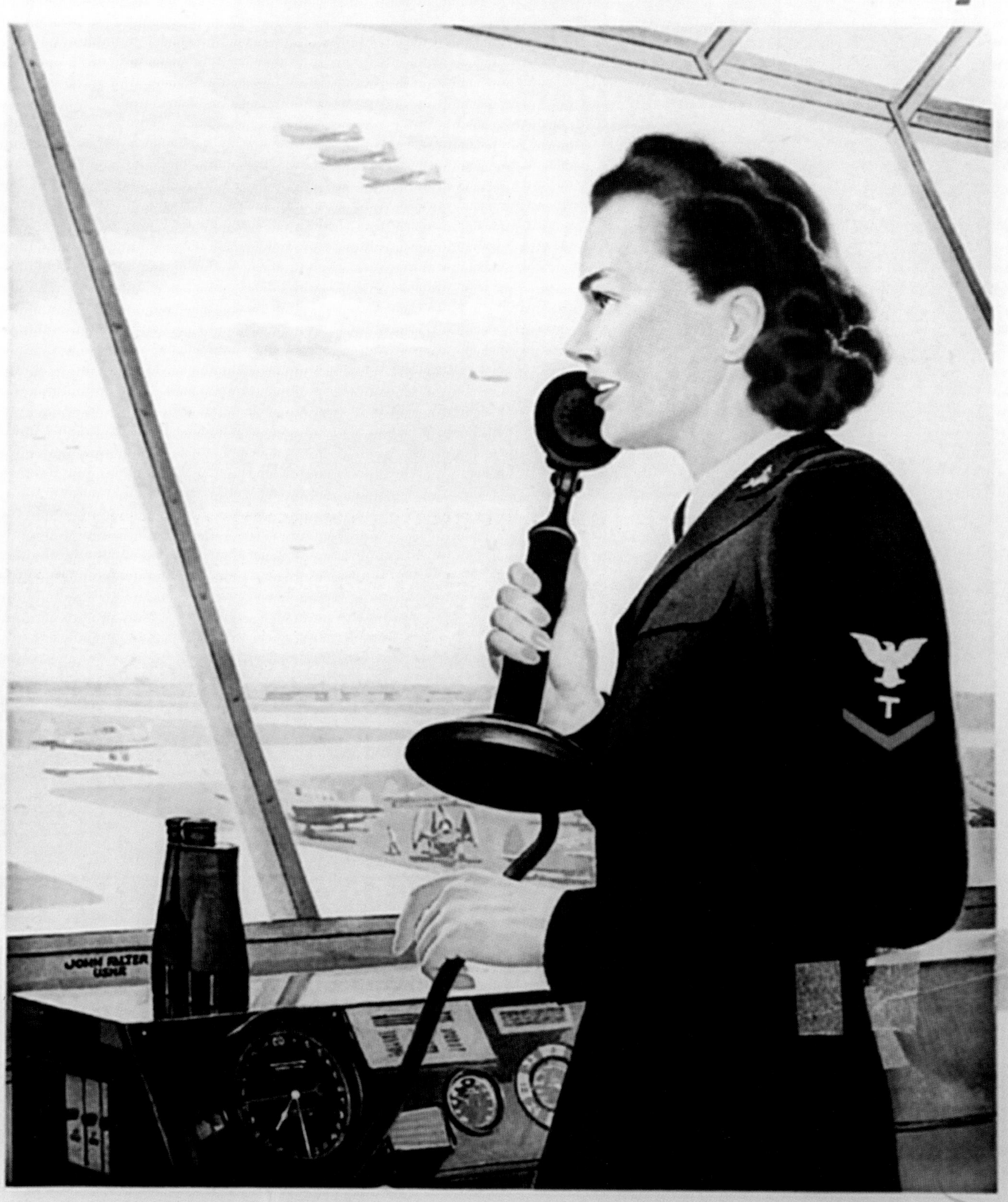

Join the WAVES

CHAPTER 5

Women in Uniform

Thousands of women joined the women's uniformed services in World War II. There was, inevitably, resistance to the idea of women in uniform, but their contribution was vital.

The Allied armed services drew thousands of women into military life, from all over the world. The United States and Britain accounted for most, employing women in all three armed forces and, in the case of the United States, in the Coast Guard and the Marines as well. Others who signed up to 'do their bit' included contingents from Canada, Australia, South Africa, India, New Zealand and Burma.

Of these, Burma, invaded by the Japanese early in 1942, was the only full-blown war zone, and here women came face to face with an enemy whose cruelty and ruthlessness were legendary. Members of the Women's Auxiliary Service (Burma) – WAS(B), known as the Wasbies – were meant to perform clerical and cypher duties for the British Army, but invasion by the Japanese only four days after Pearl Harbor meant that much more was demanded of them than a straightforward desk job.

The Japanese were experts at fighting through seemingly impenetrable jungles, a feat their British opponents believed to be impossible. This fundamental error soon became evident. The jungles of Burma did little to hinder the Japanese advance, and retreat became the only option for the British.

There was much more to modern warfare than fighting: women provided important backup, like an American WAVE shown on this poster at work in a naval air station control tower.

Excessive heat, humidity, monsoons, difficult jungle terrain, dangerous diseases, and an elusive, cunning enemy made Burma one of the most arduous battlegrounds of World War II.

THE WASBIES IN BURMA

On March 6, 1942, 300 Wasbies were hastily evacuated by sea from Rangoon, the Burmese capital. As their ship sailed, the Japanese 15th Army was already in the city. Two months earlier, in January, the British Burma Corps (Burcorps) embarked on the longest retreat in British military history – 1,000 miles (1,600 kilometres). They were joined by 65 Wasbies. All faced a gruelling journey to safety in India. Their route led them over mile upon mile of almost trackless jungle and mountain in sweltering heat and across the fast-flowing Irrawaddy River. All the way they were threatened by disease as much as by the Japanese. When the monsoon rains broke, the Japanese pursuit faded, only to be replaced by the misery of ceaseless rain that soaked the ground, the trees, the Wasbies, the men, their weapons and equipment, their clothes, their bedding, their food. It wasn't until mid-May, four months later, that they reached Assam in eastern India, by which time the Japanese controlled Burma.

But their tenure lasted only two years. In April 1944, the British returned and within six months, together with American and Chinese forces, they drove the Japanese back to Rangoon.

Founded in 1942, SPARS – The Women's Reserve of the U.S. Coast Guard – provided backup for the Coast Guard at shore establishments and bases. By 1944, 12,000 women had joined the SPARS.

CHAR AND A WAD

The Wasbies also returned to Burma, where 250 of them provided a mobile

Women Served In....

UNITED STATES

Women's Army Auxiliary Corps (WAAC), 1942-1943

Women's Army Corps (WAC), 1943

Women's Auxiliary Ferrying Squadron (WAFS), 1942

– was incorporated with the Women's Air Force Service Pilots (WASP), (1942)

Women's Reserve of the U.S. Coast Guard (SPARs, an acronym coined from their motto: *Semper Peratus,* Always Ready), 1942

Women's Reserve of the U.S. Naval Reserve (WAVES), 1942

United States Marine Corps Women's Reserve (USMCWR), 1943

BRITAIN

Air Transport Auxiliary Service (ATAS), 1938

Women's Auxiliary Air Force (WAAF), 1939

Women's Auxiliary Service (known as ATS), 1938

Women's Royal Naval Service (WRNS), 1939

CANADA

Canadian Women's Army Corps (CWAC), 1941

Canadian Women's Auxiliary Air Force (CWAAF), 1941

Women's Royal Canadian Naval Service (WRCNS), 1942

AUSTRALIA

Australian Women's Army Service (AWAS), 1942

Women's Australian Auxiliary Air Force (WAAAF), 1941

Women's Royal Australian Naval Service (WRANS), 1941

SOUTH AFRICA

Women's Auxiliary Air Force (WAAF), 1939

Women's Auxiliary Army Service (WAAS), 1939

Women's Auxiliary Military Police Corps (WAMPC), 1942

South African Women's Auxiliary Naval Service (SAWANS), 1943

INDIA

Women's Auxiliary Corps (India) (WAC[I]), 1942

NEW ZEALAND

New Zealand Women's Auxiliary Air Force (NZWAAF), 1941

Women's Army Auxiliary Corps (WAAC), 1942

Women's Royal New Zealand Naval Service (WRNZNS), 1942

BURMA

Women's Auxiliary Service (Burma) (WAS[B]), 1942

FRANCE
(FREE FRENCH FORCES IN BRITAIN)

Femmes Françaises Indépendantes (*Corps Volontaire Français* – French Volunteer Corps), 1940

THE NETHERLANDS

Women's Auxiliary Corps of the Royal Netherlands Army, 1944

NORWAY

Norwegian Women's Corps, 1940

POLAND
(FORCES IN BRITAIN)

Pomocnicza Stuzba Kobiet (Women's Auxiliary Service), 1939

SOVIET UNION
(WITH FULL COMBAT STATUS)

Red Army

Red Army Air Force

Red Navy

The Women's Auxiliary Corps (India) had full military status when formed in 1942. Open to all races, castes and creeds in India, it provided clerical, administrative, cypher and signals support.

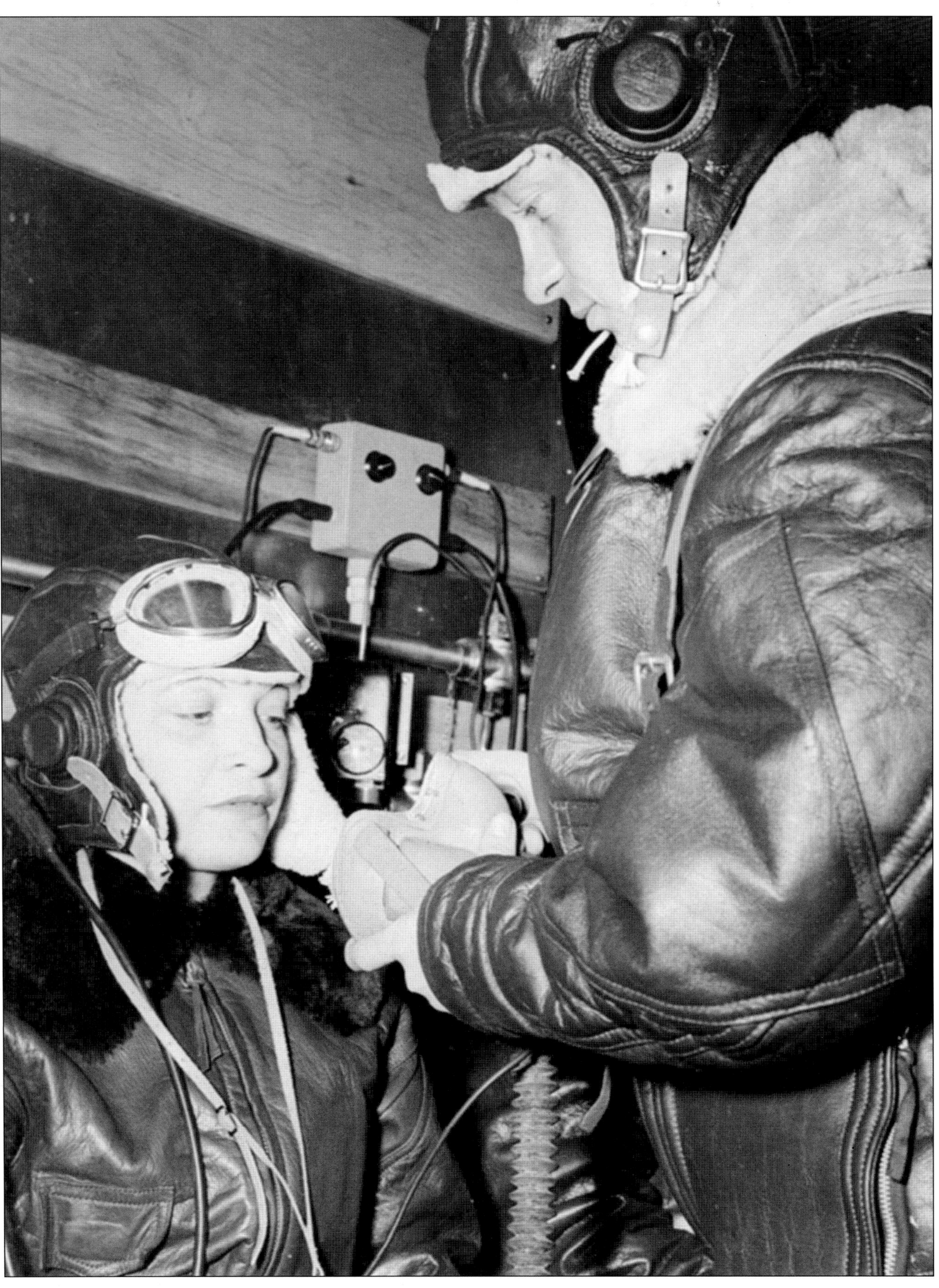

canteen service for the troops. The women moved from place to place like nomads, sleeping at night in tents. Living conditions were appalling, the tropical heat was merciless, and as they moved their canteens further and further down the road, the Wasbies often came within earshot of the guns.

To one soldier, the Wasbies appeared like a mirage, tempting them with visions of the 'char and a wad' – tea and cake – so beloved of British soldiers. But they were no mirage.

'In the distance we saw a lone lady standing by a table in the rain, and as we got nearer we saw she had lots of mugs of hot tea on the table. She gave us all tea and a packet of cigs and a wad. She was a lovely Scots lady who must have been 50 years old. I spoke to her and told her she was too near the guns, and she should go to a safer place – after all, the Japs were only 4 miles (6 kilometres) up the road. She would not leave and said, "There will be other soldiers behind you who will want tea. I am just a Wasbie." '

CONTINUING THE FIGHT

Even more intensely than the Wasbies in Burma, women from Nazi-occupied Europe knew the ravages of war first hand. Many of them enlisted as their way of continuing the fight – mainly from Britain, the only European country at war to elude German occupation.

The Free French under General Charles de Gaulle formed their *Femmes Françaises Indépendantes* (the French Volunteer Corps). After the Nazi invasion of Norway in April 1940, the Norwegian Women's Corps was established to help soldiers avoid capture by the Germans and escape across the North Sea to Britain. When an air training service was set up for Norwegian pilots at 'Little Norway' in Canada, a women's auxiliary unit of the Royal Norwegian Air Force went with them to serve as nurses and to handle the administration.

The Poles had been first among Germany's conquests in 1939, and that same year they formed the *Pomocnicza Stuzba Kobiet* (Women's Auxiliary Service). Some 4,000 Polish women joined the WAS; unlike their British counterparts, they were allowed to carry arms, frequently standing sentry alongside soldiers, SMLE (short for Short Magazine Lee Enfield) rifles in hand.

For Russian women, however, the German invasion of June 22, 1941 meant handling weapons for real, as they were drafted into the Red Army and Air Force. By 1942, women accounted for some 8 percent of Red Army personnel, a figure that rose to 10 percent by 1945, when it was estimated that 1 million Russian women had fought in the war. Three-quarters of them were conscripts.

Recruitment campaigns appealed to women's patriotism and the need to defend American freedoms. This was all the more important because there were no overt signs of war affecting the country.

The picture opposite shows a WAVE receiving help and advice from a sailor about putting on her oxygen mask before undergoing a test in a 'chill chamber' at the Jacksonville, Florida, Naval Air Station.

These members of the Canadian Women's Army Corps, seen playing cards and reading news from home at a British base, received only four-fifths the wage of their male counterparts.

COMBAT STATUS FOR RUSSIAN WOMEN

Unlike the other Allied services, there was no quibble about giving Russian women combat status, and they were never in World War II on any other basis. There were, of course, objections. Some male pilots refused to take off on learning that their aircraft had been maintained by a woman. One Soviet base commander wanted to ban women fighter pilots in his group. He was eventually persuaded otherwise by one of his men, who was in love with Lily Litvak, the legendary ace known as the 'White Rose of Stalingrad'.

Generally, however, the crisis in Russia caused by the German invasion and their early progress to the gates of Moscow was far too great to be affected by prejudice. Every person, man or woman, was urgently needed to fight – and die – for Mother Russia.

Every person, man or woman was urgently needed to fight for Mother Russia. Women were given full equality to serve as machine gunners as well as fighter and bomber pilots.

Women were given full equality to serve as machine gunners, combat engineers, anti-aircraft gunners, dispatch riders and reconnaissance scouts, as well as fighter and bomber pilots and snipers. The exploits of the top women snipers had severe effects on German morale. Four women claimed 54 confirmed kills each, and the top ace, Lieutenant Lydmilla Pavlichenko, a Ukrainian, accounted for 309 of the enemy. Pavlichenko, needless to say, became a front-page celebrity in the Soviet newspaper *Pravda*.

Russian propaganda posters such as the one opposite cast women, not as support for men, but as equal and standing with them, with a common fiercely determined expression, in the face of the German enemy.

SHOULD WOMEN SERVE?

The United States and Canada were, of course, entirely different societies, much more conscious of how the traditional roles of men and women differed and, at first, much more determined that these traditions should not be challenged. In both countries, there were strong views about not allowing women to participate in the war in any way, but in both countries, this idea had to yield to reality.

This resistance accounted for the fact that it was July 1941, nearly two years after Canada had troops in the war theatre, before the first of its women's wartime services, the Canadian Women's Auxiliary Air Force (CWAAF), was officially authorized. Seven months later, the service was renamed the Royal Canadian Air Force (Women's Division), and its members acquired the nickname of 'Wids'.

Though modelled closely on the British Women's Auxiliary Air Force (WAAF), the 'Wids' acquired a status not given to their British counterparts, who were classed as auxiliaries; they became an integral part of the Royal Canadian Air Force. Wid officers were accorded

ДА ЗДРАВСТВУЕТ
XXIV ГОДОВЩИНА
ОКТЯБРЯ!
КРЕПЧЕ УДАР ПО ВРАГУ

the same standing as their male counterparts and, like them, were entitled to salutes. The 'Wids' were nevertheless intended to perform support roles, as their motto - 'That Men Might Fly' - implied. The Royal Canadian Air Force, on the other hand, proved less idealistic; as far as it was concerned, the women were allowed to join to relieve men of 'laundry duties'.

Domestic problems impinged on the recruitment of some women. Many of them had to step in as family breadwinners because their husbands' military pay was too low.

First among the Canadian women's services, the Wids were also the first to go overseas, to Britain in September 1942. The criteria for overseas service were strict. Canadian women in uniform had to undergo three months extra basic training, enjoy good health, be over 21 with 'exemplary character...suitable temperament...appearance and general smartness'.

This was fair enough, but also present was the rather patronizing and dismissive attitude towards the so-called 'weaker sex' that was prevalent both in society in general and in the armed forces. Married women were preferred as recruits, mainly because of the general belief that, once they were away from their parents, single women would be unable to maintain the moral standards expected of them. This was a polite way of labelling single women as morally untrustworthy and, of course, there were plenty of unsavoury rumours about them that were widely taken as 'proof' of this view.

In time, 1,300 Wids succeeded in passing the morality test and other requirements needed to serve overseas. Another 300 were recruited into the service in Britain. All of them had the exclusive right to wear a special shoulder flash inscribed 'CANADA'. Initially,

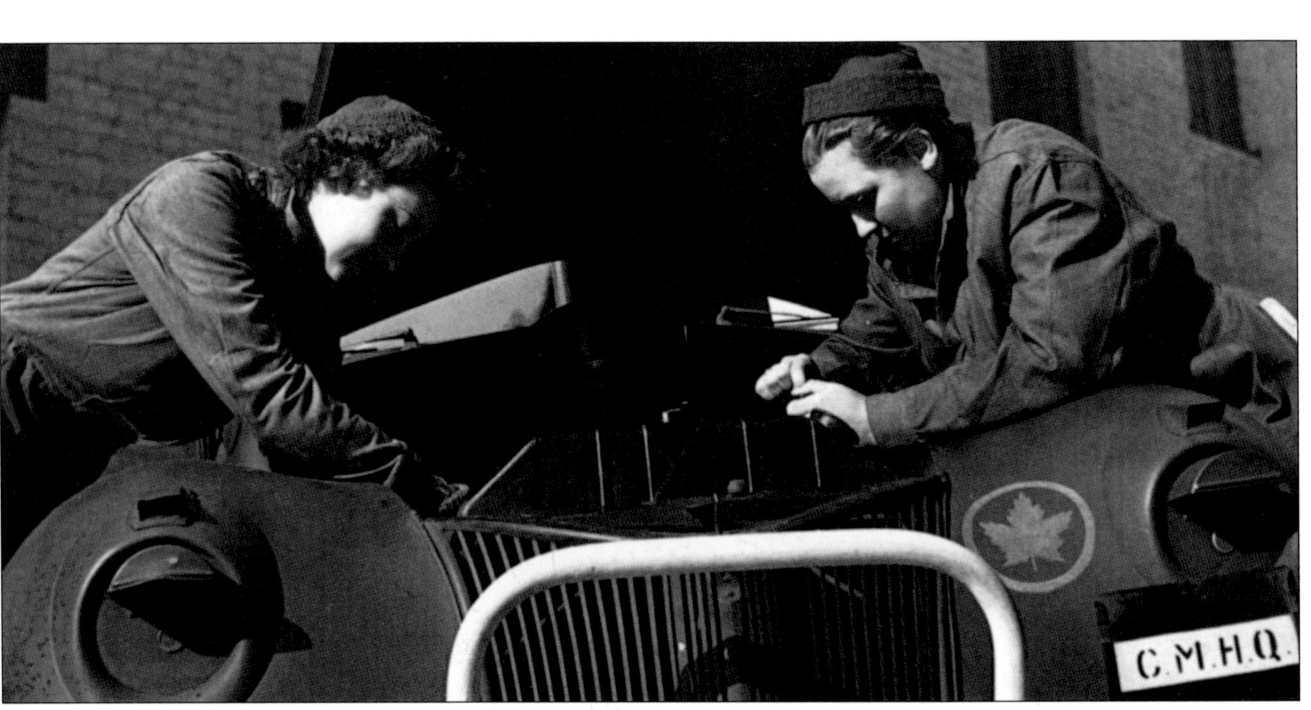

Two of the 3,000 Canadian women who served with the CWAC, learning vehicle maintenance while stationed in Britain during 1943.

despite the elevated status of their officers, the Wids were paid two-thirds of the male service rates, though this was raised to four-fifths in 1943.

CANADIAN WOMEN'S UNIFORMED SERVICES

The same pay rise applied to the Canadian Women's Army Corps (CWAC) which was officially formed in the months after the CWAAF. Largely, the CWAC operated within Canada, as a corps within the Active Militia of Canada, but by 1944 they were being assigned to clerical and other support duties in combat zones. In 1945, the 3,000 or so who were sent overseas were assigned to Britain, Italy and northwest Europe to support the Canadian forces in these areas.

By the end of the war, the CWAC made up 2.8 percent of the total Canadian Army. Like other women's services, the CWAC never acquired combat status, but their contribution to the final Allied victory was officially recognized when a special plaque in their honour was unveiled at the Canadian Force Base at Esquimalt, near Vancouver, on February 20, 2000.

The Women's Royal Canadian Naval Service (WRCNS) was the smallest of the three women's 'armed' services and also the last to be officially sanctioned, in 1942. The first class, comprising 68 'Wrens', started its training in August 1942. Within a year, there were more than 3,000 trained Wrens serving with the Royal Canadian Navy. Like the Wids, they were not auxiliaries, but part of the naval service. They earned four-fifths of male pay from the start.

Like American women, the Canadians were driven to involve themselves by taking direct action.

The women pilots of the Red Army Air Force were feared by the Germans, who called them *Nachthexen* (night witches).

Frances Mills, who joined the WRCNS in 1942, spoke for them all when she said, 'I felt, there I was, as able as any of the men, and I was being very safe. I wasn't doing anything to help. It was sort of guilt, I think, that motivated me.'

TOP SECRET

Mills, a school teacher, joined the WRCNS after one of her pupils was killed overseas. After basic training at Galt, Ontario, Mills was assigned to Ottawa where she learned about a new location radar called Loran.

The work was top secret. It involved receiving electronic signals, forwarding the data to the Massachusetts Institute of Technology, which had developed Loran, and helping in basic research on sound waves and radar beams.

Later, Mills and 24 other women transferred to Whitehead, Nova Scotia, monitoring radio signals from out at sea. On one occasion, the radio frequency became scrambled: that meant danger from an enemy submarine nearby.

'We were very frightened, very anxious,' Mills commented. 'We'd all

A petty officer serving with the WAVES gives a salute in front of the Jefferson Memorial in Washington D.C. Her rank is indicated by the 'P' on her sleeve.

been instructed that a serious problem meant we had to destroy our equipment. The girls in our hut had a revolver.... '

Four hours went by before the danger passed.

ONGOING DEBATE

In the United States, there was even more agonizing than there had been in Canada over whether or not women should be allowed to serve in the war. There was an ongoing debate over this question throughout the hostilities, and in this context the question of female service in the military was a particularly thorny one. This was not apparent, though, from the results of a series of wartime polls conducted for the U.S. Army. The first of these polls took place on September 10, 1942, and posed this question:

'The Army can either draft 300,000 single women aged 21 to 35 for the Women's Army Corps (WAC) non-fighting jobs, or it can draft the same number of married men with families for the same work. Which plan would you favour?' The answer favoured the women every time, and every time by a big majority – between 73 and 81 percent.

Dissenters were extremely vocal. Strong objections surfaced from religious groups, traditionalists and from men and families protesting about recruitment of their own women into the military. However, the whole question was not nearly as cut and dried as the poll suggested or the protesters imagined.

THE ARSENAL OF DEMOCRACY

In World War II, the United States became 'the arsenal of democracy'. This was a political term used by President Roosevelt to indicate the industrial might of the United States in the war. Although it is often thought that the Americans were surprised by the Pearl Harbor attack, the U.S. government had already been making preparations before the war actually began. The U.S. Navy was stationed at Pearl Harbor as a

Maria Lalkova of the Czechoslovak Exile Army, a much-feared sniper, disposed of dozens of Germans.

Focus on Allied Uniform

Canada

Female personnel in the Royal Canadian Navy (bottom left) performed essential shore and administrative duties, which allowed the maximum numbers of men for active service. Hence this lieutenant belongs to the paymaster section, a department identified by the white sections set into the lace on her shoulder straps. This lieutenant's uniform matches that of British ranks except, like many units of the British Empire, in the button details and hat ribbons which illustrated the country of origin. She wears a standard lightweight uniform which was shared with other ranks, but the three-cornered hat separates her as an officer from the round sailor's hat worn by NCOs and lower ranks. She carries a naval-issue bag, called a pouchette, and white gloves.

Lieutenant, Royal Canadian Women's Naval Service, London 1943 (left); Sniper, Rifle Battalion Red Army, Kursk 1943 (centre); U.S. Army Officer, U.S. Women's Army Corps, Pearl Harbor 1944 (right).

Russia

Because of chronic problems in finding the manpower to fulfil military and industrial tasks, the Soviet government recruited some 7.75 million women, of whom 800,000 served in the military. Sniping was a precision role which many women soldiers performed with expertise. Below centre is shown a female sniper deployed around Kursk in July 1943. Soviet snipers were issued with one-piece specialist overalls to wear over their standard uniforms. However, during the war these uniforms were often camouflaged, especially for snipers. This overall has a khaki base with green foliage patterns. A large hood and soft cap would obscure the face in a position of hiding. Some overalls had strips of cloth sewn to the shoulders and sleeves to break up the silhouette. This sniper's weapon is the 7.62mm (0.3in) Mosin-Nagant M1891/30 rifle.

United States

The U.S. servicewoman is wearing the cotton summer uniform issued to personnel of the U.S. Women's Army Corps. It consisted of a dark-olive tunic with open collar, broad lapels and gilt buttons with a matching peaked cap. Underneath the tunic was worn a light khaki blouse and tie. A khaki skirt and a pair of brown leather shoes completed the uniform. The WAC had their own system of insignia. The cap badge was an American eagle, usually less adorned than the standard U.S. Army cap badge, though this officer actually has the regular cap badge with the scroll and motto 'E Pluribus Unum'. WACs had the letters 'U.S.' on the upper collar and the head of the Greek goddess Pallas Athene (goddess of war) beneath. Rank would be shown on the shoulder straps and, for officers, through the contrasting olive ribbon on the cuff.

preventive measure, taken in 1940, to stop war breaking out after the European situation had escalated.

Countries like Russia could not adopt such a strong approach, since they were fighting the war on their own territory. The demands of the 'arsenal' on labour, female as well as male, were immense, and the U.S. Army had several rivals in its pursuit of female workers. The war factories needed women, as did public services and civilian government service.

Bottled gases were passed around to identify. The women went to lectures on how to defend against chemical warfare.

Domestic problems impinged on the recruitment of some women. Many of them had to step in as family breadwinners because their husbands' military pay was too low to support them. Extended families who depended for their income on businesses or farms would find themselves in dire distress if the women who ran them enlisted for war work. Agricultural work was, in any case, a vital contribution to the U.S. war effort and was recognized as such.

The U.S. military was up against rivals in the War Manpower Commission and the Office of War Mobilization, both of which objected to the Army poaching women who were urgently required for factories or farms. In this situation, the U.S. government and the Army and Navy had responded to the exigencies of war before the Gallup polls were even formulated and, somewhat un-democratically, continued no matter what opinion they revealed. Well over a year before Pearl Harbor, in 1940 and early 1941, the Army and Navy hired 60,000 women to perform important support functions such as clerical or communications work. In that same period, the federal government recruited three times that number of women, raising its complement of female employees from 186,210 to 266,407.

FORT DES MOINES

On May 15, 1942, four months before the first of the wartime Gallup polls, President Roosevelt signed a bill to set up the Women's Army Auxiliary Corps (WAAC). Its function, according to its director, Major Oveta Culp Hobby, was to 'free men for combat duty'.

Hobby's approach was very astute. She perceived how women could still perform their traditional, long-established role of helping men to succeed while serving their country at the same time.

'American women can make a significant contribution to the war effort,' Hobby said in one of her many public speeches. 'The gaps our women will fill are in those non-combatant jobs where women's hands and women's hearts fit naturally. WAACs will do the same type of work which women do in

Civilian fashions as worn by women in wartime represented a no-nonsense 'uniform' in its own right – military looking, with straight, unfussy skirts and a hat (left) inspired by military caps.

Rising Up the Ranks

OVETA CULP HOBBY (1905–1995)

Oveta Culp Hobby, wartime Director of the WAAC and the WAC, was one of those formidable women who get things done by refusing to take 'No' for an answer. The daughter of a lawyer and state legislator, and wife of a governor of Texas, William Pettus Hobby, she came from a favoured background and herself admitted that she had never had to fight for anything she wanted.

'Everything that ever happened to me,' she said. 'fell into my lap.'

Far from being pampered and softened by good fortune, Oveta Culp Hobby was a feisty woman and unafraid of danger. In 1936, when she and her husband were involved in an aircraft crash, she pulled him from the flaming wreckage and dragged him clear. Before she was appointed WAAC director in 1942, with the rank of Major, Oveta had spent ten years as editor of a Houston, Texas, newspaper, the *Post-Dispatch*. She had political experience, at both national and local levels, she was an impressive public speaker, adept at handling the press, and above all, she knew what she wanted the WAAC to do.

Hobby was no militant feminist. She refused, for example, to allow her 'ladies' to wear slacks or shorts in public. Rather, she believed in the 'power behind the throne' principle in which women supported men, using their own skills to make a good job of it. When the WAAC was replaced by the Women's Army Corps (WAC) in 1943, Hobby, who was promoted to Colonel, devoted herself to the new organization. For the rest of the war, she drove herself so hard in that role that by July 1945, when she resigned, she had to go into a hospital for rest and rehabilitation.

Oveta Culp Hobby was a woman of extraordinary drive, energy and enterprise.

civilian life. They will bear the same relation to men of the Army that they bear to men of the civilian organizations in which they work.'

By July 1942, 440 women were enrolled in a six-week WAAC officer candidate school and had begun their training at Fort Des Moines, Iowa. At the same time, another 125 enlisted women started a four week basic training course. They were the first women to undergo military training.

Elizabeth Pollock was among those women trained at Fort Des Moines. In a letter to her mother written shortly after her arrival, Pollock revealed the personal motivations that had led the women to join up.

'With some, it was because they were separated from their husbands; with others, because they had got into a rut in their jobs and wanted to get out. Some of them are like me – they were asked to volunteer because their services were needed. A lot of the girls are happily married, but joined up because they thought there was a job to do. Now that we're here,' Pollock continued, 'our purposes are all the same. And we all know we're having an experience we shall never forget.'

SERIOUS TRAINING

The training at Des Moines pulled no punches. Pollock and her colleagues were left in no doubt that this was serious training for dangerous situations. When whistles blew, they had to scramble for fire drills. Different bottled gases were passed around for them to smell for identification purposes. The women went to lectures on how to defend against chemical warfare.

Fort Des Moines was only one of the WAAC training centres. Others were opened in Georgia, Massachusetts and Louisiana. By January 1943, the first detachment of WAACs was ready to go overseas and departed for the new war front in North Africa, opened up the previous November by Operation Torch. There, they came under the command of General Dwight D. Eisenhower, Supreme Commander of the U.S. forces sent to North Africa to join the British Army in dealing with the renowned German Afrika Korps.

Although they had no combat status, the WAACs were effectively at war. Problems arose, however, due to their standing as auxiliaries: this put them with but not in the U.S. Army, and they were therefore not on the same military footing as women who served in the

This young Red Army typist was pictured working at a forward infantry headquarters on the northern front. The rifle close by her left hand shows she is ready for action, if necessary.

Keeping fit was a vital part of women's training for all services in World War II, all the more so because of the unhealthy environments involved in overseas postings.

U.S. Navy, Marine Corps and Coast Guard: those women were part of the reserves in their respective services and held military rank with all the benefits due to them.

ESTABLISHING THE WAC

This anomaly was corrected on August 31, 1943, when all WAACs were dismissed and the service was disbanded. The Army was eager for them to re-enlist in the newly formed Women's Army Corps (WAC), but encouraging them was all it could do. All the armed services faced the risk of losing female personnel altogether. In the event, 45,000 ex-WAACS joined the WAC, but almost 15,000 chose to return to civilian life. Their reasons varied; in addition to personal reasons, there were economic incentives as well: work outside the armed services was paid better.

Other explanations were not so practical – and the reasons were not pleasant. It had become almost routine for women in war work to encounter hostility and even humiliation: their efforts were trivialized and their moral character defamed. Signing up for the WAAC had, in the vast majority of cases, been an act of patriotism, but the end result was disillusionment. It was no coincidence that almost all the former WAACs who joined the Women's Army Corps held command status and were therefore too well established in the service to be easily dislodged by opposition.

COMPLEX WORK

The number of WAACs lost when that service was disbanded took the new Women's Army Corps up to six months to replace. At the same time, the demand for their particular services increased. As with all the U.S. military, there was a preference for somewhat older women, in their middle or late 20s at least, and those who were better educated, a bias justified by the complexity of some of their work. Whatever their qualifications and efficiency, though, WACs overseas could be hampered by the overprotective attitudes of some commanders. This was not entirely a matter of gallantry. The racial attitudes prevalent at the time had a lot to do with it: white males in the tropics had long been very wary about the proximity of non-European races which dominated those areas of the world, and the chance that a non-white male might 'tamper with' a white woman was always on their minds. WAC units themselves were racially segregated – like the rest of the U.S. Army – although the numbers were small: of the first 440 women accepted as candidates for officer school, 91 percent were white, and only 9 percent were black.

WACs stationed in the south-west Pacific worked up to 16 hours a day in areas heavily infested by mosquitos and other insects.

OVERPROTECTED

During the war in the Pacific, the Japanese went to extraordinary lengths to avoid capture on every island the U.S. forces conquered. If they did not commit *seppuku* (ritual suicide), they often hid in caves or jungles. In the minds of American commanders, therefore, the Pacific islands were teeming with armed Japanese on the loose, with every opportunity to seize and sully the WACs who were there under the aegis of the U.S. Army.

This probably explained why the Pacific theatre was the last to put in requests for WAC services, and several commanders were reluctant to accept any women at all. Even where they did so, the precautions they took could be

By 1943, women from the West Indies had arrived in Britain to join the WAAF: some are seen chatting to one of their predecessors, a WAAF officer from the Bahamas.

Examining feet for damage on a route march by the Auxiliary Territorial Service (ATS) in June 1940. Marching long distances was a regular part of ATS training.

stifling. On whatever captured island they happened to be, the WACs were confined within barbed wire enclosures. They had to give a day's notice before they could leave the compound, and had to be accompanied by two armed guards and be back by 11:00 PM.

Fears about the women's safety went beyond what the Japanese might do, and extended to black U.S. troops and the brown-skinned Pacific islanders. In New Guinea, for example, the WACs, all of whom were white, were placed in heavily guarded stockades with armed guards stalking the perimeters.

Yet this was not the limit of the difficulties facing the 5,500 WACs stationed in the southwest Pacific, who had the most arduous of all overseas postings. They worked up to 16 hours a day in areas heavily infested by mosquitos and other insects, with no recreational facilities, no leave, not even tropical uniforms to help cope with the intense humidity and heat – temperatures on the Pacific islands could top 100°F (38°C). Little wonder that their health suffered, with dermatitis and foot rot high on the list.

The first ATS units, comprising French-speaking switchboard operators assigned to exchanges in Paris, joined the British Expeditionary Force in France in the winter of 1939. Their stay ended very abruptly.

Despite these difficulties, 17,000 WACs served abroad during the war: 8,000 in Europe and 3,500 in North Africa and the Middle East, Burma, southeast Asia, and territories nearer to home such as Puerto Rico, Canada, Hawaii and Alaska.

IN BRITAIN

In Britain, the Auxiliary Territorial Service (ATS), the equivalent of the American WACs, was authorized by

Royal Warrant four years earlier than the WAC, on September 9, 1938, a year before hostilities broke out in Europe. The British government aimed to recruit more than 20,000 women for non-combatant duties with the Army and the Royal Air Force, mainly within Britain. It was not until June 1945, when the war in Europe was already over, that the single women among them were allowed to serve overseas.

The work done by the ATS spanned a vast array of jobs. Some women became vehicle mechanics, drivers or motorcycle dispatch riders, others were welders, carpenters or electricians. ATS tasks even included digging roads. As in the United States, there was a certain amount of resistance to the idea of women doing non-traditional work such as this, and the ATS was careful not to assign women to anything that might cause a public controversy. The British public, however, did not seem too bothered by these hard, 'unfeminine' jobs; concern arose, rather, over the danger to women operating too close to active war zones.

DUNKIRK 1940

However, regarding the realities of war, the ATS was not always in control of events. The first ATS units, comprising French-speaking switchboard operators assigned to exchanges in Paris, joined the British Expeditionary Force in France in the winter of 1939. Their stay ended very abruptly. In 1940 the women – all volunteers – made a hair's-breadth escape from the French Channel port of Dunkirk, together with the BEF and French and Belgian soldiers, while German forces were assaulting its defence perimeter.

This illustrated an aspect of the war that was peculiar to Britain: the role allotted to women might be non-combatant, but with the country under constant assault, no one could be proofed against enemy action. This situation had already been envisaged in 1938, when secret government trials were carried out to assess the performance of women on searchlight and anti-aircraft (AA) gun sites. Experiment became reality in 1941, when the first operational ATS squad was assigned to an all-woman searchlight unit. Their task was to scan the skies to light up enemy bombers overhead for the benefit of the anti-aircraft guns.

In the same year, women of the ATS got the chance to complete the job of fending off the German raiders: they graduated to

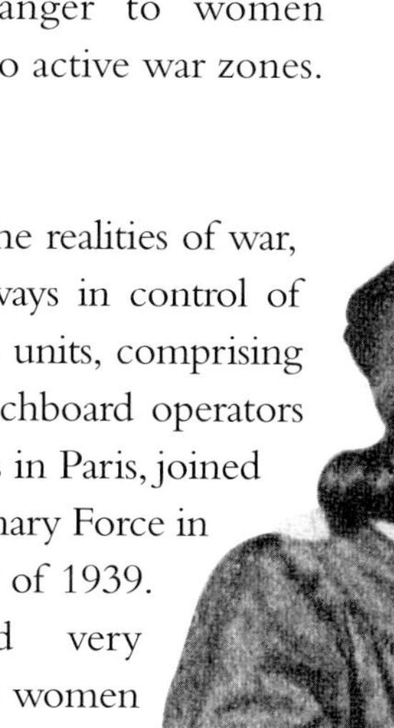

These ATS recruits were part of a mixed anti-aircraft battery, scanning the skies for enemy bombers.

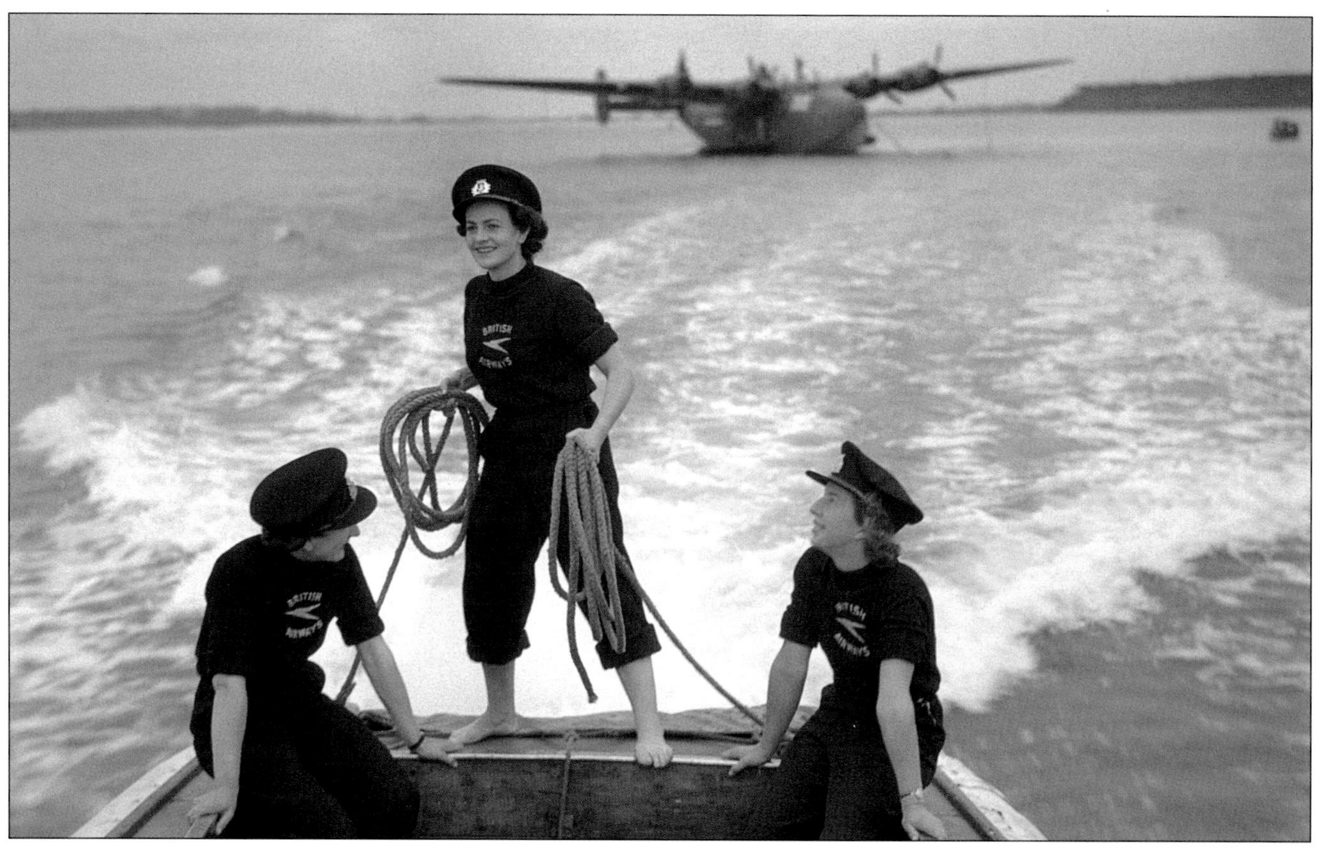

British women worked in a vast range of war jobs – as stewards, messengers, orderlies, storekeepers, air and radio mechanics and in transport roles.

the anti-aircraft batteries, whose task it was to shoot the bombers down. At this stage, the ATS served in mixed-sex AA batteries. Within two years, 50,587 women were on duty in this role, and another 9,671 operated as fire controllers.

The WAAFs worked at radar screens and plotting tables, marking and watching the progress of the aerial battle being waged over England.

OUTNUMBERING MEN

Eventually women outnumbered men in the AA batteries, and toward the end of 1944, one unit – the 93rd Searchlight Regiment – was staffed entirely by the ATS. Around this time, the ATS returned to mainland Europe in the 139th (Mixed) Heavy Anti-Aircraft Regiment, this time to take over from the male units which were due to move to the German border to support the Allied crossing of the Rhine. This was fortuitous. The existing AA units had no experience of dealing with Germany's V1 flying bombs, which had first attacked England on June 13, 1944. The 139th (Mixed) Heavy Anti-Aircraft Regiment, on the other hand, was very familiar with this threat, and when the dreaded 'vengeance weapons' started raining down on the port of Antwerp, the regiment was there to shoot down 19 of them.

In mid-1939, a year or so after the ATS was officially brought into being, some 2,000 of these women auxiliaries, organized in 48 companies, were 'on strength' in Britain with the Royal Air Force (RAF). World War II, of course, was the first in which air power was to be a crucial factor, and it was therefore logical for the RAF to have a support force of its own. When the Women's Auxiliary Air Force (WAAF) was established on June 28, 1939, most of its initial personnel were women who transferred from the ATS.

THE WAAF IN ACTION

The WAAF was mobilized and posted to RAF stations in Britain just over three months later, on September 1. The same day, the forces of Nazi Germany invaded Poland, and two days later war was declared. By the end of the war, WAAF strength had built up to 190,800 women. They served in a number of capacities, from packing parachutes and perusing air reconnaissance photographs to staffing barrage balloon sites; for the latter job, balloons resembling miniature airships, tethered to the ground, were sent aloft to entangle German raiders.

The WAAFs first became familiar with the sharp end of war in the Battle of Britain, fought between July and September 1940 – a struggle that saved the country from German invasion. The WAAFS worked at radar screens and plotting tables, marking and watching the progress of the aerial battle being waged over southern England. At times, as many as four or five plots a minute could come through, which demanded great concentration.

Work on the radar system – which used the Chain Home series of 20 British radar stations stretching from Scapa Flow in Scotland down to Portsmouth on the south coast of England – became a round-the-clock activity as the Luftwaffe took to raiding by night as well as by day. It fell to the WAAFs to plot the approach of the raiders across the English Channel. As soon as German aircraft came close to the coast of southern England, a WAAF telephonist sent a warning message, and shortly afterward the air-raid sirens started wailing in the selected towns under threat, alerting the inhabitants to an imminent attack.

PERFECT PITCH

Meanwhile, the WAAF guided the RAF's night fighters to intercept positions where they could challenge the German raiders, hopefully before they could reach their targets. In this, the women brought a particular advantage to the defence of Britain: the RAF pilots,

In this recruitment poster for the WAVES, the female image was carefully presented – attractive and feminine, but not fussy, with hair pulled back but not constrained and with a strong, confident expression.

Hanna Reitsch, First Woman Test Pilot

Hanna Reitsch, Nazi Germany's leading female pilot, made her reputation before World War II as a record breaking stunt flyer. She set the world gliding record for women, remaining aloft for five-and-a-half hours, and became one of the first pilots to glide across the Alps. Another of her exploits was to fly a helicopter inside an exhibition hall.

Reitsch's skills so impressed General Ernst Udet, who was in charge of Luftwaffe aircraft production, that he appointed her as a test pilot, something no woman flier had achieved before.

Pilot Perils

For Hannah Reitsch, extreme danger was never far away. To counter Britain's barrage balloons, an important defence that prevented Luftwaffe raiders from flying low over their targets, Reitsch tested a specially strengthened bomber designed to fly into the steel cables that anchored barrage balloons to the ground. Next, Reitsch tested the V1 flying bomb, designed to be pilotless but rigged with a special cockpit for test purposes: she found that the V1 kept veering to the right, a fault that was subsequently corrected.

Reitsch's next assignment was testing the experimental Messerschmitt 163 rocket plane (Me-163), an extremely hazardous aircraft that flew at 596 mph (959 km/h), almost half as fast again as the speediest Allied planes. The Me-163 made its first operational flight in July 1944, but this was too late in the war to make any difference to the outcome.

Reitsch's most perilous assignment was the last she performed in World War II: piloting the aircraft taking General Ritter von Greim to Berlin on April 25, 1945, so that Hitler could appoint him Commander-in-Chief of the Luftwaffe. Hitler, now hiding deep inside his bunker while Berlin was being laid waste by Russian artillery fire and air raids, was arguably insane at this point. Even so, his order was obeyed. Reitsch flew into Berlin despite Russian AA fire and managed to land in a rubble-strewn street.

Reitsch, the only woman to be awarded the Iron Cross, First and Second Class, and the Luftwaffe's Diamond Clasp, was a passionate Nazi who idolized Hitler. In the bunker, she tried to persuade him to leave and save himself, but Hitler refused and killed himself five days later. When Reitsch took off for her return flight in a barrage of gunfire, hers was the last German aircraft to leave Berlin. Hanna Reitsch died in 1979.

The woman depicted in this recruitment poster for air-raid wardens in Frankfurt, produced late in the war, shows the Nazis could no longer afford to consign women to traditional domesticity.

who had to put up with intense noise levels in their cockpits, could hear the higher pitch of women's voices very clearly above the din.

The RAF had another, cunning use for the clarity of female voices: diverting German night fighters from the flight paths of RAF bombers heading for targets in Germany. There were a number of extremely powerful transmitter sites in the UK and, using these, German-speaking WAAFs imitated the Luftwaffe's own flight controllers: piercing through the static and rising above the cockpit noises, the WAAF voices commanded the pilots' attention as they gave them wrong information or contradictory instructions.

Frontstadt
Frankfurt
wird gehalten!

Amy Johnson with the De Havilland Moth in which she became the first woman to fly solo from England to Australia in 1930. She qualified as a pilot in 1929.

WAAFs won several medals for courage during the war, including three George Crosses, Britain's highest civilian award, six Military Medals, and 1,491 mentions in dispatches and commendations for brave conduct. Despite the women's admirable record, however, the one thing the RAF never permitted them to do was to fly.

The idea of women as pilots was not considered before 1939, even though the likes of Amelia Earhart and Jean Batten had proved beyond a doubt women's ability to handle aircraft.

The idea of women as pilots was not even considered before 1939, even though the likes of Amelia Earhart and New Zealander Jean Batten, both of them record breakers before the war, had proved beyond a doubt women's ability to handle aircraft.

THE ATAS AND AMY JOHNSON

As more and more men were drafted into active service with the RAF, the secondary flying roles men had previously filled were left vacant. In 1940, women were admitted to the previously all-male Air Transport Auxiliary Service formed two years earlier. Subsequently, some 900 female pilots, all of them classed as civilians, ferried every type of plane – from light aircraft to heavy four-engined bombers – from the aircraft factories to RAF bases in Britain. Like their U.S. equivalent, the Women's Air Force Service Pilots (WASPs), the so-called 'Atas' were classed as civilians.

One of the Atas was Amy Johnson, the renowned pioneer pilot the British press dubbed 'Queen of the Air'. Johnson was a veteran of record pre-war flights to Australia, Japan and Capetown, and the first woman to hold an Air Ministry licence as a ground engineer. On the morning of January 4, 1941, Johnson took off from Hatfield, Hertfordshire, in a two-engined Airspeed Oxford Mark II, bound for Prestwick, in southeast Lancashire. There was sufficient fuel to last almost five hours, ample for the flight, but weather conditions were bad and Johnson lost her bearings in a cloud. At 3:30 PM, the Airspeed Oxford was seen way off course over the estuary of the River Thames in Essex.

By then, the aircraft's fuel tanks were almost empty. Johnson, apparently believing she was over land, bailed out. She was seen by the crew of a naval trawler, *Haslemere,* as she plunged into the water. She was not wearing a life jacket. The aircraft spiralled into the estuary and broke up. The *Haslemere's* captain, Lieutenant Commander Walter Fletcher, dived in and attempted to save her, but she slipped from his grasp and was never seen again.

The Air Transport Auxiliary Service employed over 900 women pilots, including Vera Strodl, pictured here ferrying a Curtiss P-40 fighter to a base in England in 1942.

DH
MOTH
LONDON
AEROPLANE
CLUB.

Keep mum
she's not so dumb

CHAPTER 6

The Clandestine War: Women as Secret Agents

Acting as a secret agent required an unusual degree of courage and enterprise. Women were thought to have advantages over men in this role; they were considered less noticeable and less likely to arouse suspicious attention.

There was no glamour involved in the life of a secret agent in World War II. For women and men alike, every day spent in enemy territory was potentially their last. The slightest slip or wrong word might blow their cover and reveal them for what they were. Betrayal, too, was an ever-present threat.

EXTRAORDINARY FEATS

Nevertheless, extraordinary feats were routinely required of secret agents. Nancy Wake, an Australian who was one of 39 women sent to Europe by Britain's Special Operations Executive (SOE), led successful raids in France against a Gestapo headquarters and a German gun factory. Andrée Borrel, who was French, helped British airmen shot down over France escape across the Pyrenees mountains into Spain. Yvonne Rudellat, another French agent, took part with the Resistance in the destruction of the Chiany Power Station and the Bronzavia Works at Blois, near Orléans; she also helped deactivate over 200 high-tension electricity pylons and a number of locomotive sheds.

This poster was part of a wartime British campaign to stop the public from giving away sensitive information – troop movements, ship sailings, factory production figures – where German spies could overhear them.

Training a Secret Agent

The training of secret agents in World War II was nerve-racking – and was meant to be. Every situation agents might face in enemy territory was duplicated, and they were always made to feel at risk of discovery.

Trainee agents would be asleep – for the night, they presumed – when suddenly they were awakened by menacing 'Germans', dressed in Gestapo or SS (political police) uniforms, bursting into the room. They were then manhandled out of bed and made to stand with their hands up, holding a heavy pile of books as they were roughly interrogated. They were asked trick questions designed to make them give themselves away, divulge secret information or betray other agents. On other occasions, no less stressful, they were bullied by 'friendly' interrogators into revealing the cover names or the bogus family history concocted for them by the SOE. Their cover had to be perfect, however rattled they might be – for in real clandestine life, anything less meant disaster for themselves and many others.

Two Polish women taking the oath to serve in the Home Army, formed after the defeat of Poland to harry the Germans, gather intelligence and carry out acts of sabotage.

Evading Capture

Acquiring the techniques of evading capture had a high priority. Agents were trained to stalk each other, one using the methods he or she had been taught on how to elude pursuit, the other trying to prevent escape. They received instruction on how to lay hidden traps at their bedroom doors to snare anyone who came near. Their rooms would be searched while they were away, and subtle evidence left behind to see if they could detect the intrusion when they returned.

Secret agents in the field led a peripatetic existence, and could find themselves in open countryside or too far from their safe house at nightfall. To prepare for this, trainee agents were required to sleep out in the open in all weather without being detected. In Britain, desolate and rain-soaked areas of Scotland were frequently used for this exercise.

Women SOE agents were trained to use the Welrod silencer pistol. Self-sealing leather washers, impregnated with oil in the long barrel, prevented the sound of the shot from escaping, enabling the near-silent elimination of an enemy target.

Living Rough

Agents were required to live off the land, snaring rabbits or game – in Britain, even hedgehogs if no other food was available – without being caught by the irate farmer whose land they were on, and then cook them on undetectable fires. Visible evidence that they had been living rough – rumpled, stained clothes, an unshaven chin or a disarrayed hairdo – had to be eliminated, and agents were required to return to camp neat, clean and tidy as if they had never been away.

Christine Skarbek, known as Christine Granville, a Jewish woman from Poland, helped British servicemen escape from German prisoner-of-war camps in eastern Europe. Vera Leigh, a British agent, worked on underground escape lines run by the French Resistance to aid Allied servicemen trying to get out of France.

Although women were never sent to occupied Europe to lead Resistance groups, British agent Pearl Witherington was forced to assume this mantle when Maurice Southgate, head of the so-called Wrestler Network, was arrested in May 1944, on the very brink of the D-Day landings. With only three weeks to go before the invasion, Witherington organized more than 1,500 Resistance fighters to play their parts in plaguing the Germans as they approached the landing beaches to challenge the Allied invaders.

An agent for the British SOE, Polish-born Christine Granville parachuted into southern France in 1944 to help the local Resistance and persuade Poles forced into German army service to defect.

STRINGENT CRITERIA

This was no task for ordinary women, or ordinary men. What was required, rather, was an élite, to fulfil some of the most stringent criteria ever laid down for service in war. Familiarity with the country to which they were sent and fluency in its language were obvious prerequisites. However, SOE and its American equivalent, the Office of Strategic Services (OSS), were also

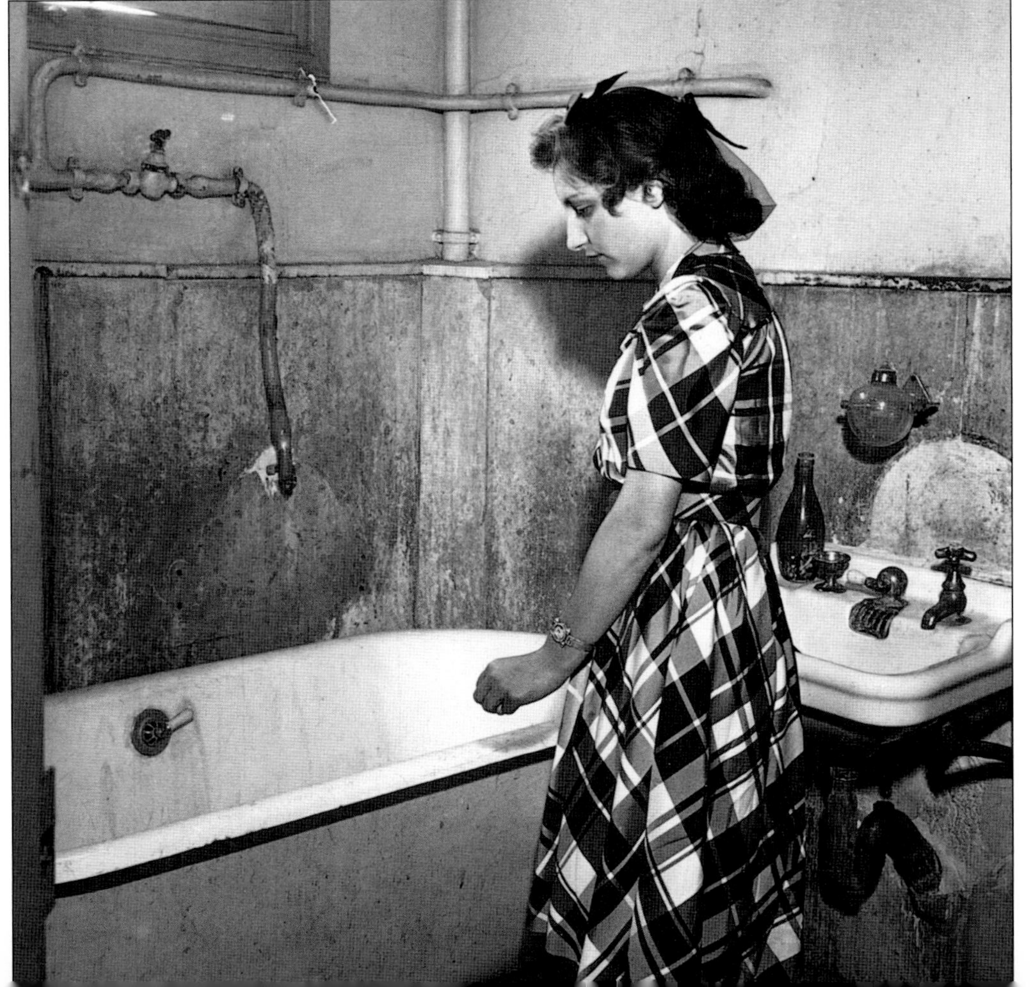

German Gestapo torture techniques included immersing agents in cold water in this bath as well as electric shocks, cigarette burns, sleep deprivation and anything else designed to make them talk.

Parachuting into occupied Europe, right, was a frequent way for SOE agents to meet up with Resistance fighters. The risks included injury on landing or landing in the wrong place.

The American poster opposite warns against revealing secret information. After 1939, FBI agents were assigned to defence plants to prevent sabotage and subversion. In 1942, 33 German spies were arrested in Florida.

The archive picture below shows trainee agents, including two women, Hanna Szena and Haviva Reik, standing on the tarmac waiting to receive instruction in parachuting from Royal Air Force personnel. Their eventual destination was Hungary.

looking for individuals of unusual enterprise and toughness. Nerves, presence of mind and alertness had to be of the highest order, for basically what was asked of agents was to set aside civilized instincts and even their own urge for survival.

Agents would have to cheat, lie, kill silently, perform acts of sabotage, use guns and explosives, keep their secrets when under torture and face the very likely chance of an early, violent death. Amy Thorpe, an American who worked for both the SOE and the OSS, aptly described an agent's life when she wrote in her diary: 'Life is but a stage on which to play. One's role is to pretend and always to hide one's true feelings.'

A WOMAN'S ADVANTAGES

In this most demanding of wartime professions, women had a certain natural advantage. Considered less conspicuous than men, women were very often used as couriers in the clandestine war in Europe. Women could also form relationships with Germans that combined sexual attraction with the task of extracting information.

Ordinary German soldiers often lived under the illusion that women posed no threat. A soldier on patrol would see a woman carrying a basket over her arm and presume that she was going shopping. It might not occur to him that she belonged to one of the numerous Resistance movements designed to fight the German occupation from inside, or that her basket could conceal secret messages, firearms or secret radios.

VIRGINIA HALL

On another level, however, the German secret police, the Gestapo, were not so easy to mislead. They knew perfectly well that the SOE and the OSS were infiltrating female agents into the occupied territories, and they made maximum efforts to find and capture them.

SILENCE

MEANS SECURITY

The resistance in German-occupied Yugoslavia was among the fiercest and most successful in Europe. Women were just as ruthless as the men in killing Germans or performing acts of sabotage.

One such agent, Virginia Hall, an American who was first an SOE and later an OSS agent code-named Diane, was the subject of a detailed Gestapo order circulated in France in 1944. Before the war, Hall had suffered a serious accident and had been fitted with an artificial foot. Though she taught herself to conceal her limp, her efforts were far from perfect and the Gestapo knew all about it.

Posing as a *New York Post* reporter while the United States was still neutral, Virginia Hall first slipped into occupied France in 1941 to organize a network of SOE agents.

'The woman who limps,' ran the Gestapo order, 'is one of the most dangerous Allied agents in France. We must find and destroy her.'

Posing as a *New York Post* reporter at a time when the United States was still neutral, Hall first slipped into occupied France in 1941 to organize SOE agents. Eventually, she roused German suspicions and had to make a hurried exit from France in 1943. However, the Gestapo had meanwhile acquired a detailed description of her from French double agents. From this, a very accurate sketch was made and distributed throughout France. It showed a good-looking woman in her late 30s, with shoulder-length brown hair, a strong chin and wide-set eyes.

After she transferred to their service in 1944, the OSS tried to convince Hall that she was too easy to identify and required a major change in her appearance. They failed. The most she would do was to dye her hair greyish-black and bundle her slim figure in the full skirts, oversized blouses and sweaters then typical of French peasant dress.

RETURN TO FRANCE

In this guise, Hall went back to France in 1944, landing at a secret location on the Brittany coast. In a suitcase specially battered by SOE to look much used but genuine, she carried a radio and identity papers they had forged for her. Renewing her contacts with the French

TELEPHONE
"....... but for Heaven's sake don't say I told you!"
CARELESS TALK COSTS LIVES

A British wartime poster showing a multitude of cartoon Hitlers gathered around a telephone box, listening in for vital information.

Any civilian in this street in occupied Poland could have been a secret agent; agents had to blend completely with the local population and appear to lead the same lives.

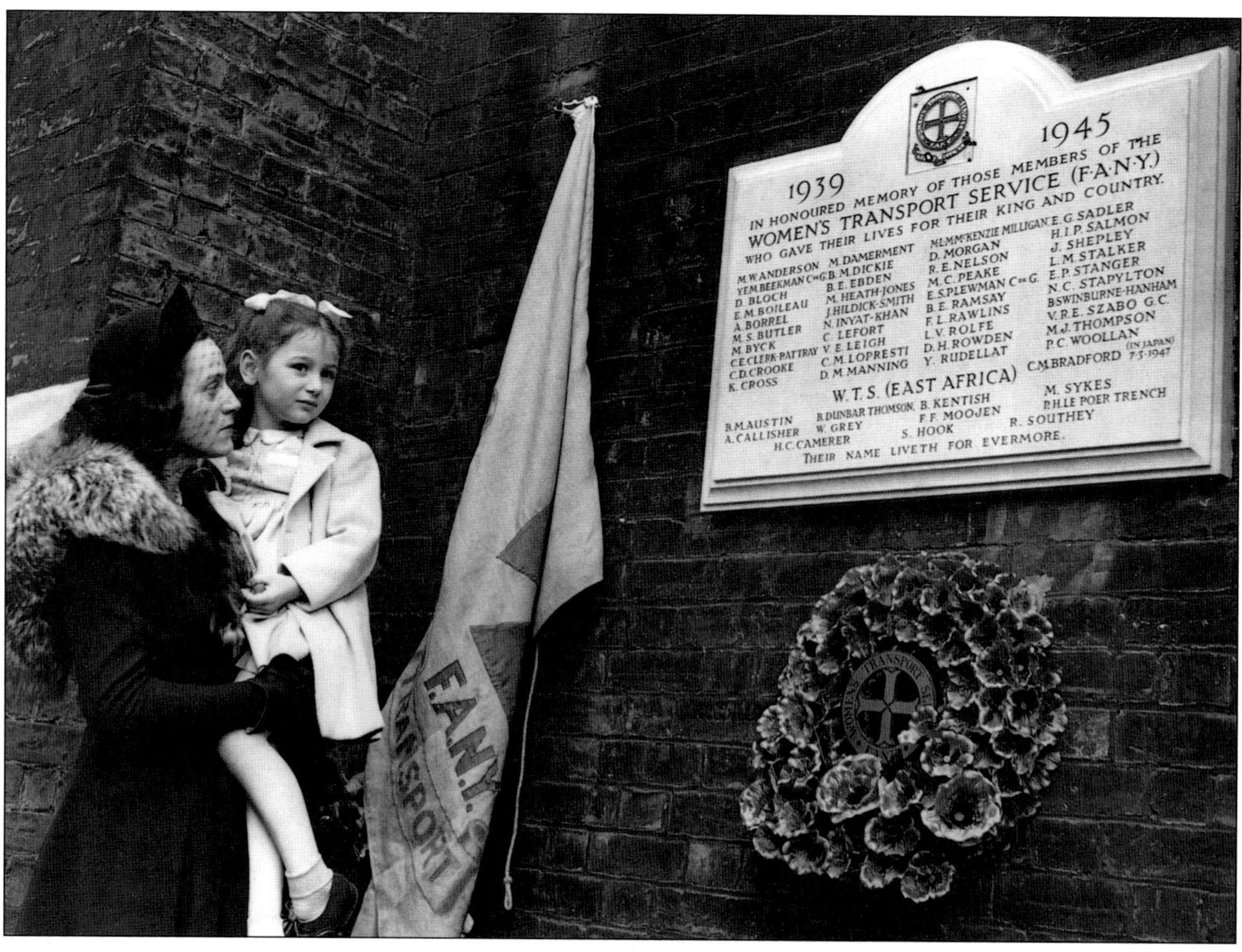

1939
1945
IN HONOURED MEMORY OF THOSE MEMBERS OF THE
WOMEN'S TRANSPORT SERVICE (F·A·N·Y.)
WHO GAVE THEIR LIVES FOR THEIR KING AND COUNTRY.
M.W. ANDERSON
Y.E.M. BEEKMAN C de G.
D. BLOCH
E.M. BOILEAU
A. BORREL
M.S. BUTLER
M. BYCK
C.E. CLERK-RATTRAY
C.D. CROOKE
K. CROSS
M. DAMERMENT
B. M. DICKIE
B.E. EBDEN
M. HEATH-JONES
J. HILDICK-SMITH
N. INYAT-KHAN
C. LEFORT
V.E. LEIGH
C.M. LOPRESTI
D.M. MANNING
M.L.M. McKENZIE MILLIGAN
D. MORGAN
R.E. NELSON
M.C. PEAKE
E.S. PLEWMAN C de G.
B.E. RAMSAY
F.L. RAWLINS
L.V. ROLFE
D.H. ROWDEN
Y. RUDELLAT
E.G. SADLER
H.I.P. SALMON
J. SHEPLEY
L.M. STALKER
E.P. STANGER
N.C. STAPYLTON
B. SWINBURNE-HANHAM
V.R.E. SZABO G.C.
M.J. THOMPSON
P.C. WOOLLAN
C.M. BRADFORD (IN JAPAN) 7·3·1947
W.T.S. (EAST AFRICA)
B.M. AUSTIN
A. CALLISHER
H.C. CAMERER
B. DUNBAR THOMSON
W. GREY
B. KENTISH
F.F. MOOJEN
S. HOOK
R. SOUTHEY
M. SYKES
P.H. LE POER TRENCH
THEIR NAME LIVETH FOR EVERMORE.
F.A.N.Y.

Tania Szabo, daughter of SOE agent Violette Szabo, with Odette Churchill at a memorial to British war heroines unveiled in London in 1948. Violette Szabo's name appears in the fourth column of the tablet.

Resistance, Hall organized, armed and trained some 300 agents for sabotage operations over the next six months. Meanwhile, as part of her cover in France, Hall lived the life of an ordinary peasant woman – or so she made it appear. She later recalled:

'I contacted farmer Eugène Lopinat who found a little house for me with one room, no water or electricity, located by the side of the road at the other end of the village from his farmhouse.… I cooked for the farmer, his old mother and the hired hand over an open fire as there was no stove in the house. I took his cows to pasture and in the process found several good fields for parachute drops.'

Remaining in one place for too long was not an option for an agent whose radio could be discovered by German direction-finders within half an hour.

A SIMPLE GOATHERD

Remaining in one place for too long was not an option for an agent, whose radio could be discovered by German direction-finders within a mere half hour. Hall relocated several times, moving from one safe house to the next and still posing as a French peasant woman. On one occasion, Hall stationed herself along a road, ostensibly tending a herd of goats, where she had a good view of German troop movements. That night, Hall transmitted the information to London.

Despite their description of Hall and the sketch they circulated, the Gestapo never caught her. Hall's cover was too good – she was a first-class actress – and she managed to keep her radio undetected. In the weeks after D-Day, between July 14 and August 14, 1944, Hall relayed no fewer than 37 messages to London containing vital information about German movements in France as they attempted to push back the tide of the Allied invasion. Hall's survival was certainly not due to luck alone. 'I was always keeping ahead of the Gestapo. I never gave them the opportunity,' she said in an interview after the war.

In 1945, Virginia Hall received the Distinguished Service Cross from President Harry Truman and an accolade from a fellow agent, Denis Rake. Rake spoke for all who knew her during the war when he commented: 'Virginia Hall in my opinion – and there are many others who share it – was one of the greatest woman agents of the war.'

VIOLETTE SZABO

After the war was over, the reputation of Virginia Hall entered the realm of clandestine warfare legend. So did stories about women like the British SOE agent Violette Szabo. The widow of a French soldier, she was captured and tortured by the Gestapo and afterwards executed at Ravensbrück concentration camp in 1945. Two years later, Szabo's parents and her young daughter, Tania, went to Buckingham Palace in London to receive from King George VI her posthumous award of the George Cross. The citation for Szabo's medal told a dramatic tale:

'With other members of her group, she was surrounded by the Gestapo in a house in southwest France. Resistance appeared hopeless, but Madame Szabo, seizing a Sten gun and as much ammunition as she could carry, barricaded herself in...and, exchanging shot for shot with the enemy, killed or wounded several of

Violette Szabo, one of 13 agents executed by the Germans in Ravensbrück concentration camp in 1945. Despite agonizing torture, she refused to give the Germans any information.

Ravensbrück concentration camp for women, situated 50 miles (80 km) north of Berlin, was first established in 1938 as a prison for Red Cross nurses. Some 50,000 prisoners died there.

Noor Inayat Khan

Noor Inayat Khan, an Indian princess and a descendant of Tipu Sultan, the 18th-century Sultan of Mysore, was probably the most unusual woman agent employed by SOE during World War II. Khan was brought up in France, and her familiarity with French life and culture and her command of the French language were obviously useful to SOE. However, she came with serious disadvantages. Although she was only half-Indian – her mother was American – her dusky skin and distinctive Indian beauty were bound to attract the attention of the racist Nazis and their French collaborators.

Telling the Truth

Worse than this, though, was Khan's inability to tell a lie, the result of her strict Muslim upbringing. Khan's SOE instructors knew that, if caught, Khan would refuse to lie to the Germans. Trained as a wireless operator, however, Khan became a valuable asset to them at a time when mass arrests of their radio experts in France had critically reduced their numbers. Khan became the first woman radio operator sent into German-occupied France. Khan arrived on June 16, 1943 and attached herself to French Resistance groups in Paris. She could not have come at a worse time: the Gestapo were in the process of arresting large numbers of Resistance personnel in the capital. Disobeying orders, Khan insisted on staying: hers was the last operational radio in France, at least for the time being.

Khan herself managed to remain free for some time, until she was betrayed by a woman jealous of her relationship with a male agent. Once she was turned over to the Gestapo, Khan's astonishing lack of concern for security was revealed. She had kept her radio set in full view in her room and had broken the strict rule, hammered home to all trainee agents, that they must never write anything down. Khan had recorded in an exercise book both the cyphers and the plain-language equivalents for every message she had radioed to London.

Dachau concentration camp in Bavaria, where Noor Inayat Khan died, was one of three camps set up by the Nazis in 1933. Dachau became notorious for its hideous medical 'experiments'. The Nazi slogan on the gates reads *Arbeit Macht Frei* – work sets free.

In Gestapo Hands

Under Gestapo interrogation, the woman who could not tell a lie would not tell the Germans anything. She remained silent about her own work and the purpose of her presence in France, and would not reveal any information about her comrades in the Resistance. Losing patience at her lack of cooperation, the Gestapo sent her to Germany for 'safe custody'. After ten months' imprisonment, mostly in isolation, she was sent to the concentration camp at Dachau. On September 13, 1944, the day after her arrival, she was executed by a shot in the back of the head. Some five years later, on April 5, 1949, Noor Inayat Khan was awarded a posthumous George Cross, Britain's highest civilian award.

Leo Marks, an SOE cryptographer during the war, knew Khan and admired her. '[She] was highly intelligent and she was fanatical,' he said. 'She probably should not have gone in, but having gone in, she was indispensable because she was so single-minded.'

them. By constant movement, she avoided being cornered and fought until she dropped exhausted.

'She was arrested and...was continuously and atrociously tortured, but never by word or deed gave away any of her acquaintances, or told the enemy anything of value.'

'Everyone tried to be a little braver than they felt. All of us had a moment of weakness, we did all cry together at one moment.'

CONCENTRATION CAMPS

French-born Odette Sansom was another legendary British agent captured and tortured by the Gestapo. She, too, told them nothing. Subsequently, on May 14, 1944, Sansom was taken to Germany, together with seven other women agents, including Andrée Borrel, Diana Rowden, Vera Leigh and Sonya Olschanezky.

'Everybody tried to be a little braver than they felt,' Sansom remembered later. '...All of us had a moment of weakness, we did all cry together at one moment, there were a few tears.... On the train, we were handcuffed...we were not free to move around.... We were frightened deep down, all of us. We were wondering what was the next thing.... Were we going straight to our deaths, were we going to a camp, were we going to prison, where were we going to.... Our only hope was maybe to be together somewhere.' It proved a futile hope.

'RELATIVES' IN HIGH PLACES

Sansom, who was sent to Ravensbrück, had already assured her survival when she was arrested together with a fellow agent, Peter Churchill: Sansom and Churchill claimed to be married and told the Gestapo that they were related to the British wartime Prime Minister, Winston

Odette Sansom's three young daughters toast their mother at a party celebrating her award of the George Cross. Peter Churchill, a fellow SOE agent, who married Odette in 1947, is seen on the right.

Wartime censorship: The letter shown right, sent from an American office in Shanghai, China, in December 1939, was examined by both German and British censors before delivery in London three months later. This is indicated by the different postmarks on the envelope.

Churchill. Although untrue, the story impressed the Germans sufficiently to prevent the couple's execution. Sansom, who was awarded the George Cross and the French Légion d'Honneur, married Peter Churchill in 1947.

Borrell, Rowden, Leigh and Olschanezky, a Jewish woman from Russia who had worked as a courier, had no such protection. They were imprisoned at the concentration camp at Natzweiler, and what happened to them there was overheard by another prisoner who worked at the ovens of the camp crematorium:

'They were bringing a woman along the corridor. We heard low voices in the next room and then the noise of a body being dragged along the floor.... At the time the body was brought past, we heard the noise of heavy breathing and low groaning.... Again and again, we heard the same noises and...groans as the insensible women were dragged away...'

The camp doctor told the four agents that they were to be inoculated against typhus, but in fact they were injected with phenol, which put them into a stupor. Still alive, Borrell, Rowden, Leigh and Olschanezky were dragged to the ovens in the crematorium and pushed into the flames. One of them regained consciousness, according to Peter Straub, the camp executioner, who was tried for war crimes in 1946. The woman reached up and scratched Straub's face, leaving deep marks.

'There!' said Straub on recounting the story when he was apparently very drunk. 'You can see how she scratched me. Look how she defended herself!'

The women who suffered this obscene death were among an estimated

These ovens at Dachau concentration camp, right, were used to cremate the bodies of Jews, gypsies and others whom the Nazis considered worthless. Captured Allied agents were also sent to concentration camps; very few survived.

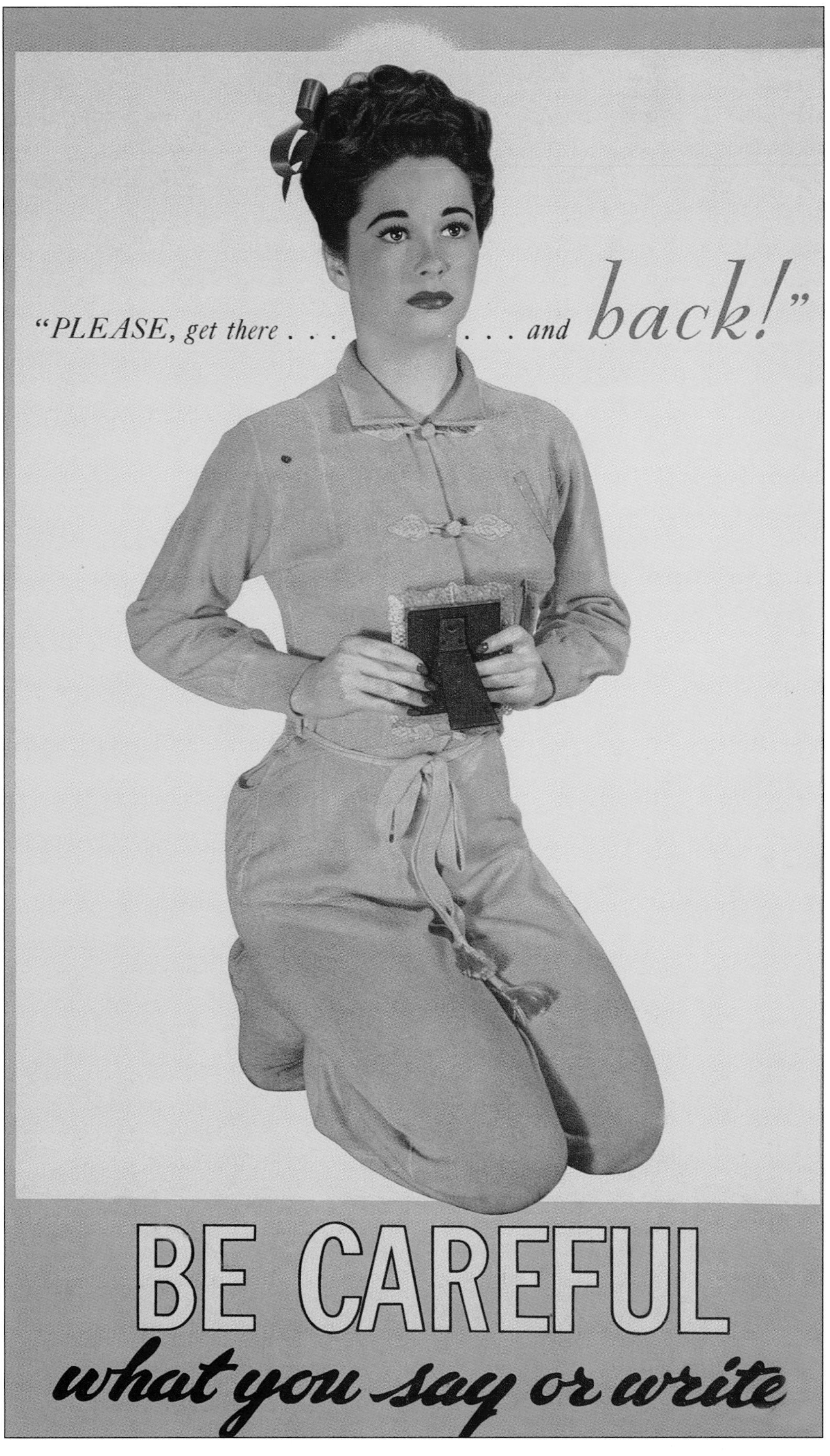

Civilian correspondents trying to elude censorship and agents sending secret information had much in common. Agents used microdots to encode letters and also employed invisible ink, artificial languages or obscure jargon. Governments were aware of the insecure nature of mailed letters, and used poster campaigns to dissuade civilians from mentioning war activities or military operations in their correspondence.

The gun shown here is the one-shot Liberator pistol. These were manufactured cheaply for use by resistance fighters and agents who needed a disposable but deadly weapon.

Deep in the French countryside, hopefully unseen by Germans, American bombers drop supplies and weapons by parachute to French Maquis resistance guerrillas waiting for them in a field (bottom left).

200 agents – over 42 percent of the total – who died or were killed in prison camps during World War II. A large number of them had operated in France, where SOE made its main effort in preparation for the D-Day landings of 1944, but other areas of occupied Europe were not neglected: SOE agents operated in most countries occupied by the Germans, including Belgium, the Netherlands, Poland, Denmark and Yugoslavia. Most agents were nationals of the European countries in which they operated, or had detailed knowledge in this respect, usually due to long-term residence. However, some came from far-distant nations. For example, French- and Yugoslav-Canadians were recruited for operations in the 'home country'. Chinese-Canadians assigned to the Far East comprised the largest contingent of Canadian secret agents during the war.

AMY THORPE

The OSS, too, had a hand in helping Resistance groups destabilize the Germans in occupied Europe. Most of this territory had been acquired by direct

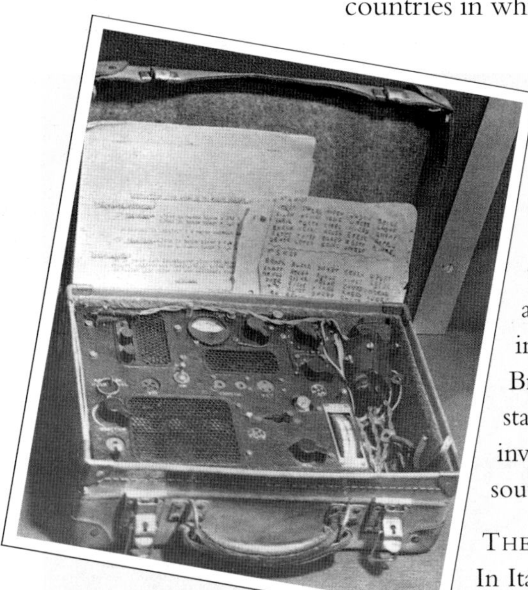

Secret radios built into suitcases were used by SOE agents to transmit coded messages. The papers at the back contain decoding tables. The suitcase was deliberately 'battered' to look inconspicuous.

FANYs in SOE

In an unusual merger of services, members of the First Aid Nursing Yeomanry (FANY) joined forces with SOE and were specially trained to work as wireless operators and coders in the Mediterranean area, part of SOE's backup for the Allied forces before and during the invasions of Sicily and Italy in 1943. The first group of FANYs left Britain for North Africa on December 22, 1942. Subsequently, FANY stations were established in Algiers, Cairo, Corsica and, as the Allied invasions proceeded and the German defenders retreated, at centres in southern and central Italy.

The FANYs in Italy

In Italy, the FANYs were close to the war zones. The incessant calls on their time and energy, especially in 1944, were made all the more challenging by poor food, no fresh fruit or vegetables, and exposure to dangerous illnesses. One of the FANY coders in Italy, Milbrough Walker, became seriously ill with suspected blood poisoning and nearly died before her life was saved by penicillin injections. The show, however, had to go on.

'You might be at death's door,' Walker later remembered, 'but you still went back to work when there was a desperate need, and on occasions – when there was no room at a table – one would sit on the floor. We were [extremely] dedicated, and once you started work you didn't notice these things.... Everything depended on getting the message right; speed and accuracy were all-important, particularly the latter, and you just never had to lose your nerve, however fast the clock was ticking towards transmission time.'

Many of the women who secretly worked on the British codebreaking effort were employed to feed information to the world's first programmable electronic computer, Colossus, of which this is a working replica. German codes cracked by Colossus were a key factor in the outcome of D-Day.

The famous German Enigma machine. The Germans never realized that the Enigma codes had been broken before the war, nor that Allied codebreakers were able to read the Enigma messages.

conquest. But after the French surrender of June 1940, southern France, previously free, came under German control through the collaborationist regime set up at Vichy. Before the United States entered the war, the OSS had a crucial advantage: American neutrality meant that Germany, Italy and the Vichy government still retained embassies in Washington – and all of them were ripe for infiltration. The agent chosen for this task was Amy Thorpe, a beautiful American woman who was herself a diplomatic wife, completely at home among embassy staff and with no qualms about using her charms to attract them.

Thorpe had a successful track record in espionage which had begun before the war. Her husband, Arthur Pack, was a diplomat stationed at the British Embassy in Warsaw, Poland, when she was hired in 1937 by Britain's intelligence organization, MI6. Thorpe informed MI6 that the German Enigma codes, used for sending fiendishly complicated secret messages, had been deciphered by Polish mathematicians. With this information, the British government persuaded the Poles to give them the codes, together with a replica of the Enigma machine. At the outbreak of war in 1939, therefore, the British were already equipped with the means of reading German transmissions. This proved an invaluable advantage to them and the Allies.

At the outbreak of war in 1939, the British were already equipped with the means of reading German (Enigma) transmissions. This proved an invaluable advantage to the Allies.

Thorpe separated from Pack in 1941 and returned to the United States, where, on behalf of MI6, she joined in the social life at the German and Italian embassies in Washington. Again the British gained an advantage when Thorpe passed to them the codes used by the Italian Navy.

Around mid-1941, Thorpe transferred her talents – and her wiles – to the service of the OSS, which needed inside information on the secrets of the Vichy regime. Once inside the Vichy embassy in Washington, Thorpe began an affair with a French diplomat, Charles Emanuel Brousse. Brousse, several times married and divorced, was highly susceptible to women, and he soon fell for the fascinating Amy Thorpe.

A still from the 1957 movie *Carve Her Name with Pride*, starring Virginia McKenna, a dramatization of the life of SOE agent Violette Szabo.

Sexual attraction was not, however, his only reason for the cooperation that followed. The French were in an agonizing position during the war: many, including Brousse, felt that the honour of France had been defiled by the Vichy government's capitulation under the aged Marshal Pétain, who had been a great hero of the First World War. Amy Thorpe found it easy to play on her lover's anti-Vichy sentiments, while he, for his part, responded by giving her information about the embassy's correspondence.

Aiding resistance to the Germans and their allies went hand in hand with a propaganda campaign designed to destroy morale.

STEALING THE CODES

Together with an expert safecracker, Thorpe and Brousse scored their greatest coup in the summer of 1942 when they stole code-books from the embassy safe, delivered them to be photographed by a special OSS team in Washington, and then returned the books, all within a few hours. By this means, the OSS obtained secret codes as well as confidential Vichy government plans and information about the defences of southern France. This was of incalculable value to undercover agents operating in the French North African colonies during the prelude to the Anglo-American invasion of 1942.

After their respective divorces, Thorpe and Brousse married in 1944.

PROPAGANDA

Aiding resistance to the Germans and their allies and undermining their war

Listening to Allied radio broadcasts incurred harsh punishments during the German occupation: here, the inhabitants of Cherbourg freely listen to the war news after the American liberation of the town in 1944.

Industrial Espionage

A great deal of slave labour was used in the war factories by the Germans, but Danes working in the plants producing the V-1 'Vengeance' weapons struck a blow of their own: they passed secret information about the V-1 to the British, enabling Allied bombers to target the factories.

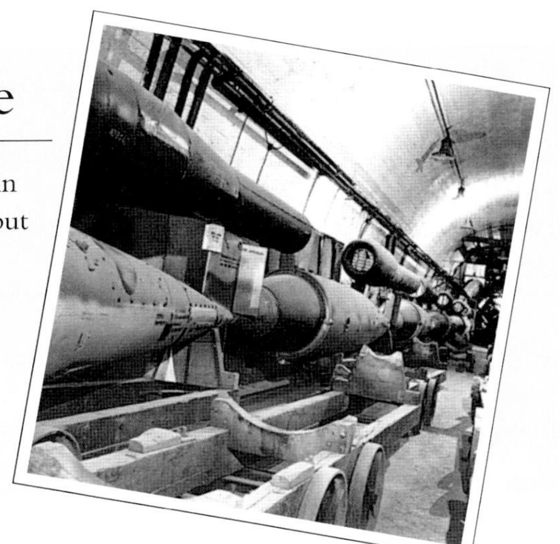

efforts went hand in hand with a propaganda campaign designed to destroy morale, sometimes making the enemy a laughing stock. One story put about by the propaganda branch of SOE claimed that Adolf Hitler was a eunuch – a slur directed at the virility-conscious Arabs in North Africa, who had been somewhat equivocal about which side they supported in the war.

The propaganda directed against the Japanese – in Japan itself and throughout their Pacific conquests – represented the main effort of the OSS in the secret war. As a result, the Japanese were bombarded with radio broadcasts and leaflets publicizing the defeats of Japan's forces and the triumphs of the United States.

The OSS campaign was carefully orchestrated to suit the Japanese mentality. Several women, all very highly educated and experts in their field, were employed by the OSS to make sure the propaganda was pitched just right.

Jane Smith-Hutton, OSS manager in Washington for Morale Operations, had spent 12 years in Japan and spoke the language fluently: she gave lectures on Japanese psychology and social structure and those cultural weak spots that could be exploited.

In a similar vein, Dr. Clare Holt, an expert on South-east Asia, lectured on the Dutch East Indies (Indonesia), the missionary Lucy

The internment of Japanese-Americans under suspicion of being potential spies was one of the great controversial issues in the wartime United States. Several were classed as 'dangerous enemy aliens'.

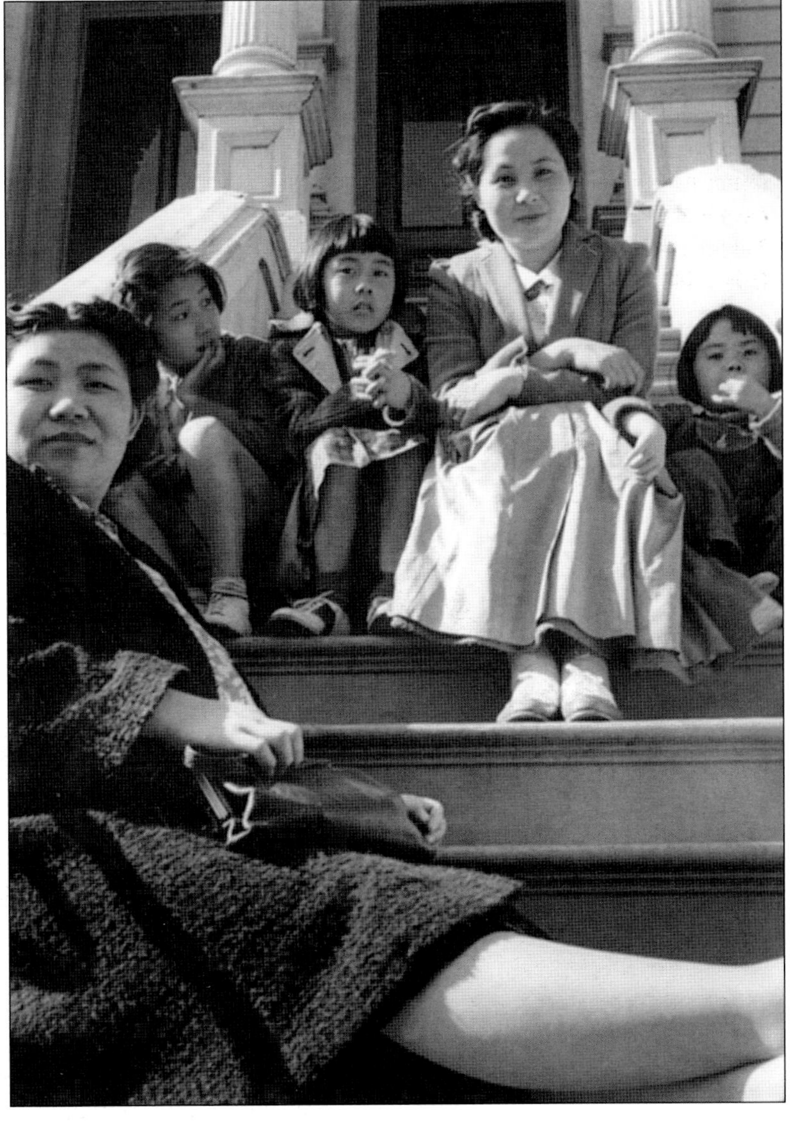

Tokyo Rose

Iva Ikuko Toguri d'Aquino was a sultry-voiced American woman of Japanese parentage whose broadcasts on Tokyo Radio during the war were aimed at demoralizing GIs stationed in the Pacific. The GIs nicknamed her 'Tokyo Rose'.

Tokyo Rose put out standard propaganda about impending counterattacks by Japanese forces, but spiced her broadcasts with snide suggestions that the GIs' wives were up to no good at home. However, in the main, the Tokyo Rose broadcasts had the opposite effect to what was intended. Reminders of home, such as American dance music, were included in the transmissions and were designed to soften up the GIs through nostalgia – but most of them loved the music, ignored the propaganda and looked forward to the next broadcast.

Arrested after the war, d'Aquino was charged with treason. Her three-month trial made headlines. She was found guilty and sentenced to ten years in prison and a fine of $10,000 (£7,000). D'Aquino served six years in the Federal Reformatory for Women in West Virginia, classified as a 'notorious offender'.

More than 30 years later, d'Aquino was granted a pardon by President Gerald Ford after she claimed that the Japanese had forced her to broadcast their propaganda. Not only had her trial been grossly prejudiced, she said, but she had been only one of a dozen women – all on air as 'Tokyo Rose' – who had broadcast from Tokyo during the war.

Starling dealt with Siam (Thailand), and Dr. Ina Telberg, who held a degree in Asian studies, dealt with Japanese military ideology and its basis in the strict samurai code of Bushido, which, among other principles, required ritual suicide for warriors faced with surrender.

JAPANESE WAR PLANS

However, while OSS operatives acquired a great deal of personal and cultural information about the Japanese, an understanding of their war plans and their activities in conquered areas was much harder to come by. Patricia Barnett, a graduate of Vassar College, was given the task of uncovering this vital information from a very small research base.

'Some of the requirements levied on me were mind-boggling at a time when our research files filled only one and a half drawers in a safe,' Barnett later commented. 'In one day, I would be asked to identify bombing targets in Southeast Asia, produce a plan to weaken the Japanese economy on the home front [and] assess political changes the Japanese occupation army had made in Indonesia.'

None of these tasks was straightforward. To select the bombing targets, for example, Barnett had to know 'what the Japanese were obtaining from [Southeast Asia], such as metals, food or fuel'. Then, she went on, 'I would try to determine where these supplies were located.'

This work required an enormous amount of digging through material just to extract a single clue, as well as quizzing people familiar with the area. All this and whatever else the OSS needed to know required long hours of labour, a very cool head and endless patience.

A warning against spies, opposite. Espionage was a distinct danger in wartime Russia; the USSR contained several groups, such as Ukrainians, who hated the dominant Russians and were only too glad to help the Germans. The poster reads 'Don't Gossip'.

БУДЬ НА ЧЕКУ,
В ТАКИЕ ДНИ
ПОДСЛУШИВАЮТ СТЕНЫ.
НЕДАЛЕКО ОТ БОЛТОВНИ
И СПЛЕТНИ
ДО ИЗМЕНЫ.

НЕ БОЛТАЙ!

The Adventures of Gertrude Legendre

Gertrude Sanford Legendre, head of the OSS Central Cable Desk in Paris, was due five days' leave starting September 23, 1944. Paris had been liberated a month earlier but the war was still close enough, Legendre reckoned, to visit the front and, as she put it, get a 'smell of the fighting'. Legendre teamed up with the equally adventurous Robert Jennings, a U.S. naval commander, and set off east. On the way, they encountered Major Maxwell Papurt of OSS Intelligence.

Ambushed

Paris, where Gertrude Legendre was afterwards stationed, was liberated on August 25, 1944; this group of happy Parisiennes greeted Free French leader Charles de Gaulle as he toured the city.

The three were heading for Wallendorf, 25 miles (40 kilometres) from Luxembourg, in the mistaken belief that it was in American hands, when their Jeep ran into a German ambush. Papurt was badly injured, and they were forced to bring out a white flag and surrender. In the time it took the Germans to reach the Jeep and arrest them, the Americans agreed on their cover stories. Jennings could admit to being what he was, a U.S. naval officer, but Legendre and Papurt were to conceal their identities: she was to be an American Embassy filing clerk, he would pose as an ordnance officer. Amazingly, Legendre had had enough time to burn and bury the incriminating papers they carried revealing their OSS connections, but there was one document Papurt had not given her: it contained a list of 30 agents, together with the names of the intelligence organizations that employed them.

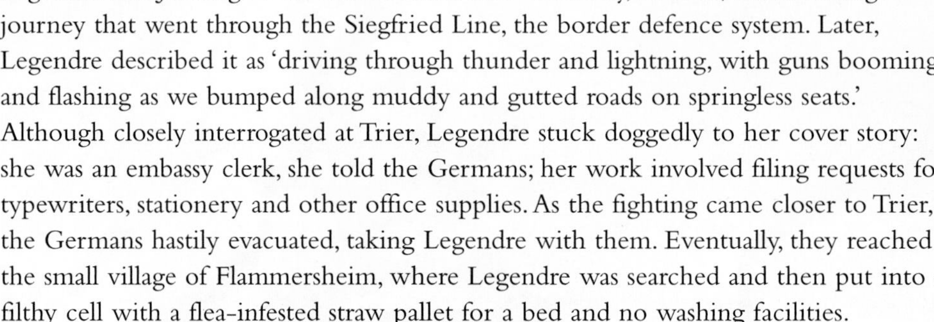

The Germans took the injured Papurt to a nearby field medical station. Legendre and Jennings were taken further into Germany, to Trier, a hair-raising journey that went through the Siegfried Line, the border defence system. Later, Legendre described it as 'driving through thunder and lightning, with guns booming and flashing as we bumped along muddy and gutted roads on springless seats.' Although closely interrogated at Trier, Legendre stuck doggedly to her cover story: she was an embassy clerk, she told the Germans; her work involved filing requests for typewriters, stationery and other office supplies. As the fighting came closer to Trier, the Germans hastily evacuated, taking Legendre with them. Eventually, they reached the small village of Flammersheim, where Legendre was searched and then put into a filthy cell with a flea-infested straw pallet for a bed and no washing facilities.

A Dangerous Spy

Legendre was questioned again, but soon realized the Germans did not believe her. The incriminating list Papurt carried had been taken off him at the field medical station. Legendre, the Germans assumed, had been in league with him, and they now regarded her as a spy. Legendre was told as much by an SS officer, Lieutenant Wilhelm Gosewisch, who interrogated her after she was moved again, this time to the Wehrmacht (German Army) headquarters in a castle close to the German village of Diez.

'He came right to the point,' she reported later, 'and said I was considered a very dangerous spy. If I didn't tell him everything, he would get it out of me. The Germans had ways of making people talk.'

The interrogation continued far into the night. Legendre denied everything: she professed to have no knowledge of the list or the people and organizations named on it. She was fortunate, however, that Gosewisch was a civilized man: though an SS officer, he had none of the brutality normally associated with the German political police.

As time went on, the two of them became quite friendly, and soon they were on first-name terms.

'Bill would come down to my cell...and take me upstairs to his office,' said Legendre. 'Here, over cognac or wine, we would chat from about nine o'clock till two or three in the morning.' Gosewisch told Legendre that his wife was American, and that he had lived and worked in the United States for 18 years. He went further and revealed that he had never been in favour of the war and hoped that the Allies would win it.

A Convincing Fiction

Then Gosewisch was suddenly ordered to the front for three weeks. His departure from Diez Castle was the cue for the Gestapo, who had been angling to get their hands on Legendre and interrogate her. The day after Gosewisch left, Gestapo agents came to the castle and took Legendre to Gestapo headquarters in Berlin.

Under interrogation there, she repeated her cover story yet again and found, somewhat to her surprise, that Gertrude Legendre the filing clerk had taken on the aspect of reality.

'My imaginary life as an embassy clerk was real,' she said. 'I could see the room, the steel filing cases, a table littered with requests for typewriters...manila folders.... Even [the] women colleagues I invented began to assume a personality of their own.'

Legendre was kept in Wansee Prison in the suburbs of Berlin, but Allied bombing and the proximity of the Russians meant that she had to be hurriedly moved twice more, until she finally arrived at Kronberg, near Frankfurt, where she was lodged with Dr. Hans Greime, an industrialist. Greime had contacts at the German Foreign Office, and with his help Legendre managed to contact Gosewisch, who was now back in Diez Castle. He came to see her almost at once, and arranged for her to escape into neutral Switzerland.

Spared at the Border

Legendre's way out was a train that left Konstanz, close to the Swiss border, late in March 1945. A short time after departure, though, it came to a halt while still inside Germany. Legendre leapt down onto the tracks and sprinted toward the white gates indicating Switzerland and freedom. A German border guard shouted at her to halt, but she kept on and managed to get through the gates while he stood yelling and gesturing with rage behind her. Why he failed to shoot her in the back Legendre never discovered.

Legendre's dangerous adventure lasted six months before she finally returned to Paris on her birthday, March 29, 1945. She appeared contrite about her escapade and made no attempt at excuses. However, her career in Paris was over. Sworn never to reveal anything about the OSS or her experiences, she was sent back to Washington soon after her return.

In 1950, five years after the end of the war, Legendre learned that, back in Germany, Lieutenant Gosewisch and his family were destitute. She arranged for them to travel to South Carolina, where she and her husband ran a plantation, and gave Gosewisch a job. Legendre and her former jailer met often to reminisce, and every holiday he brought her a bouquet of red roses.

CHAPTER 7

Women as Prisoners

Millions of women became prisoners during the war. Jewish, gypsy and Polish women became victims of Nazi atrocities, while others were caught up in the rapid Japanese advance across Southeast Asia and the Pacific.

In 1940 and 1941, civilians trapped by the swift conquests of the Germans in Europe and the Japanese in Southeast Asia had little time to comprehend the crisis that had suddenly engulfed them and to arrange their escape. Those who managed to get away were few compared to the millions with nowhere to go or no time to reach safety.

In Europe, the Nazis had long planned to 'cleanse' society of racial and other categories of 'undesirables' and leave the continent free for their own Aryan 'master race'. To this end, non-Aryans – mainly Jews and gypsies – were rounded up and transported to concentration camps. Some escaped by going into hiding. Most, however, were starved or worked to death in the concentration and slave-labour camps, subjected to obscene medical experiments, or were murdered, thousands at a time, in the Nazi gas chambers. They were then cremated in ovens built for the purpose.

The Nazis used zyklon-B crystals to effect these mass killings. With 250 gypsy children serving as guinea pigs, they tested the efficacy of the toxic substance in June 1940. All 250 died. Ultimately, the routine of mass murder became so efficient that, at its peak, on August 1,

Some British women taken prisoner by the Japanese endured over three years of hard physical labour. Here civilian prisoners in Singapore dig their own drainage ditches using primitive slate tools and a single hoe.

Local Germans were made to view these cremation ovens at Belsen concentration camp after its liberation in 1945; out of 60,000 survivors of Belsen, 28,000 died within a few weeks.

1944, 4,000 gypsies were gassed and cremated in a single session. In all, 6 million Jews and up to 5 million gypsies perished by this means. So did some 4,500 Poles who, as Slavs, also failed to fit the Nazi image of racial perfection.

Zyklon-B (hydrocyanic acid), the deadly gas originally intended as a vermin killer and disinfectant, which was used to kill thousands at a time in the concentration camp gas chambers.

EUROPEANS UNDER THE LASH

Civilians, mainly Europeans, trapped by the war in Southeast Asia, were similarly affected by a harsh racism linked with the politics of empire. Much of the influence the Japanese hoped to exert over their conquered territories was premised on the fact that they, an Asian people, had vanquished the hated European imperialists. The Europeans they took prisoner might be only minor colonial officials, businessmen, plantation owners, office workers, missionaries, or their wives, husbands and children, but they represented empires – British, French, Dutch – which had oppressed and exploited Asian subjects for a century or more.

Now it was the turn of Europeans to feel the lash. And the Japanese made them feel that lash every day over the next three years. Disease, malnutrition, starvation or simply despair did the rest, and thousands of Europeans died or had their health irreparably damaged in Japanese captivity.

CHANGI JAIL

The greatest single symbol of Japanese brutality was Changi Jail in Singapore, where prisoners languished in atrocious conditions of squalor and degradation. Sheila Allen, the 17-year-old daughter of an Australian mining engineer and a Malayan mother, was imprisoned in

The Captives' Hymn

During World War II, Margaret Dryberg, an English Presbyterian missionary, was captured by the Japanese and confined in the prison camp at Ngambur in the Dutch East Indies (Indonesia). Soon joined by other women, mainly Dutch, Dryberg, a talented musician, created a 'voice orchestra' as a means of taking the inmates' minds off their captivity. Dryberg was also a poet, and she wrote a special song for four voices, The Captives' Hymn, which was first performed in the camp on July 5, 1942:

Father, in captivity
We would lift our prayer to Thee,
Keep us ever in Thy love,
Grant that daily we may prove
Those who place their trust in Thee
More than conquerors can be.

Give us patience to endure,
Keep our hearts serene and pure,
Grant us courage, charity,
Greater faith, humility,
Readiness to own Thy will,
Be we free or captive still.

May the day of freedom dawn,
Peace and justice be reborn.
Grant that nations loving Thee
O'er the world may brothers be,
Cleansed by suffering, know rebirth,
See Thy kingdom come on earth.

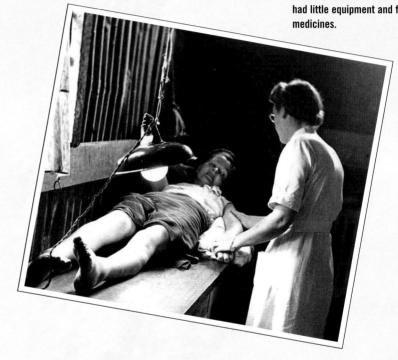

Prisoners of the Germans and the Japanese suffered starvation, malnutrition and numerous epidemic diseases and infections. Nurses and doctors, themselves suffering, had little equipment and few medicines.

Changi after the colony surrendered on February 15, 1942. On the way there, Allen witnessed an example of what was to come. A woman lay dead or dying by the roadside. Her baby, however, was still alive. Hearing its cries, a Japanese soldier tossed it high into the air and speared it on his bayonet as it descended. The child died instantly. Allen saw its blood trickling down the bayonet and saw, too, how the soldier smiled with satisfaction.

Thousands of Europeans either died or had their health irreparably damaged by their Japanese captivity. In Singapore, prisoners languished in atrocious conditions.

The prisoners bound for Changi had been told to bring sufficient supplies for ten days. It did not occur to them that the supplies should include food. It was the start of over three years of near-starvation. Red Cross parcels supplied some food, but all too often they were appropriated by the Japanese. For the rest, Allen and the other prisoners in Changi lived by scrounging what they could, even eating worms at times, but otherwise going hungry. One day, Allen learned first-hand what shocking things hunger could do to ordinary, civilized people. She found a nest of newborn mice, so tiny that they slid easily down her throat. Afterwards, in disgust and remorse, she attempted to make herself sick.

Sheila Allen lived in perpetual terror that they would find her secret diary. Had they done so, she would have been executed immediately. Luckily, the diary was never discovered.

LIFE IN CHANGI

Every day in Changi was a day of trepidation. The tone was set when the first Japanese commandant, a kindly man who gave sweets to the children, was charged with treason by his subordinates and executed. The Korean guards, however, were never anything but brutal. They barged into the prisoners' quarters any time of the day or night to conduct searches, tossed the women's few possessions around the huts, and threatened to beat them up or kill them if they protested. Sheila Allen lived in perpetual terror that they would find the secret diary she was keeping. Had they done so, she would have been executed immediately. Luckily, the diary was never discovered. Supplies of every kind were short in Changi, and she had to scrounge around for scraps of paper on which to write it.

Despite the danger, writing the diary was therapeutic. 'I had to do something to keep my sanity…' Allen commented. 'What better option than to record…how we lived, what we did to keep ourselves from getting bored, and how the camp was running as near to a civilized manner as an uncivilized situation would allow.'

Deliberate humiliation was a part of the ill-treatment in the Japanese prison camps; at tenko – the twice-daily roll call – these prisoners were forced to bow in reverence to their captors.

Women prisoners in the Japanese wartime camps had to grow their own food – or otherwise starve. After living in peacetime luxury, many Europeans were unused to such humbling, back-breaking work.

Overcrowding was endemic at Changi. At night, a sleeping prisoner only had to turn over to invade someone else's space. Nerves were so taut that arguments and even fistfights occurred. The women banded together, though, when it came to protecting the children: they would crowd around the youngsters or cover them up when the Korean guards were near.

The Changi quilts had a clandestine purpose – they were ideal for sending messages to other prisoners.

The prisoners made every effort to keep themselves occupied. They formed several committees – for teaching the children, performing music, playing cards, making quilts. The Changi quilts had a clandestine purpose: they were ideal for sending messages to other prisoners. One woman, Elizabeth, used a quilt to conceal a secret letter she sent to her husband Jack, who was imprisoned in the male section of the jail.

HUMILIATION

During their nightmare years of imprisonment, the 'colonial' women in Changi – many of whom were accustomed before the war to a life of ease, with servants to attend their every need – learned what it meant to do the most menial chores and live in filth and

want, terrorized by their jailers and always in dread of execution. The Japanese, in fact, played on these fears, by taking women under sentence of death to see the rooms in which they were to die, then returning them to prison camp to brood on the prospect.

When the Japanese conquests began, some women were living far enough away from the initial hostilities to have time to escape. Not all of them took advantage of the opportunity.

This descent from privilege to degradation was the ultimate exercise in humiliation, as the Japanese intended it should be, and it was an experience shared by women prisoners all over the conquered territories of Southeast Asia and the Pacific.

When the Japanese conquests began, some women were living far enough from the initial hostilities to have time to escape. Not all of them took advantage of the opportunity, however. Some were unwilling to abandon their silver, china, fine linen and other luxury items, and perhaps imagined that somehow they could keep their possessions intact even if the Japanese came. However, a far greater imperative was keeping the family together. Rather than split up, with no guarantee of ever being reunited, many women stayed where they were, despite the consequences.

One of them was Agnes Newton Keith, the American wife of a British civil servant and the mother of a son, George. In the early days of the war in Europe, Keith had followed events closely as they unfolded, and she knew perfectly well that what had happened there could also happen where she lived, in Sandakan in the north of the faraway British colony of Borneo.

'Homes like ours were being blown to bits,' Keith wrote. 'Babies like George were being killed, lives like our own were destroyed.... Thus, in the shadow of Europe's destruction, we waited with dreadful certainty for Pearl Harbor.'

THE JAPANESE IN BORNEO

Keith did not have to wait long before the aftermath of Pearl Harbor reached her doorstep. The Japanese invaded Borneo only six days later, on December 13, 1941, and on January 19 they reached Sandakan. With that, the comfortable expatriate life – with its exclusive golf, tennis and social clubs, its plethora of parties and other social events – vanished overnight. At Sandakan,

Epidemics of typhus were virtually endemic in the Japanese camps. These nurses, prisoners in Singapore, cut down lulang plants to eliminate the natural environment of tick-infested rats which spread typhus.

For over three years, these two women prisoners, seen here doing household chores, made their prison camp home in a ramshackle hovel roofed by pieces of rusty corrugated iron.

the Japanese first seized all the men and put them in prison. The women, Agnes Keith among them, were allowed to remain in their houses, but the Japanese were never far away. She was pregnant and ill with malaria when three soldiers came to the house to question her. They pushed her around, knocked her to the floor several times and beat her. That afternoon, Keith suffered a miscarriage.

The Japanese, meanwhile, were making their arrangements. On May 12, 1942, all Europeans in Sandakan – and Agnes Keith – were ordered to report to internment camps. Keith and her son were sent to a camp for women and children on Berhala Island, off the coast of Borneo.

An American poster designed to inspire hatred and disgust of the Japanese enemy. The poster graphically illustrated the perceived extent of Japanese atrocities as inflicted on women – murder, execution and rape.

RAPE

On Berhala, the Japanese regarded white 'Caucasian' women as members of a 'fourth-class nation', and this may have been a reason why, generally, they did not interfere with them: the purity of their own superior race might have been at stake had they done so.

Another explanation may have been the traditional Japanese respect for the family ideal, as represented by mothers and their children. It was a paradox, though a gratifying one, that rape was not usually on the agenda, even though the Japanese did not shrink from mistreating their white women prisoners, beating them, torturing and killing them.

Women who bore the brunt of rape were more likely to be Asians, whom the Japanese used for prostitution: Chinese women were raped as a matter of routine, and the Japanese kept 200,000 women, most of them Koreans, as 'comfort' for their soldiers. Another vulnerable group were the American, British and other nurses, 'single' women seen as living outside the family context. One group of British nurses in Hong Kong, captured by the Japanese on December 25, 1941, spent Christmas day and night in a small room where their Japanese guards took turns raping them over and over again. Three of the nurses were murdered after the Japanese had finished with them.

Although the women on Berhala Island were spared the spectre of rape, the rest of the scenario still applied. Agnes Keith described the conditions:

In Japanese 'samurai' culture, there was nothing more shameful than surrender; rather than this, many Japanese preferred suicide and had contempt for prisoners who had allowed themselves to be captured.

'There was no furniture,' Keith wrote, 'and we slept and ate on the floor.... Centipedes lived under us, and rats lived over us. The rats were so numerous that the noise of their fighting, play, eating and copulating kept us awake at night.'

WORKING FOR THE JAPANESE

Like all prisoners, Keith was soon put to work. Labour in the camps varied from cleaning out a guardhouse, dusting the entire length of a wharf using only handkerchiefs, or working in the fields, to the back-breaking task of clearing a patch of jungle to make it fit for cultivating food. In any case, after four hours, Keith was absolutely exhausted.

'I could scarcely walk back to my barracks,' she recalled. 'I would be so filthy that I could not sit down inside and so tired I could scarcely stand up to bathe.'

On Berhala and elsewhere, simply staying alive was a major effort for women unaccustomed to fending for themselves and reliant all their lives on the support of men. Being a lone mother never had more dire connotations than it did under Japanese imprisonment. Agnes Keith's greatest concern was her son George and the need to be strong for him. The fear, exhaustion and apprehension Keith suffered in the first week of internment would have been sufficient, in other circumstances, to reduce her to hysteria and tears. Instead, for George's sake, she disciplined herself into a calmness she did not feel and never let her son see a moment of weakness.

TRIAL BY BAYONET

Psychological strength was, in fact, the only weapon the women had to use against the Japanese. Gwen Dew, a

Japanese soldiers had respect for mothers, as representatives of the family ideal which they themselves revered, but single working women, such as nurses, became targets for rape, as did many Asian women.

journalist later imprisoned in Hong Kong, was initiated into the mentality of terror when the newly arrived Japanese came to the hotel where she and other civilians were staying. A soldier drew the blade of his bayonet across her throat, repeating the exercise several times, probably to see how she reacted. Dew managed to keep her expression impassive and shrugged at the soldier to show how little she cared. He tired of the game and put the bayonet down.

In addition to the physical and psychological pressures of Japanese captivity, the struggle merely to survive required maximum ingenuity and women had to resort to desperate means of obtaining food.

In addition to the physical and psychological pressures of Japanese captivity, the struggle merely to survive required maximum ingenuity, and women like Agnes Keith had to resort to desperate, even dangerous, means of obtaining food. The food provided by the Japanese was never sufficient, consisting mainly of thin rice gruel, a small amount of cooked rice, and sometimes salt, sugar and tea. Needless to say, malnutrition was rife on Berhala, but prison rules forbade prisoners to obtain food or supplies from outside.

Keith broke the rules. She managed to make contact with a local fisherman named Saleh, who agreed to deliver a supply of eggs sent to her by a man who had once worked for her husband, Harry. This was the start of a regular supply arrangement which put both Agnes Keith and Saleh at enormous risk.

BLACK MARKET

As a small island, Berhala was much more accessible than Kuching, a camp on the mainland of Borneo where Keith and other women prisoners were transferred late in the war. In Kuching there was no way smugglers like Saleh could reach them, and the only recourse was a three-way black market. The pattern was established in 1945. Local Chinese merchants were forced to sell food to the Japanese guards for cash. The guards in turn bartered the food with the women in exchange for such valuables as they still possessed. Keith, for example, exchanged her sorority pin for 40 eggs and a bottle of coconut oil, which ensured nourishment for herself and George for the next three weeks.

Eventually, on September 11, 1945, Australian troops liberated Kuching and the Keith family was reunited. Agnes and Harry Keith were gaunt, pale, utterly weary and suffering from malaria and malnutrition, but she was still able to record the joys of their newfound freedom. The Australians, she wrote in an understandable mood of euphoria, 'were for that time a part of all goodness and virtue, a part of all love. They brought us liberty and freedom and something even greater – belief again in the decency of men.'

HORRORS BEYOND IMAGINATION

The belief in 'the decency of men' had been brutally challenged in Europe the previous year, on July 22, 1944, when the concentration and extermination camp at Majdanek, near Lublin, was discovered by Russian troops advancing into Poland. Majdanek was only the first chapter of a story so horrific that, when fully revealed, it defied the imagination with its examples of profound and systematic evil.

Over the next ten months the Allied armies overran almost 30 more camps, and the hideous sights that confronted them were everywhere the same. In the camp compounds, emaciated corpses

Prisoners of the Gestapo

The most terrifying fate in Nazi-occupied Europe, and in Germany itself, was to become a prisoner of the Gestapo, the sinister secret police which used brutal interrogations and torture to drag information from its victims. In Paris, the Gestapo headquarters at the Avenue Foch became known as a place of the most fearful suffering and death. It was here that several Allied agents, including Odette Sansom who was tortured by having her fingernails drawn out, were interrogated. Odette survived but many others never emerged alive.

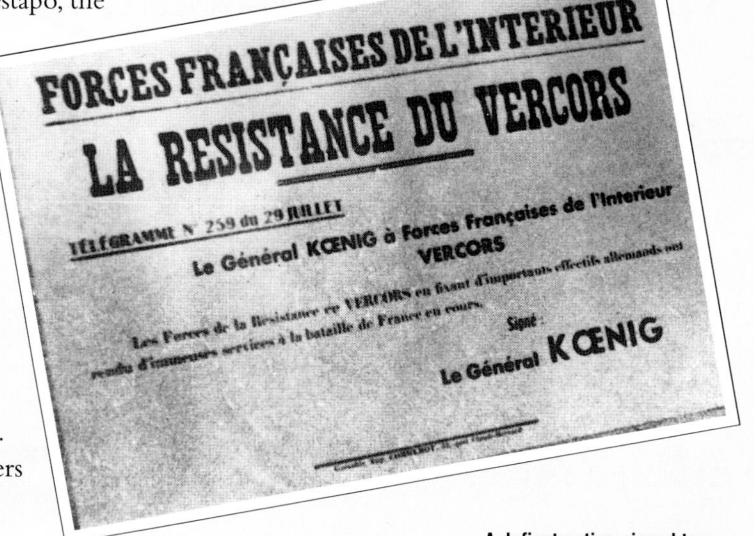

A defiant notice pinned to a wall in Vercours encouraging the French Resistance and signed by General Marie-Pierre Koenig, a leading member of Charles de Gaulle's Free French forces.

The Avenue Foch was only one of several places where horrific brutalities were practised. In 1997, the El-De House, Gestapo headquarters in Cologne, opened its doors as a museum. Exhibits graphically revealed the extent of the terrors that once went on behind its walls. A gallows in the courtyard marked the place where prisoners were executed. In the squalid, cramped cells where prisoners were held, some 1,800 inscriptions were scratched on the walls with pieces of chalk, coal or nails. Some prisoners wrote poems, others desperate pleas for help or letters; one was a complete message from a French girl to her mother, which read: 'I don't know why I'm here. I haven't done anything, but they have already held me for 15 days and I can only pray that somehow I will get out of this terrible place.'

It was all too easy for people to find themselves in Gestapo hands. Rivals could settle old scores by denouncing acquaintances or neighbours for supposedly anti-Nazi activities. Anyone coveting some valuable possession could get the owner out of the way by reporting them to the Gestapo. Some were given a chance to avoid this fate. They received a warning to stop their anti-Nazi activities, and if they heeded it, nothing further might happen to them. If they did not, they were arrested 'for the security of the State'. Those considered the most dangerous by the Gestapo were interrogated and, frequently, beaten to death. Sometimes, a semblance of legality was needed to justify the Gestapo's actions; to this end, prisoners were taken before the Volksgericht (People's Court) which held sessions in a chamber decorated with big swastika banners and statues of Adolf Hitler. In these daunting surroundings, prisoners were bullied, denounced as traitors and usually sentenced to death, with no appeal allowed.

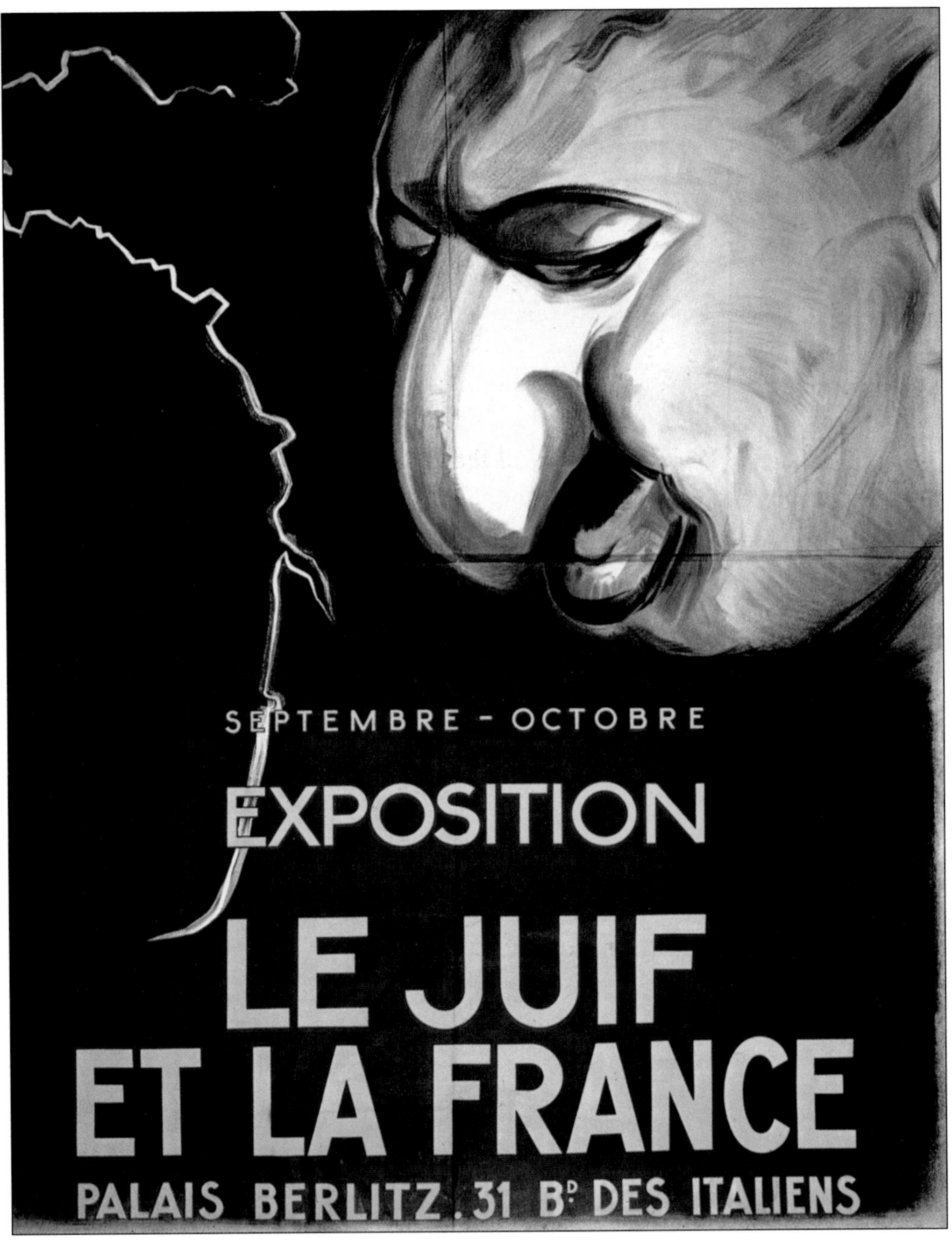

SEPTEMBRE - OCTOBRE
EXPOSITION
LE JUIF
ET LA FRANCE
PALAIS BERLITZ. 31 B^D DES ITALIENS

Exhibition poster, 'The Jew and France', featuring a supposedly typical Jewish face, with an exaggerated hooked nose, thick lips and shifty-looking eyes; Nazi anti-Semitic propaganda featured similarly gross images.

were heaped atop one another in huge piles. One, consisting of naked women, was discovered by British soldiers at Belsen concentration camp near Hanover: it measured 80 yards (73 metres) long, 30 yards (27 metres) wide and 4 feet (1.2 metres) high. More bodies were heaped in gutters. Skeletal survivors, barely alive, sat by – hollow-eyed, expressionless and ghastly pale.

'Belsen,' wrote one British journalist, 'is the nearest thing I know to a spectacle of absolute evil.... Outside one of the huts, I stopped to talk to a woman. She told me she was 21. She was twisted and wizened.... Her head had been shaved. She was so small and emaciated that she looked rather like an undernourished girl of 16; but her face was that of a woman of 60.'

JEHOVAH'S WITNESSES

The first of the Nazi concentration camps, Dachau, near Munich, had been opened on March 22, 1933, seven weeks after Adolf Hitler came to power in Germany. Initially, it was meant to house political prisoners – socialists, trade unionists and other enemies of the Nazi Party. But there were others, such as Jehovah's Witnesses, who also figured on the Nazis' hate list.

The feeling was mutual. Jehovah's Witnesses had openly condemned the Nazis even before their assumption of power in Germany. Afterwards, they went on doing so, totally fearless and convinced that the Nazis were agents of the Devil. Vicious persecutions followed, but armoured by their faith, the Witnesses refused to give in. Details, descriptions and diagrams of the concentration camps appeared in their publications, together with denunciations of the atrocities. The publication described Hitler as 'a perfect child of the Devil [whose] speeches and decisions flow through him like water through a well-built sewer.'

Jehovah's Witnesses openly condemned the Nazis even before their assumption of power in Germany. Afterwards, they went on doing so, totally convinced that the Nazis were agents of the Devil.

'This brood will be exterminated in Germany!' an enraged Hitler promised.

Jehovah's Witnesses were sent to the concentration camps as early as March 1934, and were among the first there. Ten years later, Witnesses were still in the camps, still refusing to bend. Geneviève de Gaulle, niece of the wartime Free French leader General Charles de Gaulle and a member of the French Resistance, was in Ravensbrück camp near Berlin, where she met a group of women Witnesses:

'It was absolutely forbidden for them to talk about their beliefs,' Geneviève de Gaulle later remembered. 'Or to have any religious books, and especially the Bible, which was considered [by the Nazis as] the supreme book of sedition.... I knew of [one Jehovah's Witness] and there were others, I was told, who were executed for possessing a few pages of Bible texts....

'What I admired a lot in them was that they could have left at any time just by signing a renunciation of their faith. Ultimately, these women, who appeared to be so weak and worn out, were

The perpetrators of the Nazis' most heinous atrocities were not always men. These guards from the Belsen concentration camp were put on trial for their crimes in September 1945.

stronger than the [Nazis] who had power and all the means at their disposal.... [They] had their strength and it was their willpower that no one could beat.'

[The Witnesses] could have left at any time by signing a renunciation of their faith. These women, who appeared to be so weak and worn out, were stronger than the Nazis.

THE WITNESSES AND THE JEWS

Though suffering themselves, Jehovah's Witnesses made a point of comforting Jewish inmates in the camps, often giving their miserly bread ration to the old and hungry and going without food themselves.

'They were a brave people who bore their fate patiently, ' said one Jewish woman. 'Though gentile [non-Jewish] prisoners were forbidden to talk to us, these women never observed this regulation. They prayed for us as if we belonged to their family, and begged us to hold out.'

Jews and gypsies were, of course, the Nazis' prime targets for persecution. This was nothing new for either community, which had suffered fierce depredations for centuries. But these outrages had been sporadic and, though terrorized and diminished, both communities had managed to survive. The Nazi persecutions of World War II were of a different and much more sinister calibre, however: more

Jews from the Warsaw Ghetto, mostly women, lined up against a wall; they are about to be shot by a German firing squad, 1942.

systematic, more widespread and intent on extermination rather than random killing. Their approach was evident as early as 1933, when gypsies were interned in concentration camps and forcibly sterilized under the Law for the Prevention of Hereditarily Diseased Offspring.

Numerous anti-gypsy laws, some of them centuries old, were already in place in Germany when the Nazis came to power, but these were not sufficiently severe for the Nazis' purposes. By 1938, the Nazis had formulated their own policy, as set down in *The Final Solution to the Gypsy Question,* which predated by four years a similar plan to exterminate the Jews. From there, the Nazis' campaign of 'cleansing' Europe escalated into the abominations the Jews called *shoah,* the Holocaust, and the gypsies termed *porajmos,* the Great Devouring.

NETWORK OF RESCUE FOR JEWS

In 1940, as the Germans acquired their empire in Europe, thousands of Jews went on the run, hoping to escape their clutches. For most, their only option was to find a safe place to hide; help came both from the Catholic Church and from individual families, who put their own lives at risk in order to shelter them.

Le Chambon-sur-Lignon was an isolated village hidden away in a forested plateau in south-central France. From Le Chambon, Magda Trocme and her husband André, a Protestant minister, organized a network of villages that provided safe havens for around 5,000 Jews. While some managed to reach neutral Switzerland, others remained in hiding: in many villages, there was not a single house or farm which was not sheltering a Jewish family.

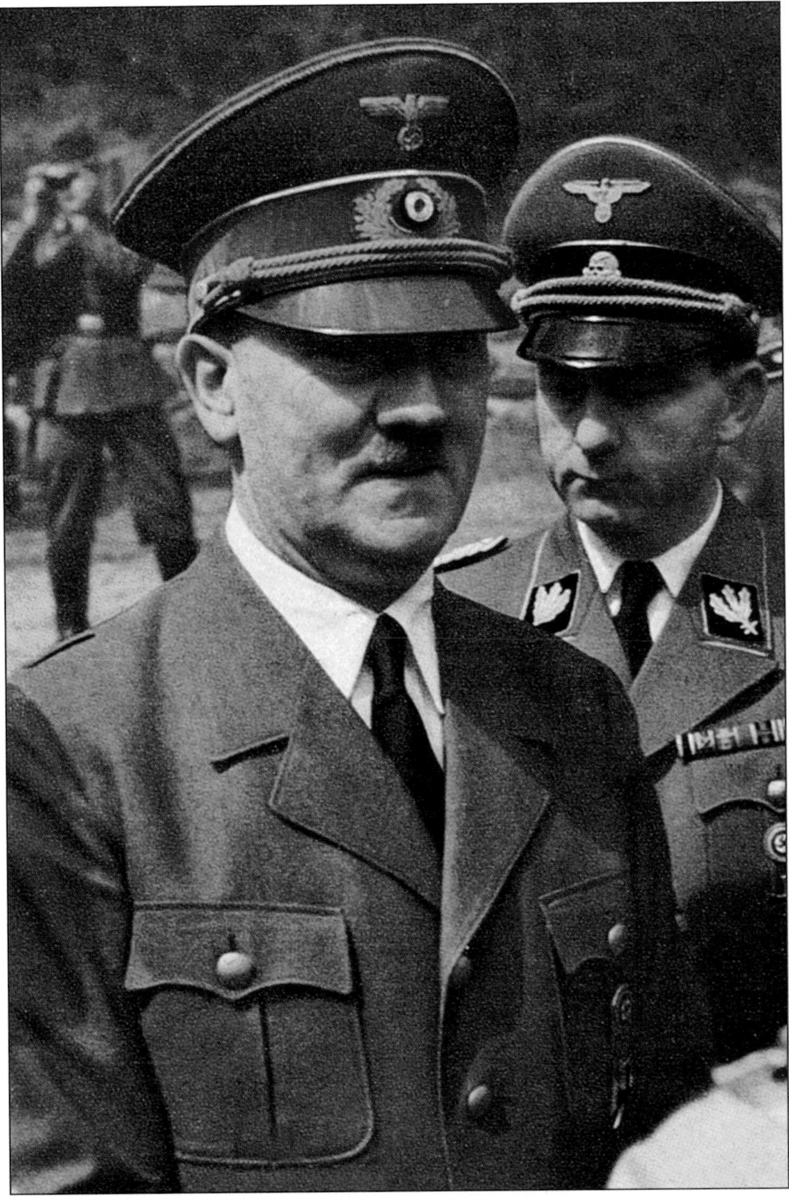

Hitler's rabid anti-Semitism and his resolve to rid the world of Jews was a basic tenet of Nazi policy.

The safety of these families depended, of course, on the collusion of entire village communities.

'The village was [concealing] at least 30 Jews,' wrote Nicole David, a Jewish girl sheltered by a Catholic family at Besines, in Belgium. 'The villagers saved many lives, providing the Jews with false papers and food.'

When Gisela Konopka, a German Jew from Berlin, came to the village of Norauban in northern France, she soon realized that the situation she found there was 'like a miracle'.

'Catholics, Protestants, the entire village opened its homes,' she said.

'[They] gave us false papers, rations, all the things you needed…and the farmers gave us milk.'

CONVENT CAMOUFLAGE

Convents were ideal hiding places. So were orphanages, monasteries and other Church institutions which were scattered across Europe from Poland and the Balkan countries to Belgium, France and Italy. The refugees, often children whose parents had been taken to concentration camps, received new identities, food and medical care. Jewish women, too, took on new identities by disguising themselves in nuns' habits, the best possible camouflage for diverting the suspicion of the Gestapo.

In Poland alone, there were some 190 convents where the nuns not only sheltered Jews, but went out into the streets of nearby towns to rescue them. They became known for their willingness to take any number of Jewish children, including the 2,500 whom Irene Sendler, a social worker, rescued from the Warsaw Ghetto.

'I knew I could count on the Sisters,' Sendler said. 'No one ever refused to take a child from me.'

The Nazi SS (Schutzstaffel or Elite Guard), originally Hitler's personal guard, was instrumental in hunting down Jews, gypsies and other victims and administered both the concentration and the extermination camps.

IN THE GHETTOS

Initially, Jews and gypsies were sent to ghettos – the ghetto at Lodz in Poland was used for both communities – on the assumption that they would starve to death or die of disease, thus saving the Nazis the trouble of disposing of them. In the Warsaw Ghetto in Poland, where 400,000 Jews were confined in 1940, only 60,000 were still alive by 1943. Their diet made subsistence look plentiful: they were allowed no more than 6.3 ounces (180 grams) of bread a day, 8 ounces (220 grams) of sugar a month, and just over 2 pounds (1 kilogram) each of jam and honey. Extra food was smuggled in, despite Nazi attempts to stop it, and this helped supplement rations that amounted to less

than 10 percent of a normal diet.

Despite these conditions, the women of the Warsaw Ghetto made every effort to perform the traditional task of keeping up their religion in the broken-down slums that passed for home.

'We lit candles on Friday evenings for the start of the Sabbath,' recalled Esther Pshybysh, a Polish Jew who managed to survive both the ghetto and the concentration camps. 'We lit them for the holy days, too. On Yom Kippur, the Day of Atonement in the autumn, we did our religious duty and fasted.'

When Passover came around in April, Jews ate unleavened bread – containing no yeast or other raising agent – for the eight days it lasted to commemorate the exodus of the Hebrews from Egypt in biblical times. There was little or no unleavened bread in the ghetto, but to mark the event the Jews gave up their

On the way to death: Jewish women and men being marched out of the Warsaw Ghetto in 1942, destined for a rail journey by cattle truck to the extermination camps.

Brigadeführer (Major General) Juergen Stroop (third from left) commanded the German troops during the Warsaw Ghetto Uprising in 1943 when 16 of his men were killed and another 190 wounded.

meagre ration of ordinary leavened bread, even though their hunger was intense.

HEROIC BATTLE

Eventually, in 1944, the Warsaw Ghetto was emptied by the SS and the surviving Jews were taken away for extermination in the camps. Before they went, however, the Jews used weapons that had been smuggled into the ghetto to hold the SS troops at bay. The ferocious battle that ensued lasted a month, destroyed the ghetto, and killed 180 Jews and 16 Germans, with another 90 wounded.

Jews and gypsies were shut into ghettos on the assumption that they would starve to death or die of disease, thus saving the Nazis the trouble of disposing of them.

SS Brigadeführer Juergen Stroop, in command, wrote in his official report, entitled *The Warsaw Ghetto Is No More,* how astounded he was that the Jews, 'this trash and subhumanity' as he called them, could put up such resolute resistance. Stroop noted that the Jewish 'battle groups' consisted of about 20 men and 20 women, and that the women 'had the habit of firing pistols with both hands, and concealing hand grenades in their bloomers'.

But their resistance could never have been anything but futile. The fate of the Jews of the Warsaw Ghetto was concentration, extermination or slave-labour camps. It was a destiny they shared with Jews from all over Nazi-occupied Europe.

THE BITCH OF BUCHENWALD

The career of Ilse Koch as one of the most wicked women concentration camp guards of the war began after her marriage in 1936 to SS-Standartenführer Karl Koch. Three years later, Koch's husband, already a notorious criminal, became commandant of Buchenwald, near Weimar. Buchenwald, termed 'an extermination factory' in a postwar American congressional report, was tailor-made for Ilse Koch to exercise her sadistic instincts.

Stroop noted that the Jewish 'battle groups' consisted of about 20 men and an equal number of women, and the women 'had the habit of firing pistols with both hands'.

Soon known as the Witch or Bitch of Buchenwald, Koch was a heftily built red-haired woman whose favourite sport was to ride on horseback through the compound, touting a large whip. Any prisoner who made the mistake of glancing at her was viciously lashed. While at Buchenwald, Koch had a collection of gloves, lampshades and book covers made from the skin of murdered prisoners, and ordered that skins with 'interesting tattoos' should be specially reserved for her.

Being commandant of Buchenwald did not prevent Koch's husband from pursuing his criminal activities, and in

Russian Prisoners of War

A Russian woman paratrooper captured after landing behind the German lines. Her nationality was more important than her gender: communist Russian prisoners were treated harshly as a matter of routine.

Russian prisoners of war, whether women or men, received no mercy from the Nazis. They held a special hatred of Russians as communists and regarded the failure of the USSR to sign the 1929 Geneva Convention on the treatment of PoWs as 'permission' to mistreat them as they chose. Russian PoWs were poisoned, shot or otherwise executed. In 1942 in the Ukraine, Heinrich Himmler, head of the SS, issued a secret order that 'Russian war prisoners must be branded with a special mark…kept in concentration camps under severe conditions...poorly fed [and] subjected to moral outrages'. Supplying proper food to Russian PoWs was considered by the Germans 'an unnecessary humanitarian act'.

Starvation, deprivation, terror, squalor – these were the means by which the Nazis made Jews suffer in the Warsaw Ghetto, before they were marched away, hands up in surrender, to die in extermination camps.

1944 he appeared before an SS tribunal charged with racketeering and murder. He was executed early in 1945. The same court found Ilse Koch not guilty of receiving stolen goods.

RETRIBUTION

The tide finally began to turn against Koch in 1947, when an American military tribunal found her guilty of murder. The tribunal sentenced her to

Partisan Campaigns in Greece

Women partisans in wartime Greece were tough and played their full part in guerrilla ambushes and acts of sabotage. It was a rough life, living off the land and sometimes sleeping in caves. One woman guerrilla from the Peloponnese, known as Annetta, singlehandedly captured a group of German soldiers. Another, Lisa Theodorido-Sozopoulou, was an active partisan while still at school and later became commander of the 9th Company of Women Partisans. Another, Eleftheria Drosaki of Thessalonika, carried messages for prisoners when she was only 15, and helped one of them escape.

Like the Russians, these Greek women had never known a soft or easy life and served during the war as partisans fighting the Germans who invaded their country in 1941.

life imprisonment. This was reduced to four years by the American General Lucius D. Clay, Deputy Military Governor of the American Zone of occupied Germany, in a decision that roused a furore of protest over its leniency. But the following year, further investigations into Koch's past were carried out by a committee of the U.S. Senate.

On December 27, 1948, the committee came to the conclusion that Koch had participated in the killing or beating of hundreds of inmates at Buchenwald. 'This bestial woman's guilt in specific murders is irrefutably established,' ran the committee's report.

Ilse Koch was arrested again in 1949 and tried for war crimes by a West German court. On January 15, 1951, for a second time, she was sentenced to life imprisonment. Koch claimed she was innocent and appealed to the International Human Rights Commission, which refused to help her. Psychiatrists who examined her came to a totally damning conclusion, describing her as 'a perverted, nymphomaniacal,

Jews being removed from the Warsaw Ghetto: from an album kept by German commander Juergen Stroop which was presented as evidence by the U.S. prosecution at the Nuremberg Trials (1945–1946).

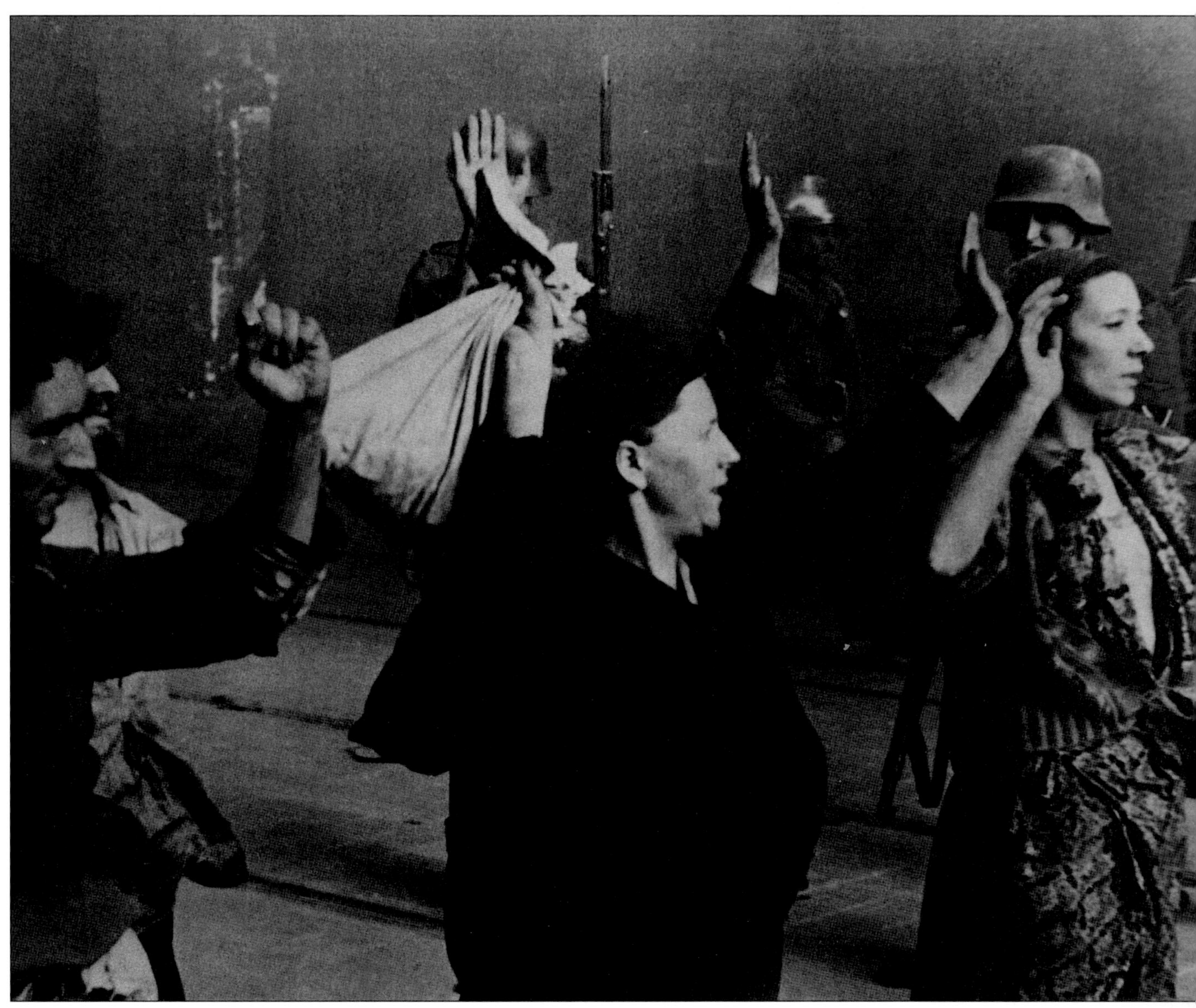

hysterical, power-mad demon'.

Koch continued to insist on her innocence, but by 1967 she had exhausted all avenues and finally gave up hope. On September 1, 1967, she tied a bed sheet to the door of her cell at Aichach Prison in Bavaria, southern Germany, and hanged herself.

She left a last note for her son, Uwe. 'I cannot do otherwise,' it read. 'Death is the only deliverance.'

THE STORY OF STELLA MARCUS

In June 1944, Stella Marcus, a Dutch Jew aged 14, and her mother were among a group of women loaded into a railway cattle truck and taken from Vught concentration camp in the Netherlands to Auschwitz in Poland. As the train approached Auschwitz, Marcus later remembered, she noticed 'chimneys with smoke and flames coming out of them and a very strange odour in the air'. What she had seen were the chimneys of the Auschwitz crematoria.

The fact that prisoners were murdered and their bodies burned was unknown to Marcus at the time, but she was able to sense the sinister, brooding atmosphere of Auschwitz and had the feeling that terrible things were happening there.

'SS officers were running around, I was very scared,' she recalled. 'I said, "Mother, I am so scared. I don't want to die." ...We were given rags to wear. The barracks was a huge block and the walls were lined with three shelves, with

A large contingent of prisoners, the sexes already separated and the children placed with the women, waiting at Auschwitz station for transfer to the concentration camp.

one...for every six people to sleep in. If one person turned, everyone had to turn. There were no blankets. The latrine was a big trough with wooden planks with holes.'

WORK AND SURVIVAL

On arrival at Auschwitz, all the women had to strip naked. Their heads were shaved to prevent lice, and their underarm and pubic hair was also removed. As a matter of routine, all prisoners were tattooed for identification and sorted: those who were fit enough were selected for work; the old and the very young were picked for death. Marcus and her mother were lucky – they had experience in electronics and were selected for work in the Telefunken electronics factory. The work was arduous and exhausting, the hours long, the conditions appalling and the prisoners constantly hungry, but at least work meant a chance of survival.

Meanwhile, the Russians were inexorably advancing towards Germany from the east and, as 1944 neared its end, artillery fire was audible in Auschwitz. In February 1945, the concentration camp was hastily evacuated and its occupants relocated. Marcus later recalled the semi-nomadic life that followed. The prisoners were marched from place to place or shoved into cattle trucks and shunted to labour camps. They were never in one place for long, but were soon tramping across the countryside again through rain, sleet and the snow of winter. Before long, Marcus's hard wooden clogs cut and tore at her feet. The scars remain to this day.

The French Resistance had strict rules about relationships between French women and Germans: these women, with their hair shaved off, were publicly disgraced at Cherbourg for collaborating with the invaders.

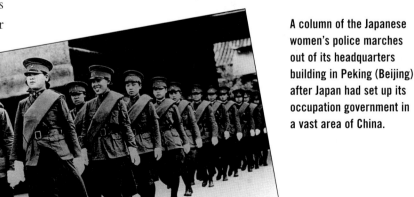

Stragglers and others who collapsed from exhaustion or stopped for a rest found themselves left behind. Those prisoners who managed to keep up the pace were constantly on the move for over two months, through rain, snow and sleet.

MAKING ROOM BY MURDER

There were more train journeys by cattle truck which, according to signs painted on the sides, were meant for 'eight horses or 40 men'. Into these, some 200

A column of the Japanese women's police marches out of its headquarters building in Peking (Beijing) after Japan had set up its occupation government in a vast area of China.

The prospects for these women and children arriving at Birkenau concentration camp in 1944 were nothing but filthy living conditions, inadequate food and clothing and death in the gas chambers.

people were crammed in tightly, unable to move, lie down or sometimes even to breathe. The SS guards had their own way of dealing with the overcrowding.

'Every day,' said Marcus, 'they picked out a few people to kill to have more room, and at night they murdered them and threw them out of the truck.'

For those who survived, there was no food for days on end, and very little water. Eventually, someone managed to get hold of some red cabbage leaves: one leaf had to be shared by four people.

Eventually, on May 1, 1945, Stella Marcus and her mother were liberated in Denmark. After recuperating in Sweden, they went back to their home in the Netherlands in August. The last Marcus had seen of her father was on March 20, 1944, in Vught concentration camp, three months before she and her mother were taken to Auschwitz. Once free and at home again, Marcus kept hoping that her father, too, would return.

'Whenever I walked down the street,' she said later, 'I looked for my father, hoping to [see him].'

Hope lasted only three months. In November 1945, news came that Marcus's father had died in the concentration camp at Flossenburg near Nuremberg, Germany.

A Canadian War Heroine

Mona Louise Parsons (1901–1976), born in Nova Scotia, lived in the Netherlands during the war. She might have spent the years of the German occupation in relative ease: a one-time actress with the Ziegfeld Follies in New York, she was now the wife of a wealthy Dutch businessman, Willem Leonhardt Parsons, and a well-known socialite admired for her beauty, grace and charm.

Instead, she put everything at risk, including her life, in order to help Allied airmen escape detection after they had bailed out onto Dutch soil. In September 1941, Parsons was arrested by the Gestapo near Amsterdam and was sentenced to death. She appealed the sentence, managed to get it commuted to life imprisonment and was taken to a series of prison camps in Germany.

The last prison in which Parsons was kept was at Vechta in northwest Germany. On March 24, 1945, the men' s section at Vechta was devastated as the Allied armies pushed across the River Rhine. The women' s section was relatively untouched, but the prison commandant nevertheless opened the gates and let the inmates go. Parsons fled with a fellow prisoner, Baroness Wendelien van Boetzelaaer, who, fortunately, spoke several languages including German. Parsons and the Baroness decided to pose as aunt and niece. Parsons spoke little if any German. She decided to use her acting experience to pose as a half-witted woman with a cleft palate, which excused her from speaking at all.

The two women headed north, for the Dutch border. It was a harrowing two-week journey through foul weather. Their feet were bare and became blistered and infected. They did physical labour in return for food and shelter. Parsons lost weight at an alarming rate, until she weighed just over 85lb (38kg), far too little for her height of 5 feet 8 inches (1.72m).

Then, just as they were nearing the Dutch border, the two women became separated as Canadian and Polish troops surged into Germany. Parsons pressed on, alone, until a Dutch farmer agreed to lead her to British troops, where she at last found safety.

As units of the Ukrainian Front advanced on Vienna, this young Russian woman was on duty on the road, controlling the military traffic. Vienna was captured on April 7, 1945.

'The War Illustrated,' May 2nd, 1941 Registered at the G.P.O. as a Newspa

Vol. 4 ★ INTO BATTLE WITH THE 'FORCES OF THE EMPIRE' ★ No. 8

THE WAR ILLUSTRATED

4d Weekly

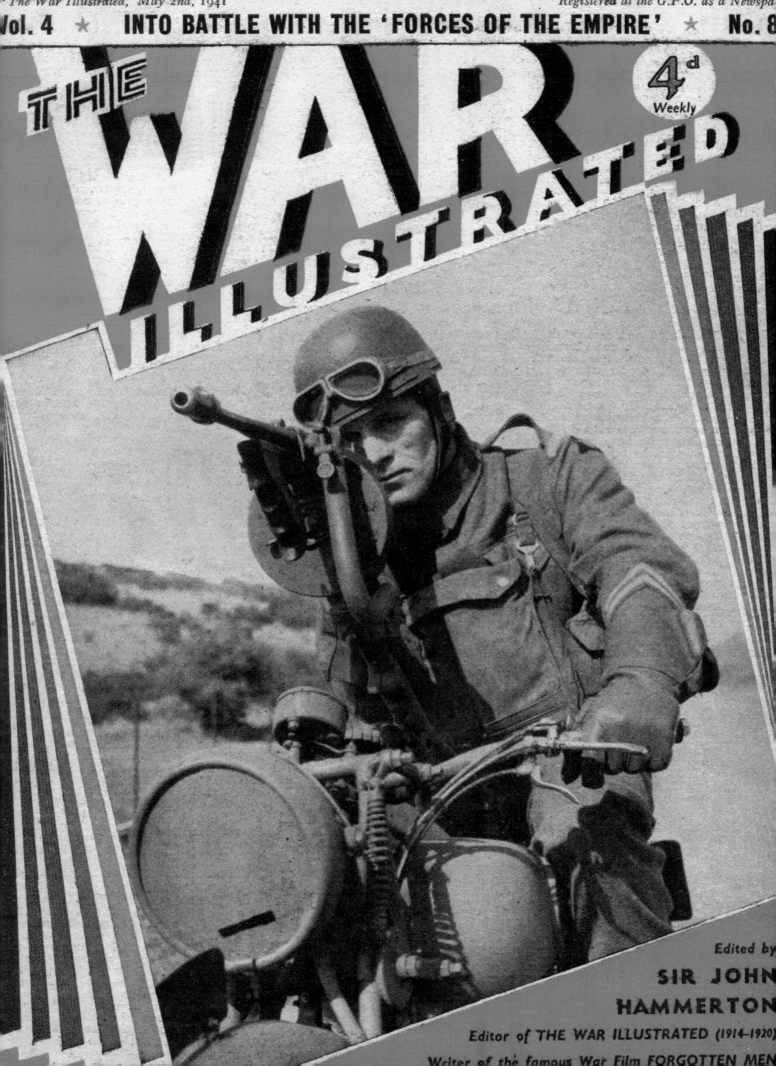

Edited by
SIR JOHN HAMMERTON
Editor of THE WAR ILLUSTRATED (1914–1920)
Writer of the famous War Film FORGOTTEN MEN

CHAPTER 8

Women Report and Photograph the War

More than death and misery, the war brought new opportunities for some. This was particularly true of women journalists and photographers, even though they had to fight against prejudice and obstruction to get their jobs done.

The invasion by women of formerly exclusive male domains characterized World War II more widely than with any other single event in history. However, where it occurred in journalism and its ancillaries, news photography and broadcasting, the rivalries that ensued were coloured by the peculiar nature of the media. Journalists, whatever their area of expertise, have always been individualistic, energized in pursuit of professional success, more willing to take risks – including wagering their lives – and much more alert to the activities of rivals who might beat them to that Holy Grail of their profession: the scoop. World War II generated more news and more scoops than journalists of either sex had ever known before, heightened by modern technological means of conveying their reports to their newspapers – yet their rivalries remained as intense as ever.

A NEST OF SNAKES

Colonel Barney Oldfield was the U.S. Army Air Force public relations officer

This British magazine was published throughout the war and afterwards until 1947. Though heavily censored for security reasons, it kept the public informed about the way the hostilities were going.

They Reported the War

A total of 127 American women reporters were accredited during World War II. Here are some of them, together with the publications or organizations they represented and the war zones in which they operated:

In 1942, Margaret Bourke-White became the U.S. Army Air Corps' first female official photographer. She worked at the front in World War II and during the Korean war (1950–1953).

Marjorie Avery, *Detroit Free Press* (France, Germany, Norway)
Margaret Bourke-White, *Time* (North Africa, Russia, Germany)
Georgette M. Chapelle, *Look* (Iwo Jima, Pacific Ocean/ Okinawa, Japan)
Ruth B. Cowan, Associated Press (North Africa, France)
Virginia Cowles, North American Newspaper Alliance (Britain, France, Italy)
Catherine Coyne, *Boston Herald* (Belgium, France, Germany)
Peggy Hull Deuell, *Cleveland Plain Dealer* (China, Pacific theatre)
Barbara M. Finch, Reuters (Pacific theatre)
Janet Flanner, *The New Yorker* (France, Germany)
Martha Gellhorn, *Colliers'* (France, Germany, Far East)
Marguerite Higgins, *New York Herald Tribune* (Germany)
Josephine Herbst, *New York Post* (Germany)
Annalee Whitmore Jacoby, *Time* (China)
Helen Kirkpatrick, *Chicago Daily News* (Britain, Italy, France, Germany)
Mary P. Lochridge, *Women's Home Companion* (Iwo Jima, Germany)
Lee Miller, Conde-Nast (France, Germany)
Shelley Mydans, *Time* (Philippines)
Eleanor C. Packard, United Press (Albania, France, Italy)
Anne Stringer, United Press (Germany)
Dorothy Thompson, *Chicago Tribune* (Germany)
Sonia Tomara, *New York Herald Tribune* (North Africa, France, Germany)
Mary Welsh, *Life* and London *Daily Express* (Britain, France)
Lael Tucker Laird Wertenbaker, *Time* (Britain, Germany)

who established press camps for journalists reporting the campaigns of the 1st, 3rd and 9th U.S. Armies in Europe after 1944. The clash of egos there was deafening.

'The press camp became a capsule of extraordinary life along the front,' Oldfield recalled in a postwar interview. 'There was gung-ho competition [and] much character assassination.... It was like being housemother to a nest of snakes....'

In all, Colonel Oldfield handled 1,828 correspondents during the course of the war. In this very high-powered environment, there was little difference between the sexes, and the women had to be just as diligent, enterprising and extraordinary as the men in competing for news. Many were rebels against convention, spurning a woman's traditional, domesticated role for a freer, more exciting and more dangerous life at large in the world. Many of them found contemporary American society stifling and regarded the conflict in Europe as their escape route to personal freedom. Many of them even sacrificed their marriages in order to get there and report the war.

In this high-powered environment, women had to be just as diligent, enterprising and extraordinary as the men in competing for news.

MARRIAGE A CASUALTY

Top female war correspondents such as Dorothy Thompson, Margaret Bourke-White, Josephine Herbst, Janet Flanner and Martha Gellhorn all had brief, unsuccessful marriages in their background. Gellhorn, who was married to Ernest Hemingway between 1940 and 1945, objected strongly to being known simply as the third wife of the famous novelist or, as she put it, 'a footnote to someone else's life'. Bourke-White foresaw the clash her career might cause even before she married the novelist Erskine Caldwell in 1939, and she devised a form of prenuptial contract which included the demand that Caldwell not interfere with her work. Their marriage lasted only three years, and for much of that time Bourke-White was working abroad. There were subsequent romances, but she never married again, declaring that she had no time for love.

It is not surprising that several women correspondents of World War II who were physically attractive and sexually motivated had numerous liaisons outside their own marriages. Temperamentally, they were unsuited to the passive background role society expected them to play. That said, their drawbacks as wives were virtues as journalists: they were pushy, fearless and single-minded and were often driven by

This *New Yorker* cartoon shows the crude but effective way materials – in this case a bag of wartime U.S. mail – were transferred from one ship to another while at sea.

strong political beliefs. They could not afford to be squeamish or rely on chivalrous protection from the horrors of war that would shield them from reality. What they needed, and in many cases possessed, was a strong stomach for doing the job, whatever sickening sights or dangers they might encounter.

Among the first correspondents into the newly liberated concentration camps, for instance, was Margaret Bourke-White, the *Time* magazine correspondent who photographed the charred bodies of prisoners lying beside the electrified perimeter fence that halted their attempts to escape. Clare Boothe Luce was in Maymyo, Burma, in 1942 when battle casualties came in. 'My insides had not stopped quivering,' she later admitted, but she took her pictures just the same.

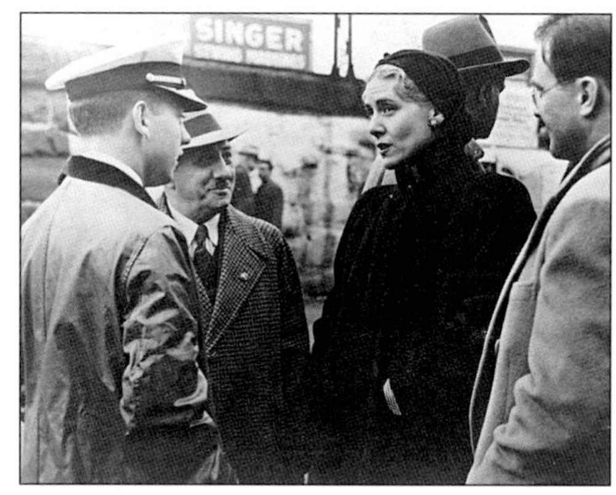

Clare Boothe Luce, right, was a pioneering news photographer who campaigned for women's rights both before and during the war.

THE DEFIANT MARTHA GELLHORN

Martha Gellhorn openly defied military regulations about where correspondents might venture. Eager to get to where the action was in Italy in 1944, but lacking the proper credentials

British soldiers in action in Burma. Burma was a particularly punishing battlefield, but the feisty Clare Boothe Luce willingly faced its dangers and discomforts to photograph some of the action.

D-Day preparations: Martha Gellhorn defied regulations and pulled every trick she knew to reach the Normandy beaches.

for a combat zone, Gellhorn climbed a wire fence, hitched a ride to a military airfield and, after convincing the pilot that she was desperate to see her fiancé, managed to get on board an unauthorized flight to Naples.

Once in Naples, Gellhorn had no backup: 'No papers, no travel orders, no PX [personal supply] rights, nothing,' she later revealed. 'I was a gypsy in that war in order to report it.'

Gellhorn's back-door method of getting to the war zone in Italy was not her only exploit of this kind. On June 7, 1944, the day after the D-Day landings, she stowed away on a hospital ship leaving England for Normandy across the English Channel.

'You could always [tell the] military police, "I'm just going on board to interview the nurses," ' Gellhorn said in a postwar interview. 'It was the woman's angle. You could get anywhere saying you were doing the woman's angle. So I just locked myself in the toilet....' Once off the Normandy beaches,

Martha Gellhorn and the novelist Ernest Hemingway on their honeymoon in 1940. Their marriage would founder when Gellhorn went to Europe to cover the war.

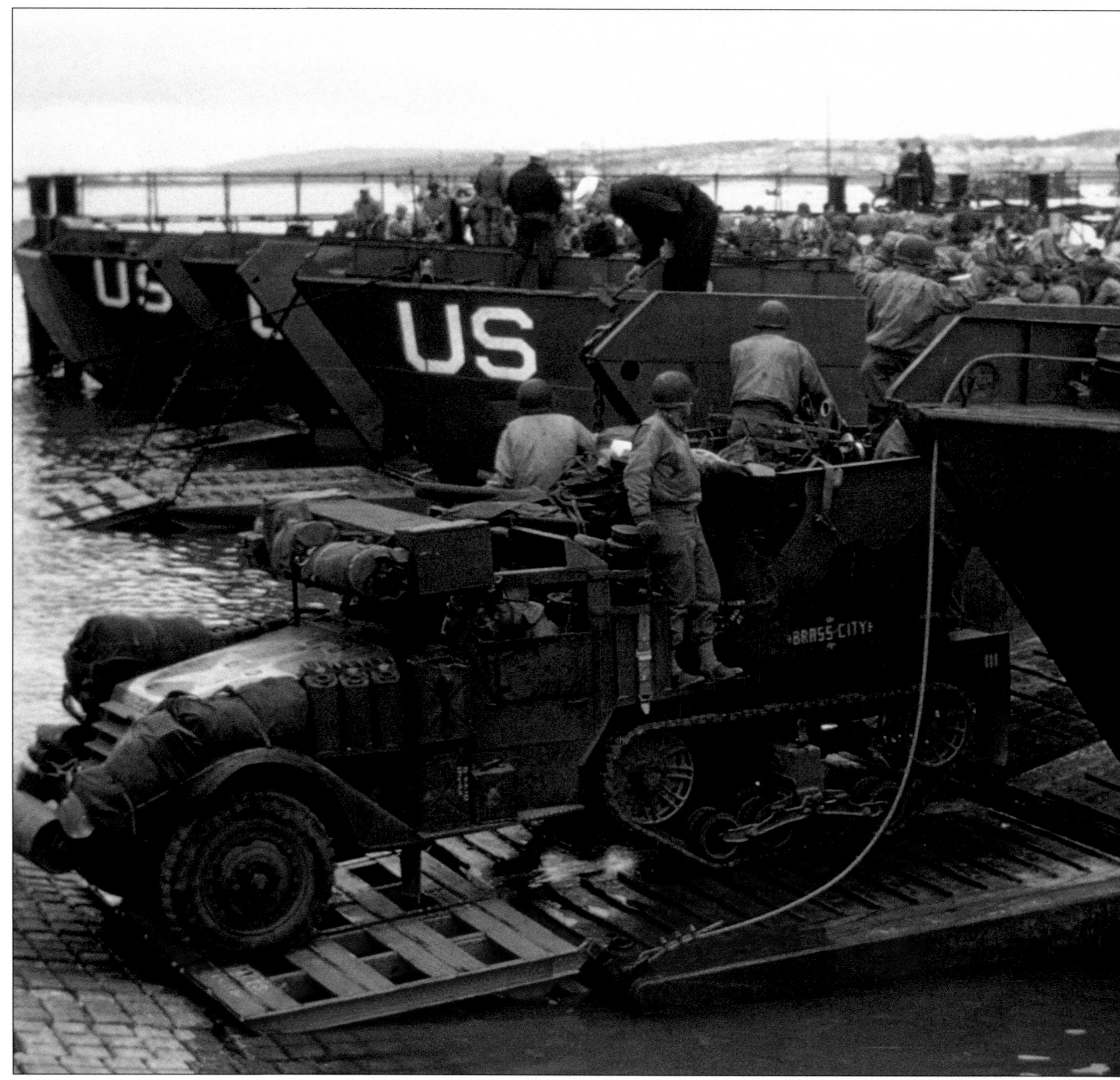

with savage fighting only yards away and distant gunfire thundering in the air, Gellhorn joined in as a stretcher bearer when the ship's personnel 'went on the beaches to get the wounded, and then I was found out and was told that if I disobeyed orders again, I would be deported.'

Colonel Barney Oldfield understood and respected the mindset that drove Gellhorn and others to seek out the worst the war had to offer.

'If they wanted to take those risks,' he said, 'and if getting the story meant that much to them, if their future professional status was worth these

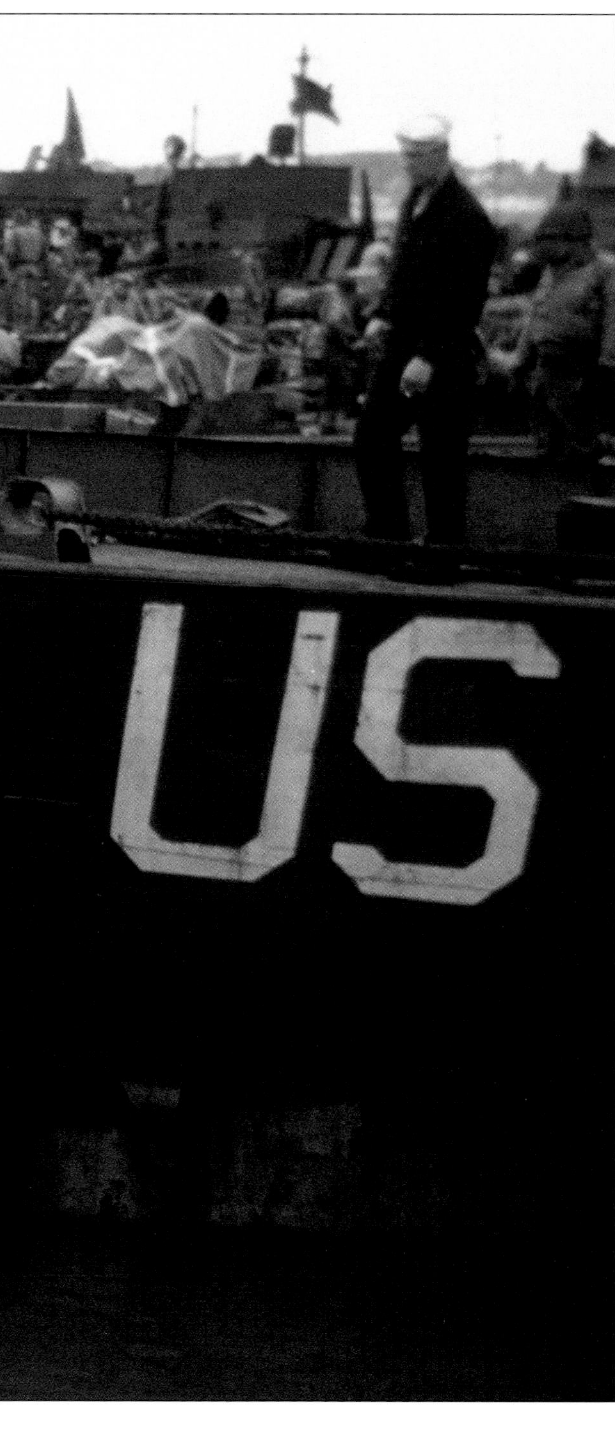

U.S. forces preparing for the Allied invasion of Normandy on D-Day, June 6, 1944. This was the most critical event of the war and featured the largest amphibious invasion force ever assembled.

kinds of risks, why should we stand in the way?'

OBSTACLES

Despite those like Oldfield who supported women correspondents, a great deal stood – or was placed – in the way of their getting a story.

'If the battalion aid medical teams included a nurse or more,' Oldfield remembered, 'the women correspondents could get as close to the front as the battalion headquarters, and that was as close as you needed to get unless you wanted to be captured.... [However], every time allocations for spaces came up, someone was bound to suggest that the women stay with the field hospital units where nurses were already provided for, or not go at all.'

It was an achievement for women correspondents to get as close to the fighting fronts as they did, considering the other difficulties they faced. Women were barred from press briefings almost to the end of the war. Some important military men, like Britain's General Bernard Montgomery and America's General Douglas MacArthur, stoutly resisted the idea of female correspondents in combat zones. It was not until February 1945 that MacArthur permitted them to report the Battle of Iwo Jima – and then only from

U.S. troops approaching Omaha Beach, one of the five Normandy invasion beaches. A few minutes later, these Americans were embroiled in the bloodiest, most costly battle of D-Day.

Algiers, North Africa, was a useful base for journalists, but it was dangerously close to the front line.

General Bernard Montgomery (1887–1976) fought hard to ban women from the battlefront.

hospital ships moored offshore.

But problems also began at square one, with women journalists encountering difficulties while still in the United States, hoping to acquire the necessary papers to go abroad. Neither the State Department, which issued passports, nor the War Department, which handled press accreditation, was all that eager to accommodate them. Only after American press organizations leaned on them did they finally give in.

Even after getting around this official reluctance, women could face open opposition from bureau chiefs like Wes Gallagher of the Associated Press in Algiers. Gallagher was a declared misogynist. Even though Ruth Cowan had worked for AP since 1930, he refused to give her any assignments or the transport she needed to get to war zones in North Africa. Instead, Gallagher suggested, Cowan should return to the United States immediately.

Britain's General Bernard Montgomery and America's General Douglas MacArthur stoutly resisted the idea of female correspondents in combat zones.

MOVING INTO THE NEWSROOM

Wartime America offered women more entries into serious journalism than ever before, as men went abroad or joined the armed forces. This enabled many women to graduate from the periphery – covering fashion, children, cooking and other home-based subjects or the society pages – to reporting hard news. This, though, was not good enough for Ruth Cowan, and she refused to return to the States as Gallagher had suggested. Too eager to get a piece of the action and far too stubborn to take this easy way out, she remained in North Africa – only to find herself ostracized: refused entry into the press dining room in Rabat, Morocco, on the grounds that it was a men-only mess, Cowan had to eat alone in her room. Nevertheless, she stuck it out, found her own transport, made her own contacts and later reported the war not only from North Africa, but also from France after the D-Day invasion and from Paris after the liberation of the French capital in August 1944.

Certainly the most fortunate female war correspondents were those unaffected by obstruction because they happened to have based themselves in Europe before World War II began – sometimes long before. Dorothy Thompson, for instance, had left the United States towards the end of the First World War and established herself in Paris and, later, in Vienna as a publicity writer for the American Red

The brilliant and daring General Douglas MacArthur (1888–1964), Supreme U.S. Commander in the Pacific.

U.S. transports on their way to Iwo Jima, 750 miles off Japan, in February 1945.

Therese Bonney specialized in photographing the sufferings of civilians in war zones. This photograph was taken in Finland in 1940, during the Russo-Finnish War – Bonney is wearing a Finnish medal awarded for bravery.

Cross. On the side, she freelanced for the *Philadelphia Public Ledger.*

Vienna, in the period after the First World War, was a fortuitous location for a writer seeking to be at the centre of political affairs. Central Europe had been convulsed by the conflict, and defeat in the war had shattered the Continent at its very heart, dismembering the empires of Germany and Austria-Hungary. In 1918 the Austrian Emperor Karl I had been forced to abdicate, and both countries, much reduced in size, became republics. Then, in 1921, an abortive attempt by royalty to regain power provided Dorothy Thompson with a very big story. Her account impressed the editors of the *Public Ledger,* giving her the leverage she needed to apply for a permanent position. Astutely, Thompson even made a special journey to the newspaper's Paris office to stake her claim. She got the job.

Berlin was without doubt the place to be for big news stories, as the Nazi Party and Adolf Hitler relentlessly ascended the heights of power.

DOROTHY THOMPSON IN BERLIN

Thompson was now launched as a bona fide foreign correspondent. She rose rapidly within the Curtis Syndicate, which owned the *Public Ledger* and the *New York Evening Post.* In 1925 she became central European bureau chief for both newspapers, a position that required her to move to Berlin. Thompson accepted the promotion, undeterred, it seems, by her recent marriage to the Hungarian writer Josef Bard. Predictably, the marriage failed, and in 1928 Thompson took a second husband, the American novelist and future Nobel Prize winner Sinclair Lewis. This relationship, too, was destined to founder on the rocks of Thompson's career.

Berlin in the mid-1920s was without doubt the place to be for big news stories, as the Nazi Party and Führer Adolf Hitler rebuilt their fortunes after their failed putsch in 1923 and relentlessly ascended the heights of power in Germany. The Nazis attained that height in 1933, when Hitler became chancellor. Thompson had watched the rise of fascism, with its strong-arm

Dorothea Lange

Photographer Dorothea Lange, born in Hoboken, New Jersey, in 1895, brought home to the rest of the United States the misery and fortitude of Californians whose lives had been ruined by the Great Depression of the 1930s. From 1935 to 1942, Lange produced photographs for the California Rural Rehabilitation Administration, which aided those impoverished by the Depression. In 1942, Lange's sympathy was caught by the plight of Japanese-Americans who were regarded by the U.S. government as potential security risks after Japan's attack on Pearl Harbor. Japanese-Canadians, the Nikkei, who were also interned to prevent them becoming Japanese agents, suffered the same fate. Lange's pictures dissipated the idea that they were furtive, deceitful would-be spies and depicted them as worthy citizens of courage and dignity. Dorothea Lange died in 1965.

The picture below shows Dorothea Lange in California in 1936. She was already well established as a professional photographer.

Fortune
NOVEMBER 1938

Dorothea Lange's images appeared in many publications including on the front cover of this 1938 issue of *Fortune* (left). Below, Lange can be seen at back right photographing Japanese-Americans assembled at a San Francisco control station prior to evacuation and internment.

Dorothea Lange's photograph above shows a young Japanese-American, one of 664 such Americans removed from San Francisco and rehoused inland in June 1942.

***Cosmopolitan*, right, was a glossy, glamorous woman's publication, but it also had a serious side. It was this magazine that published a remarkable scoop - Dorothy Thompson's interview with Hitler in 1931.**

tactics, rampant anti-Semitism, glorification of the Aryan 'master race' and other extreme right-wing policies, and her reports for the Curtis Syndicate were full of alarm and warnings about the future which a Nazi Germany would create. Despite her views, Thompson was curiously dismissive of Hitler himself, misjudging his potential when she interviewed him for *Cosmopolitan* magazine in 1931.

'I was a little nervous,' Thompson wrote. 'I considered taking smelling salts. And Hitler was late. An hour late. Waiting upstairs in the foyer of the Kaiserhof Hotel, I saw him shoot by, on the way to his rooms, accompanied by a bodyguard who looked like Al Capone. Minutes pass. Half an hour.... When finally I walked in...I was convinced that I was meeting the future dictator of Germany. In something less than 50 seconds, I was quite sure that I was not. It took just that time to measure the startling insignificance of this man who has set the whole world agog.... He is inconsequent and voluble, ill-poised, insecure. He is the very prototype of the Little Man.'

During the Nazis' ten-year rise to power, supporters made their presence felt by spectacular marches through the streets and large, emotional public meetings.

Burying Coventry's Dead

In the heavy Luftwaffe raid which destroyed much of Coventry, England, on the night of November 14, 1940, some 554 persons were known to have been killed and 865 injured. Tania Long, of the *New York Herald Tribune* and *New York Times,* covered the mass funeral:

'There was nothing beautiful about this mass funeral. It was grim – as grim as the expression on the pale faces of the drably clothed mourners who had walked 2 miles [3.2 kilometres] in a drizzling rain from the city where they once had homes to the cemetery set among the fields.... The Bishop of Coventry led a brief service from a heap of muddy earth, his purple robes flying in the wind. The people stood below him, facing the common grave.

'When the service was over, the people walked slowly along the length of the grave, casting their flowers on the pine boxes below. Death was anonymous – many of the victims were never identified....'

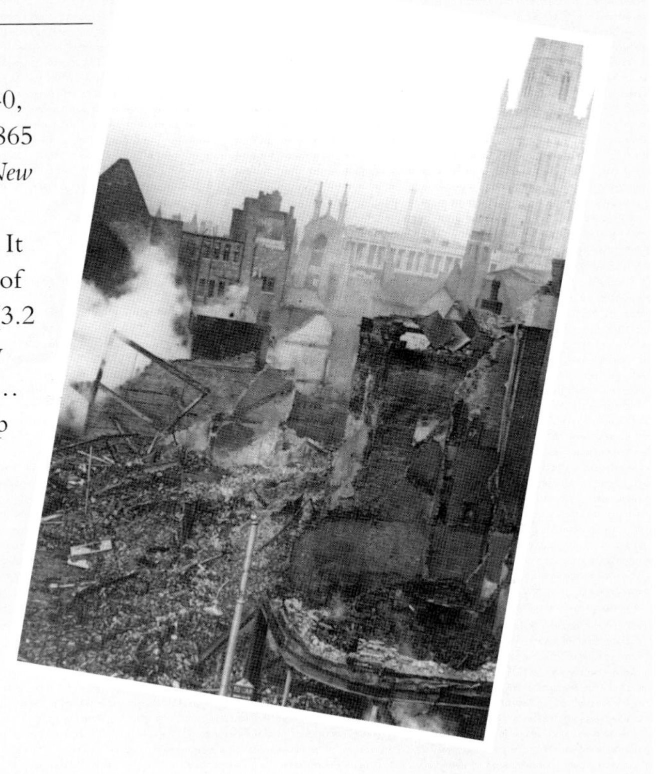

RETURN TO GERMANY

Shortly afterwards Thompson went back to the United States with Sinclair Lewis and their son, who had been born in 1930. She was still there in 1933 when Hitler became chancellor and when he authorized, the following year, the 'Night of the Long Knives', the blood-stained purge of his perceived enemies within the Nazi Party. For Thompson, the Nazi news story, always big, had just got bigger. Leaving her son in Vermont in the care of her domestic staff – and her husband, presumably, to his own devices – she then returned to Germany. The atmosphere, she discovered, was intensely sinister: the telephones in her hotel were tapped, fear was in the air and, as Thompson soon discovered, the Nazis knew she was back.

'When I walked in I was convinced that I was meeting the future dictator of Germany. In less than 50 seconds, I was quite sure I was not....'

The Gestapo, the Nazi secret police, had a long memory. Despite the fact that Thompson's earlier warnings about the dangers German fascism posed to world peace had made little impact in the United States, in Europe her views had marked her as a dangerous enemy of Nazism. Within days of her return to Germany, the Gestapo gave her 48 hours to leave the country. Thompson left for Paris. Later, when she returned home to Vermont, she defiantly framed the expulsion order and hung it in a prominent place.

Eleanor Roosevelt (centre), the first lady, pictured here at a meeting to discuss the welfare of women just after the war, was a great asset to the American war effort through her magazine articles and public speeches and radio broadcasts.

Thompson's colleague, Sigrid Schultz, had wired her own newspaper, the *Chicago Tribune,* with news of the expulsion, adding that it was due to Thompson's 'numerous anti-German articles in the American Press'. Thompson herself believed her 'crime' had been less dramatic.

'My offence,' she said, 'was to think that Hitler was just an ordinary man. That is a crime against the reigning cult in Germany, which says that Mr. Hitler is a Messiah sent of God to save the German people.... To question this mystic mission is so heinous that if you are German you can be sent to jail. I, fortunately, am an American, so I merely was sent to Paris. Worse things can happen....'

Shortly after the First World War, women were still obliged to find backdoor ways into news reporting.... They had to rely on their own ingenuity [and] a certain amount of bluff.

GOERING'S DRAGON LADY

Sigrid Schultz risked many worse things in her contacts with the Nazis. For example, in 1935, at a Foreign Press Association luncheon held in honour of Field Marshal Hermann Goering, head of the Luftwaffe, and his new wife, Schultz angered Goering by complaining about Nazi harassment of foreign correspondents. Goering struck back with an insult at Schultz's birthplace, Chicago, calling it 'that crime-ridden city'. Afterwards Goering always called Schultz 'the dragon lady from Chicago'.

Schultz, as it happened, knew little about Chicago. Born into a family of Norwegian descent, she moved to Paris with her parents when she was eight. Shortly before the outbreak of the First World War in 1914, she graduated from the Sorbonne and joined them where they then lived, in Berlin. Schultz was a talented linguist, fluent in French, Dutch, German and Polish, and in 1919 this earned her a place as an interpreter for the *Chicago Tribune* in Berlin.

At that time, shortly after the First World War, women were still obliged to find backdoor ways into news reporting. It would be years before Helen Reid, vice-president of the *New York Herald Tribune,* and First Lady Eleanor Roosevelt actively promoted women news reporters. Until then they had to rely on their own ingenuity, a certain amount of bluff and, sometimes, a great deal of chutzpah. Dorothy Thompson had found her way into news reporting as a freelancer. Sigrid Schultz's position as an interpreter did the same for her, but she was also an expert in German politics. Once established at the *Chicago Tribune* offices in Berlin's Hotel Adlon, Schultz mixed socially with German professionals, diplomats and government officials and was not averse to charming them with her pretty face and fetching manner.

RIDING HER REPUTATION

Before long, Schultz acquired a reputation as a knowledgeable young woman. Ministers of the ruling Weimar Republic frequently called at the Adlon to elicit her opinions and discover the American viewpoint on how Germany and Europe had been shaping up after the war. Ultimately, Schultz's expertise and her widespread contacts paid off professionally: late in 1925, she became Berlin bureau chief of the *Chicago Tribune,* when her predecessor was reassigned to Rome.

Schultz's image as a charmer was something of a ruse. While ostensibly enjoying the company of diplomats and sometimes flirting shamelessly with

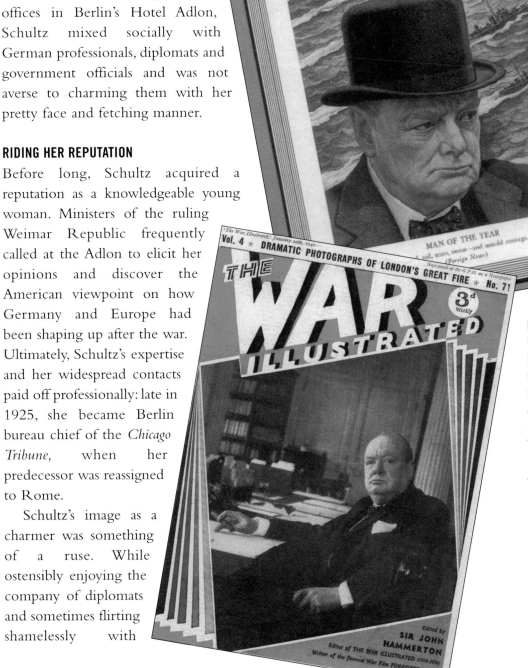

Prime Minister Winston Churchill inspired the British with his dramatic speeches and attitude of stubborn defiance. To Americans, he came to symbolize Britain's role in the war. Here he is seen on the cover of the January 1940 issue of *Time* (above), and the January 1941 issue of *The War Illustrated* (left).

them, she never let herself be fooled about the malign nature of the Nazi Party and its policies or the potential danger to world peace they represented. Eventually, in 1929, the subterfuge paid off when Schultz's connections enabled her to arrange a meeting with Goering at a Berlin restaurant. They met, had lunch, and talked – the upshot was that Goering introduced Schultz to Hitler.

The Führer kissed her hand, Austrian-style, and to Schultz's intense discomfort, fixed her with his somewhat hypnotic eyes. Unlike Thompson, Schultz never believed for a moment that Hitler was of no consequence, but she hid her dislike sufficiently well to become part of a small group of journalists who had regular access to the Führer during the 1930s.

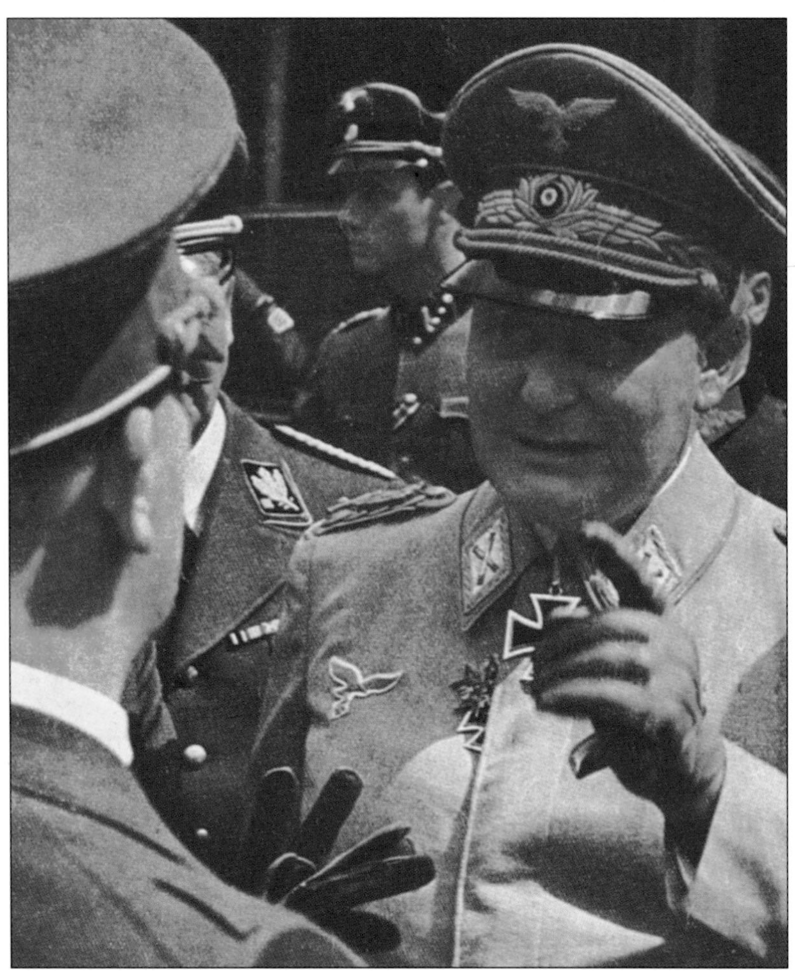

Field Marshal Hermann Goering, the flamboyant, buccaneering head of the Luftwaffe, lost favour with Adolf Hitler after the defeat of his air force in the Battle of Britain in 1940.

HIDDEN SENTIMENTS

Schultz was always conscious of what had happened to Dorothy Thompson in 1933 and took care not to go as far as she had and get herself thrown out of Germany. However, remaining in Germany after Hitler attained power meant Schultz came to know much more than Thompson about the pall of fear generated by Nazi rule, the scale of Nazi censorship and their surveillance of foreign correspondents like herself. She was aware of being watched. Berliners with whom Schultz had once been friendly were now afraid to be seen talking to her. Despite attempts to conceal her sentiments, Schultz soon found herself identified as anti-Nazi. It was only a matter of time before she became the target of a favourite Nazi ploy to discredit her.

One day in 1935, a large sealed envelope was delivered to Schultz's widowed mother, with whom she lived in Berlin. Schultz was at work at the time, but her mother recognized the trap and telephoned her daughter, who came home immediately. The envelope contained an aircraft engine design, something that would have been classified as a state secret by any government. Schultz burned the incriminating material and headed back to her office at the Hotel Adlon. Before she got there, however, she encountered a man she recognized as a Nazi agent. She confronted him, as well as his two guards, and told them the envelope sent to her apartment had already been destroyed. A taxi happened to be passing. Schultz got in and made sure the agent and his guards heard her give the driver the address of the American Embassy. There, they might have presumed, she was going to lodge an official complaint.

Schultz, however, picked a better and more direct target for her protest: Hermann Goering. When she told him of the Nazi agents' tactics, he replied, scowling, that it was just her imagination and told her she should have more respect for state authority. Schultz was well aware of what Goering, the highest-placed Nazi next to Hitler, meant by respect for the state and its authority.

The 'Battle of the Bulge' (1944) was the last Nazi organized stand. In this U.S. Army picture, supply trucks pass through Bastogne, Belgium, which was captured only after ferocious fighting.

'JOHN DICKSON'

Nevertheless, the real story behind Nazi rule in Germany had to be told, and for this the *Chicago Tribune* supplied its Berlin bureau chief with a ploy carefully crafted to protect her from even the all-seeing eyes of the Gestapo and its agents.

On May 15, 1937, the first of a series of articles appeared in the *Tribune,* written from Paris by John

Battle of Britain

Virginia Cowles reported for Hearst Publications in the United States and Britain's *Sunday Times* on the Battle of Britain in 1940, when the Royal Air Force fought off the German Luftwaffe and helped save Britain from Nazi invasion:

'In front of you stretched the blue water of the Channel and in the distance you could distinguish the hazy outline of the coast of France.... You lay in the tall grass with the wind blowing gently across you and watched the hundreds of silver planes swarming through the heavens like clouds of gnats. All around you, anti-aircraft guns were shuddering and coughing, stabbing the sky with small white bursts. You could see the flash of wings and the long white plumes from the exhausts; you could hear the whine of engines and the rattle of bullets. You knew the fate of civilization was being decided 15,000 feet [4,500 metres] above your head in a world of sun, wind and sky.'

Allied pilots race for their aircraft during the Battle of Britain in 1940.

Dickson, a trained correspondent who, it seems, had been sent 'into Germany to obtain facts which [the newspaper's] accredited correspondents in...the Berlin bureau have been unable to cable to America'. The series revealed several facts about the Nazi regime which its leaders had been careful to conceal: their own self-aggrandizement and growing personal wealth, the manipulation of young men in the Hitler Youth organization, the weakening of Christian values and the detailed watch it kept on every German citizen. The series created a terrible picture of a brutal police state which sought to expunge every freedom, including freedom of thought, which Americans held dear.

It was only a matter of time before Schultz became the target of a favourite Nazi ploy to discredit her.

'John Dickson' was, of course, Sigrid Schultz, and her personal writing style was all over every article in the series. Nevertheless, if her fellow journalists guessed the truth, they never revealed it, and Schultz herself kept the matter a secret from everyone. She was still in place as bureau chief in Berlin until 1940, when she took a risk that eventually made her departure from Germany a matter of urgency.

August 17, 1940
5¢ A COPY
Collier's
How to Build Airpower By W. B. Courtney

A 1940 issue of *Collier's* magazine. Though published before the United States entered the war, the article on air power had clear connotations. Later, Martha Gellhorn became *Collier's'* war reporter.

ESCAPING FROM GERMANY

Schultz became a broadcaster for the American Mutual Radio Network, alternating with author William Shirer in late-night live news programmes timed to coincide with Royal Air Force raids on Berlin. It was during one such raid that Schultz suffered a leg injury from a large piece of shrapnel and had to make her broadcast fighting the pain and attempting to staunch the flow of blood.

Schultz had long ago determined, and agreed with the *Tribune,* that she should get out of Germany if she felt herself to be in real danger. However, her injury, although quite serious, was not

American news journalist May Craig talking with a bomber crew after they had just returned from raiding Germany. An intrepid reporter, Craig provided, among other vivid eyewitness accounts, reports on V-bomb raids on London.

the only reason she had to leave the country. The Nazi authorities had become increasingly suspicious of her and, despite all precautions, seemed to have guessed the truth about 'John Dickson' and the information 'he' had passed on to the *Tribune*. The Nazis had many traps at their command. Their ploy with the aircraft design sent to her apartment may have failed, but there was always the chance of a convenient 'accident', perhaps, or arrest for some minor infraction of air-raid regulations.

The bottom line was that Schultz knew and understood far too much of the truth about Nazi Germany. When she attempted to leave in 1941, the authorities were loath to let her escape their control and did all they could to delay her departure. The United States was not yet in the war at this point, and it was only after the American Embassy in Berlin began putting on the pressure that Schultz managed to get away. She headed first for Switzerland, then through southern France into Spain and eventually, after a nasty bout of typhus, back to New York. Schultz did not return to Germany until 1945, when the once omnipotent Nazi state was fast collapsing and ordinary Germans were denying they had had anything to do with it.

MARTHA GELLHORN IN GERMANY

Martha Gellhorn was there at the time. 'No one is a Nazi, no one ever was,' she wrote sarcastically in *Collier's* magazine. 'To see a whole nation passing the buck is not an enlightening spectacle. It is clear that all you have to do in Germany, in order to lead the country, is to be successful; if you stop

The fiery, fearless Martha Gellhorn, primarily a novelist, never intended to become a war reporter but ultimately proved herself as one of the most brilliant.

being successful, no one will admit they ever heard of you.'

Gellhorn had first arrived in Europe 15 years earlier, in 1930, when she settled on the bohemian *rive gauche* (Left Bank) in Paris as correspondent for *Vogue,* the United Press and a newspaper in her home town, the *Saint Louis Dispatch.* On her initial encounter with young Nazis during an invited visit to Germany, she thought them intellectually barren and ridiculous, but before long she realized how dangerous they were.

Gellhorn was principally a novelist and already a celebrity for *The Trouble I've Seen,* a series of stories containing observations gleaned while travelling around America during the Great Depression. *The Trouble I've Seen* was published in 1936, the same year the civil war in Spain began. This conflict, between fascist Nationalist forces and socialist republicans who had unseated the king, Alfonso XIII, in 1931, had political impact outside Spain and came to exemplify the struggle between dictatorship and democracy that dominated the 1930s in Europe. Martha Gellhorn was a fervent republican. Spain, where she arrived as a special correspondent for *Collier's* magazine in March 1937, came to trigger her transition to war reporter, something she had never intended.

Gellhorn was principally a novelist, and already a celebrity for *The Trouble I've Seen*, a series of stories containing observations gleaned while travelling around America during the Great Depression.

'AN UNSCATHED TOURIST OF WARS'

'I had no idea you could be what I became, an unscathed tourist of wars,' Gellhorn remarked. 'I found out about the Spanish war because I was in Germany when it [began],' Gellhorn later recalled. 'The German papers [which supported the Nationalists] always described the Spanish republicans as "the Red swinedogs". I didn't know anything about it except that, and that was all I needed to know.

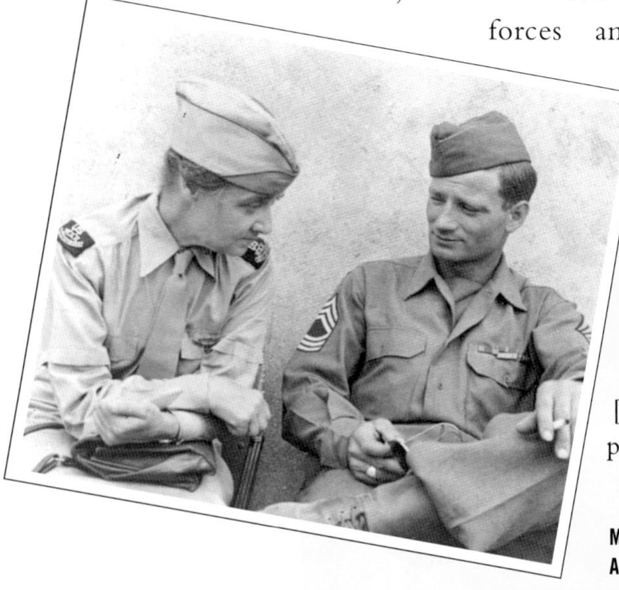

May Craig interviewing an American soldier in 1945.

May Craig

May Craig reported the war for newspapers based in Maine. She waged her own battles against male obstruction and once said:

'When I die, there will be the word "facilities" [engraved on my heart], so often has it been used to prevent me from doing what men reporters could do.'

Machine-gunners of the British Battalion of the International Brigade practising targetry in 1937, during the Spanish Civil War, in which Martha Gellhorn earned her spurs as a war reporter.

[Spain] was the only place that was fighting fascism.... Spain was my cause. Spain was what I loved and believed in.'

Spain not only introduced Gellhorn to the realities of the fighting front, but it also provided her with her first experience of modern mechanized warfare, with its accompanying destruction and death, horrors which would become all too familiar during World War II. Gellhorn was at the Hotel Florida in Madrid when the Spanish capital was shelled by Nationalist artillery.

Spain not only introduced [Martha] Gellhorn to the realities of the fighting front, it also provided her with her first experience of modern mechanized warfare, together with its accompanying destruction and death.

'Suddenly, a shell landed and there was a fountain of granite cobblestones flying up into the air, and the silver lyddite smoke floating off softly,' she wrote. '...I went back to my room and again...there came that whistle-whine-scream-roar and the noise was in your throat and you couldn't feel or hear or think, and the building shook and seemed to settle.... [On] the floor above, we went into a room in which the lyddite smoke still hung mistily. There was nothing left in that room, the furniture

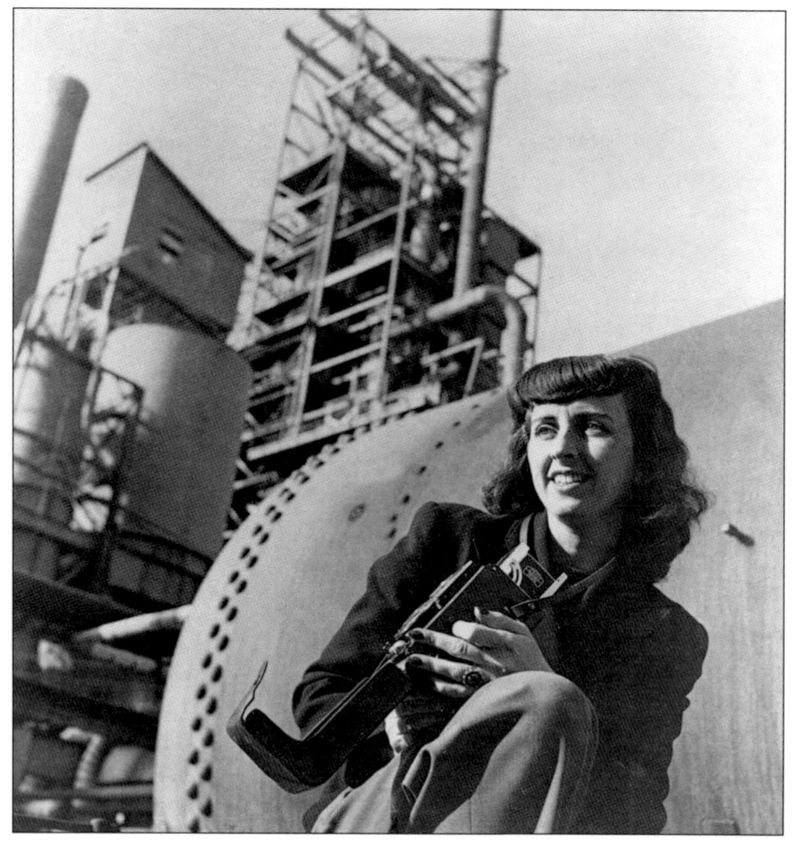

Esther Bubbley, U.S. Office of War Information photographer, in New Jersey. Her career ended abruptly after she married a diplomat: her pictures were considered potentially subversive by the U.S. government.

was kindling wood, the walls were stripped and in places torn open, a great hole led into the next room and the bed was twisted iron....'

Madrid finally fell on March 28, 1939, and though the fighting continued for another four months, the Spanish Civil War was over. To Gellhorn's chagrin, the Nationalists had won.

Magazines waged their own publicity 'war': this 1942 *Life* cover features a WAAF. The inscription 'This above all...' comes from Shakespeare's *Hamlet* and continues: '... to thine own self be true.'

MORE BATTLEFIELDS ON THE HORIZON

Although she still wrote novels, Gellhorn was now firmly set on the path that made her the most indomitable of war correspondents, reporting on fighting as far distant as the war against the Japanese in China, which began in 1937, the Russian assault on Finland in 1939, the invasion of Normandy in 1944, the subsequent drive into Germany and the liberation of the concentration camp at Dachau.

Ultimately, Martha Gellhorn, the unexpected war correspondent, covered more major conflicts than almost any other journalist of her time. Throughout, her reports were steeped in her passionate concern for the defence of liberty against the evil encroachments of fascist dictatorships and the fate of ordinary people caught up in the turmoil of war.

Gellhorn was in Czechoslovakia in 1938 as this small and ultimately doomed country mobilized its army to fight against the territorial demands of Adolf Hitler. In October of that year, Nazi Germany absorbed the Sudeten German area of Czechoslovakia, a prelude to its takeover of the whole country five months later. Gellhorn's article 'Obituary of Democracy', in which she conveyed the grief and isolation of the Czechs as they were terrorized by their new Nazi masters, appeared in *Collier's* magazine on December 10, 1938.

Martha Gellhorn was reporting from Finland when the Russians attacked at the end of November 1939. In February 1941, now married to Ernest Hemingway, Gellhorn

Murder in the Cathedral

Helen Kirkpatrick of the *Chicago Daily News* entered Paris with the French liberation troops on August 26, 1944. Suddenly, all the joy and celebration were cut short when an attempt was made to kill General Charles de Gaulle, head of the Free French forces, and three other generals.

'The generals' car arrived on the dot of 16:15 hours. As they stepped from the car, we stood at salute and at that very moment, a revolver shot rang out. Within a split second, a machine gun opened up.... It sprayed the pavement at my feet.

'The generals entered the church, with 40-odd people pressing from behind to find shelter.... [They] were cowering behind pillars. Someone tried to pull me down.... Suddenly an automatic opened up from behind us – it came from behind the pipes of the organ...for one flashing instant, it seemed that a great massacre was bound to take place as the cathedral reverberated with the sound of guns. Outside, machine guns were rattling. There was a sudden blaze and a machine gun sprayed the centre aisle, flecking the tiles and chipping the pillars to my left.

'Time seemed to have no meaning. Spontaneously, a crowd of widows and bereaved burst forth into the 'Te Deum', as the generals stood bare-headed before the altar.... I saw one man killed. He stood beside me in the main aisle. A woman behind me fainted, but otherwise the only other person I saw killed was a [gunman] who was trapped by the police....'

De Gaulle's great day: entering (front right, in uniform) liberated Paris in 1944 after four years as leader of the Free French armies which pioneered French resistance against Nazi Germany. The event was reported by Helen Kirkpatrick.

arrived with him in China, where the war against Japan had been going on for four years. Late in 1943, Gellhorn arrived in London, interviewed Royal Air Force bomber pilots and refugees from Nazi-occupied Poland and the Netherlands, and visited military hospitals where she saw, but did not flinch from, the ghastly, disfiguring results of burn injuries.

GELLHORN IN ITALY

However, for Gellhorn, a woman of icy courage, this was war at second hand. What she wanted was to go where the serious action could be found. She was by now accustomed to the discomforts that came with getting the best stories – the cold, the damp, the rough living, the lack of civilized facilities, the dirt, the danger – and in 1943 she got her wish. After their victories in North Africa and Sicily, Allied forces had invaded Italy on September 3, 1943. In 1944, from a nearby hill, Gellhorn and a group of other correspondents watched a battle in progress at the Gothic Line, the German defences north of Florence.

By this time, Gellhorn had acquired a reputation for war reporting so vivid that, as Hemingway himself wrote, 'The things that happen to her people really happen, and you feel it as though it were you and you were there.' Gellhorn's report from the Gothic Line was a good illustration of what he meant:

'Suddenly, you see ant-like figures of infantry outlined against the sky,' Gellhorn wrote in *Collier's* magazine. 'Probably, they are going in to attack

American GIs pictured during the fighting in Italy in 1944. The Italian battlefront was an especially dangerous area for war reporters such as Martha Gellhorn.

The Liberation of Dachau

Marguerite Higgins, of the *New York Herald Tribune,* accompanied by Peter Furst of the U.S. Army magazine, *Stars and Stripes,* described the scene at Dachau concentration camp, in southern Germany, after it was liberated by troops of the U.S. 7th Army on April 29, 1945:

'There was not a soul in the yard when the gate was opened. As we learned later, the prisoners themselves had taken over control of their enclosure the night before, refusing to obey any further orders from the German guards, who had retreated to the outside.... The prisoners maintained strict discipline among themselves, remaining close to their barracks so as not to give the [Germans] an excuse for mass murder.

'But the minute the two of us entered, the jangled barrage of "Are you Americans?" in about 16 languages came from the barracks 200 yards [183 metres] from the gate. An affirmative nod caused pandemonium.

'Tattered, emaciated men, weeping, yelling and shouting "Long Live America!", swept toward the gate in a mob. Those who could not walk limped or crawled. In the confusion, they were so hysterically happy that they took one [German] for an American. During a wild five minutes, he was patted on the back, paraded on shoulders and embraced enthusiastically by prisoners. The arrival of American soldiers soon straightened out the situation.

'I happened to be the first through the gate, and the first person to rush up to me turned out to be a Polish Catholic priest...who was not a little startled to discover that the helmeted, uniformed, begoggled individual he had so heartily embraced was not a man.'

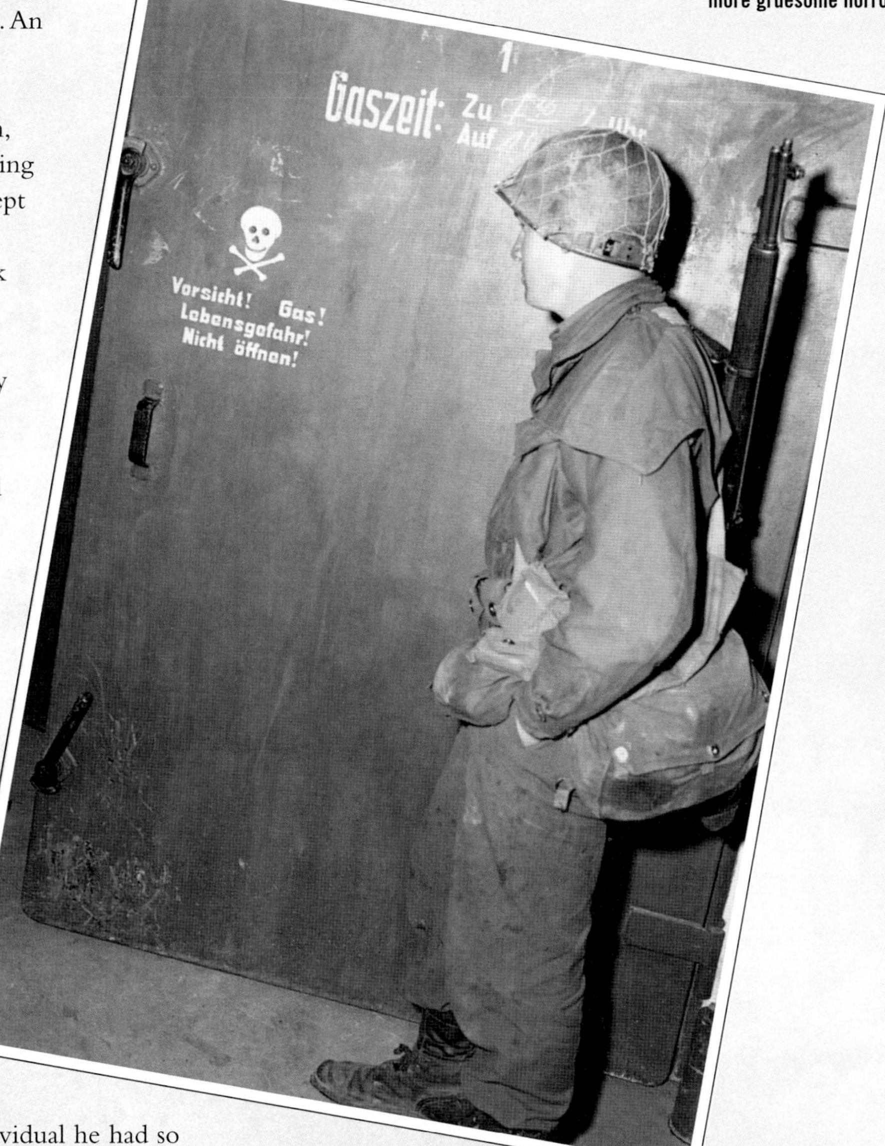

A U.S. 7th Army soldier examining the doors of the Dachau concentration camp gas chambers. Reporters and photographers such as Margaret Bourke-White had to witness and record much more gruesome horrors.

that cluster of farmhouses. Then, they disappear and you do not know what became of them. Tanks roll serenely across the crest of a hill, then the formation breaks, you lose most of them from sight, and then in what was a quiet valley, you unexpectedly see other tanks firing from behind trees. On a road that was quite empty and therefore dangerous, because nothing is more suspect at the front than the silent places, you see a jeep racing in the direction of a town which may or may not be in our hands.'

'The wagons were filled with hay and the [Russian] soldiers lay on top of the hay like an army taking a holiday and going on a mass hayride.'

VICTORY IN SIGHT

Virginia Irwin, of the *Saint Louis Post-Dispatch,* travelled with Russian soldiers heading for Berlin after they had met up with U.S. troops at Torgau on the River Elbe in Germany on April 25, 1945:

'We hit highways clogged with the great body of the Russian Army, beating along in its motley array of horse-drawn vehicles of all sorts. There were Russian troops riding in American 2½-ton [2.3-tonne] trucks. There were Russian troops riding in two-wheeled carts, phaetons, in old-fashioned pony carts, in gypsy wagons and surreys with fringed tops. They rode in everything that could be pulled.

'The wagons were filled with hay and the soldiers lay on top of the hay like an army taking a holiday and going on a mass hayride.…The fierce fighting men of the Red Army in their tunics and great boots, shabby and ragged

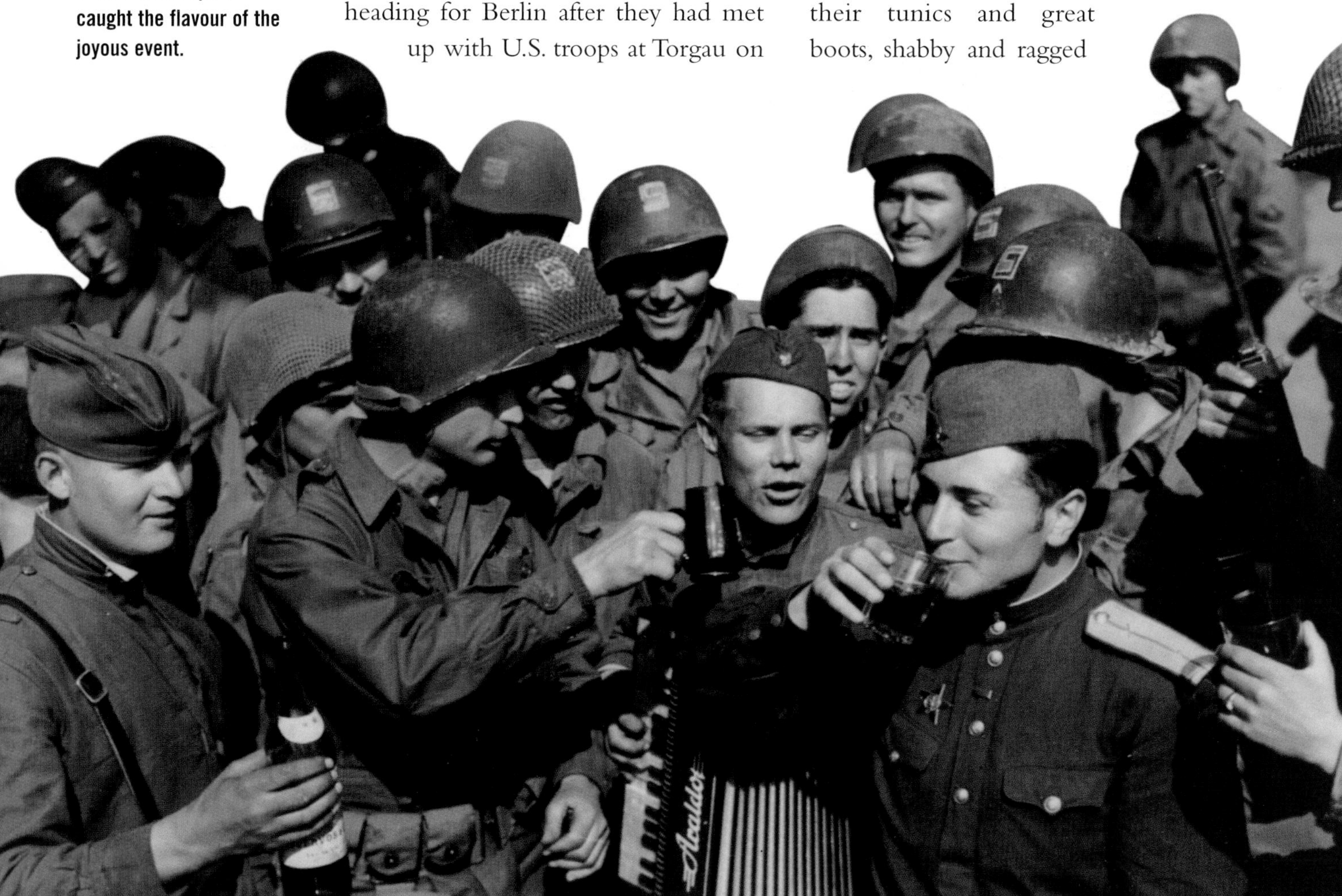

The American and Russian forces meet at Torgau. Unfortunately, no reporters, male or female, were present to record this meeting, but Virginia Irwin's later reports caught the flavour of the joyous event.

Paris Rejoices

Janet Flanner, who had been reporting from Paris for *The New Yorker* since 1925, was there on May 8, 1945 – VE (Victory in Europe) Day – to witness the celebrations of its ecstatic citizens:

'The babble and the shuffle of feet drowned out the sound of the stentorian church bells that clanged for peace, and even the cannon firing from Les Invalides and the precincts of the Louvre were audible on the nearby Place de la Concorde only as rumbling explosions, muffled by the closer noise of feet and tongues that were never still.... Restaurants were closed, apéritifs were scarce, beer was feeble. Peace and spring found the Parisians as badly victualled [fed] as they had been during the war and the winter, but now no one thought or cared about being hungry. All anyone cared about was to keep moving, to keep shouting, to keep singing snatches of the *Marseillaise* [the French national anthem] – *"Le jour de gloire est arrivé...marchons, marchons...."* (The day of glory has arrived...let us march, let us march....)'

Janet Flanner, the veteran *New Yorker* reporter and novelist, is seen here with fellow reporter Ernest Hemingway relaxing at the Deux Magots café in Paris in the last months of the war.

Flanner, left, had lived in Paris since 1925. In addition to 'Letter from Paris', her regular column in *The New Yorker* during the war, she wrote important articles on Adolf Hitler and the Nuremberg trials, and broadcast from Paris after its liberation.

after their long war, riding towards Berlin in their strange assortment of vehicles, singing their fighting songs, drinking vodka, were like so many holidaymakers going on a picnic.'

NUREMBERG

After Italy, after the D-Day landings in France, after the Battle of Bastogne – the last gasp of Nazi resistance before the Allies reached Germany – and the ghastly sights of Dachau, Martha Gellhorn's war ended with the Nuremberg trials of 21 major Nazi war criminals in 1945–1946.

'These 21 men,' Gellhorn wrote, 'these nothings, these industrious and once-confident monsters were the last left alive of that small gang which had ruled Germany.'

CHAPTER 9

Women as Entertainers

Big names in the show business industry – film, stage and singing stars – gladly gave their services to entertain the troops and civilian audiences in a much needed effort to take the edge off wartime tensions.

Keeping morale high in wartime has always been seen as crucial to victory. During World War II, this need to boost people's spirits was the cue for famous stars of the entertainment industry, as well as lesser-known performers, to do their part to divert troops, and also civilians under the extraordinary pressures of wartime. Organizations such as the Red Cross and the Salvation Army created their own entertainment groups, but the major effort came from two official units: ENSA (Entertainments National Service Association), formed in Britain in 1938 by the theatrical producer, director and filmmaker Basil Dean, followed in 1941 by the American equivalent, the USO (United Services Organizations). By the end of the war, ENSA shows had been seen by over 500 million people, with USO shows reaching 172 million.

PROBLEMS

The successes of ENSA and the USO were achieved despite difficulties. Performers were not exempt from wartime restrictions. The best transport – by coach – was reserved for the larger units. Smaller ENSA units had to content themselves with lorries that not

Films and theatre during the pre-war years, such as the 1935 comedy *Oh Daddy* starring Frances Day, opposite, had been purely escapist, with the accent on glamour. This emphasis continued in wartime, when audiences needed to be distracted from the grim realities of warfare.

All-women orchestras, like this British ATS Dance Band seen performing in 1944, were an innovation in wartime, giving a chance for female instrumentalists and singers to shine.

only served as transport but as stages as well. Private motoring was severely restricted in Britain, and petrol rationing was very tight. One ENSA performer, Robina Hinton, managed to get hold of a small caravan and a car, but she and her husband and stage partner, Reg, had to be very careful how they used it.

'We found that variety people [like us] could get coupons for petrol through the Showman's Guild, but these were severely rationed to the exact mile, so care had to be taken not to take a wrong turning. My husband coasted down all the hills to save petrol.'

'Costumes had to be contrived.... We used stuff from secondhand shops.... A new production could apply for an extra allowance of clothing coupons, but there was a limit on these.'

SEQUINS AND STAGES

Stage costumes, which had to be glamorous to make an impact on the audience, posed a particular problem.

'Costumes just had to be contrived,' Hinton remembered. 'We used stuff from secondhand shops, cut down and reused. A new production could apply for an extra allowance of clothing coupons, but there was a limit to these. Sequins soon became scarce.... I had one costume pre-war that was like a complete skin covered all over in hand-sewn sequins. The sequins had to be replaced almost every performance. [So] when I started with ENSA, I persuaded Wardrobe to give me a costume in place of the sequined one, and they came up with a [brief] silk leotard and a chiffon long split overdress.'

Hinton also encountered hazards when ENSA shows took place in

The Forces' Sweetheart

In Britain, radio – then a monopoly of the BBC (British Broadcasting Corporation) – became a major means of mass entertainment and an ideal platform for programmes featuring the current style of popular music: sentimental love ballads spiced with patriotism. One of the greatest exponents of this genre was Vera Lynn, who broadcast a regular half-hour programme on Sunday evenings named *Sincerely Yours, Vera Lynn.* In addition to singing, Lynn passed on messages to and from soldiers overseas and their families at home. These broadcasts earned official disapproval because the authorities believed the sentimentality of *Sincerely Yours* sapped military morale, making troops feel maudlin about being far from home. The programme was able to continue only with difficulty.

Despite this, the broadcasts remained enormously popular, as did Vera Lynn. Lynn's songs may have been sad in tone, reflecting as they did the pain of lovers' partings and the self-sacrifice imposed by war, but they also contained an element of hope for a better future.

Wartime entertainment gave troops the chance to see their favourite performers – like popular British singer Vera Lynn – close up and in person.

Icon of Hope

'We'll meet again,' ran one of Lynn's best-known songs, 'don't know where, don't know when, but I know we'll meet again some sunny day…'

A similar song, *The White Cliffs of Dover,* also promised future contentment. 'There'll be bluebirds over the white cliffs of Dover, tomorrow, just you wait and see. There'll be love and laughter, and peace ever after, tomorrow, when the world is free.'

Other British wartime singers may have had better voices and been much more glamorous, but Vera Lynn had a special appeal: her husband, Harry Lewis, was in the Royal Air Force. She was soon seen as the epitome of the brave wartime wife keeping up her spirits despite enforced separation.

Vera Lynn, who reached even wider audiences when she toured India and Burma for ENSA, soon became known as 'the Forces' Sweetheart', a name she retains to this day. Though long since retired, Lynn has made several televised appearances on the occasion of anniversaries and commemorations of wartime events, such as for D-Day in 1994 and for VE Day (Victory in Europe) in 1995.

improperly maintained theatres. At the time, Dover, on the Southeast coast of England, was being bombed by the Luftwaffe and shelled by German artillery fire from across the English Channel. Hinton was working on stage when the floor gave way and she plunged through it up to her waist. On another occasion, less serious but discomfiting nonetheless, Hinton's act at a Navy land base required her to roll over on a stage which, unknown to her, had not been swept: she got up covered with dust and dirt.

British film actress Frances Day, seen here in period costume, was one of the most popular stars before and during the war and was much admired for her beauty and glamour.

TOO MUCH THE LADY?

Other problems afflicting ENSA during the war arose from the sort of entertainment they provided: mainly light comedy, floor shows, comic patter or spectaculars like high-wire acts, which tended to exclude film and stage stars who had built their reputations on more 'serious' acting. With this as its standard approach, ENSA envisaged problems with stars like Anna Neagle. Neagle – not an obvious glamour girl – was best known for her films, in which she played 'heavy' parts like the aged Queen Victoria in *Sixty Glorious Years* (1938). Ultimately, she proved to be one of their most enthusiastic and tireless performers. Unlike many other top stars who were too vain to sink their prestige in ENSA uniform, Neagle wore hers with pride and was willing to help in any way, from signing autographs to posing for pictures with soldiers.

Even though Neagle could dance and sing as well as act, ENSA feared she was too decorous and ladylike to appeal to the troops. To complicate matters, her husband and mentor, the film producer Herbert Wilcox, was greatly concerned about his wife's professional reputation as a serious actress and turned down ENSA's suggestion that she perform hit songs from musicals. Instead, he devised a much more up-market show.

'The first half,' Anna Neagle recalled, '...had Mae Coffey, who was an opera singer, and an actor reciting scenes from Shakespeare, a lovely ballet dancer and her partner doing...semi-ballroom dancing, and me doing a couple of musical comedy numbers. The second half was taken up with one act from [the play] *Victoria Regina* and ended with Mae Coffey singing *Rule Britannia.*'

This wasn't the sort of show ENSA wanted. They demanded *Victoria Regina* be dropped. Herbert Wilcox insisted on retaining it and Billy Milton, the pianist for the show, remembered what happened after a dress rehearsal at London's Drury Lane Theatre.

'"Anna Neagle?" they said. "She'll be no good for the troops at all. Oh no, they won't like her." [All the same], we opened on a Monday at Bulford Camp [on Salisbury Plain]. And the reception Anna got! It raised the roof. Every bigwig at [ENSA] said, "My God, what a surprise!"'

FROM MILAMENT TO SCARLET

Wilcox had judged the show's audience astutely, and it helped set a standard for a more serious slant to ENSA entertainment. Subsequently, Neagle appeared with great success in Terence Rattigan's play *French without Tears.* Veteran actress Sybil Thorndike performed in plays by Shakespeare in France, Belgium, the Netherlands and Germany.

Edith Evans, one of the great stars of the British stage, appeared in one of her most admired roles, as Milament in *The Way of the World* by 17th-century dramatist William Congreve. When Evans appeared on stage in full period costume, the audience assumed they were watching the slapstick comedy of a traditional British pantomime and began to laugh – only to have their amusement frozen into silence by the immensely dignified, steely-eyed actress. Nevertheless, at the end of Evans's performance, the men burst into loud applause.

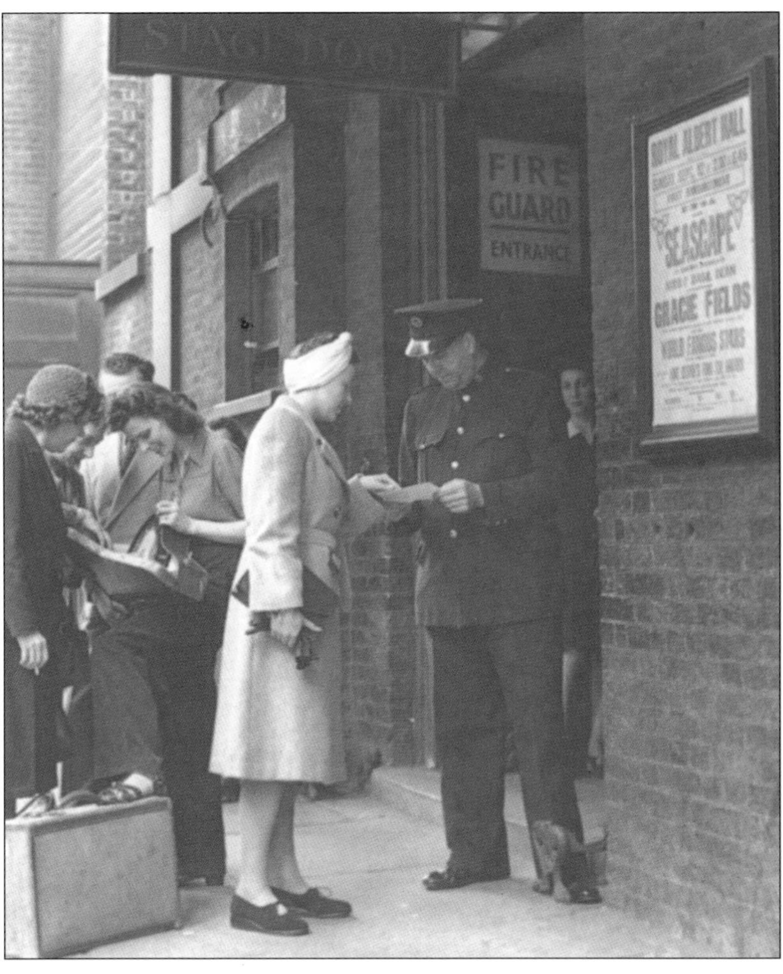

Muriel Miller, a member of ENSA, has her identification papers examined by the doorman at the stage door of the ENSA headquarters at the Drury Lane Theatre in London, 1944.

The film and stage actress Vivien Leigh received a similar reception when she appeared with the Spring Party, the first ENSA star company to arrive in North Africa. Dressed as Scarlett O'Hara, the role she had made famous in the 1939 film *Gone with the Wind,* Leigh bewitched her audience, according to Roland Coombs, a performer with the Kairotics, an RAF concert party.

'Perhaps my most vivid recollection of any show during the war,' Coombs recalled, 'was sitting in an intolerably hot and overcrowded theatre...watching Vivien Leigh on stage performing scenes from *Gone with the Wind.* As

Myra Hess

Myra Hess had become a world-famous concert pianist several years before the start of World War II and was much admired for the spiritual quality she gave to her music. She was about to set off on a tour of the United States in 1939 when war broke out in Europe. Hess at once abandoned her engagements and her international career and concentrated instead on providing concerts during the German Blitz for the hard-pressed people of London.

'All the public buildings were closed,' she commented. 'Concerts had stopped. Nothing was going on, and the blackout made it so difficult for people to get home.'

Classical music provided more intellectual entertainment for wartime audiences. The need to be entertained was such that many people who attended concerts had never previously heard this kind of music.

LUNCHTIME CONCERTS

It was also difficult for people to get to London for an evening's entertainment. To get around this problem, Myra Hess conceived the idea of lunchtime concerts in the National Gallery at London's Trafalgar Square. The concerts were a tremendous success, despite the danger of daylight air raids. Once, a performance was in progress when a bomb exploded outside the National Gallery. The whole place shook and people started running for the exits, but Myra Hess played on as if nothing untoward had occurred.

Hess specialized in the music of Robert Schumann, but was also noted for performances of Bach, Beethoven and Mozart. In the course of her lunchtime concerts, she played all 27 of Mozart's piano concertos. After five years, by 1944, she'd given a total of 1,300 classical music performances at the National Gallery. Already a Dame (the female equivalent of a Knight, an honour bestowed by the British sovereign), Myra Hess received the greatest professional honour of all in 1941: the Gold Medal of the Royal Philharmonic Society, awarded only to the greatest musicians.

Scarlett O'Hara, her cool, striking beauty was breathtaking. It aroused an aching nostalgia, a feeling of homesickness....'

This level of entertainment had figured in ENSA's assessment as too élitist and highbrow for ordinary soldiers. ENSA was wrong. The soldiers not only loved it and cheered the performers loud and long, many of them admitted that they had acquired a new taste for serious theatre.

CLASSICAL MUSIC

It was the same when classical musicians undertook ENSA tours. Most of their audiences had once shied away from 'long-haired' concertos, operas, chamber music and symphonies. Many had never even heard classical music before. Some of the musicians themselves doubted the likelihood of its appeal, especially as so much of the great classical repertoire had been written by German composers. They need not have worried

The message of this British poster was that anyone and everyone, male or female and regardless of which service they belonged to, would find fun and entertainment at the wartime ENSA shows.

on either score. When the first of the experimental Good Music concerts was given at Aldershot, Hampshire, in October 1940, the performers – who included the opera singer Maggie Teyte and the pianist Eileen Joyce – were given such an enthusiastic reception that the exercise was repeated. Soon, there were seven Good Music concerts on tour with ENSA, including tours by large symphony orchestras.

John Foskett, a stage technician for a Good Music concert at RAF Halton, was convinced beforehand that the event would be a disaster.

'I was proved wrong,' he later recalled. 'It attracted an audience of between 500 and 700 for every performance.... I still remember Eileen Joyce playing *Jesu, Joy of Man's Desiring* on the grand piano, stage drapes lit deep purple and a pale blue spot playing on her and the piano. She looked quite ethereal.'

'This level of entertainment figured in ENSA's assessment as too élitist and highbrow for ordinary soldiers. ENSA was wrong.'

UNIQUE BATTLEGROUND

This sort of appreciation was not always shared by commanders in overseas battlefields, who saw ENSA shows as too much of a distraction. For a start, the presence of women seemed an intrusion into an all-male society that needed to be constantly ready to make war.

It was true, of course, that the presence of civilians close to the battlefront posed a danger not only to themselves, but also to the conduct of the fighting and the performance of the soldiers. Besides this, in North Africa, the focus of the land war between 1940 and 1943, military morale and discipline were much more difficult to maintain than in more conventional battle areas. As a battleground, North Africa was unique: there was little but endless miles of desert, no towns, few inhabitants except for nomads, no available local women, no places of entertainment – nothing, in fact, to see, do or enjoy. In this environment, the impact women could have on men so far removed from their normal surroundings had very unsettling potential. All the more so because the

Luxuriously dressed women, like this singer entertaining hospitalized soldiers in 1941, were the epitome of glamorous femininity and took audiences into a fantasy world far distant from wartime realities.

women in question were British and, as actresses and dancers hired for their physical attractiveness, they were women of the most desirable kind.

CONFINED TO CAIRO

The first attempts by the military to keep soldiers away from female temptations resulted in confining the ENSA units to the Egyptian capital, Cairo, and the Suez Canal Zone, with only a few allowed to venture to the fringes of the desert. Thus the only men with access to entertainment were the wounded in hospitals and those given rest time behind the lines. The situation changed, however, in 1942 as the British 8th Army's campaign against Rommel's Afrika Korps built up to its great defining moment: the Battle of El Alamein. As the British troops advanced steadily across the desert, ENSA units followed.

As always, where men far from home came into contact with pretty girls, there had been hints of sexual impropriety; this particularly applied to British officers, who tended to monopolize the girls during after-the-show socializing. However, Reg Lever, leader of the Hello Company, which worked under the ENSA aegis, insisted that sex and having a good time were not the girls' purpose or significance.

'We used to live with the troops in the orange groves of Tunisia,' Lever remembered, '[but] we never had any trouble. This was respect for the girls, because it so happened I had very nice girls with me. I suppose if I'd had one or two tarty types, we might have got that sort of thing, but I didn't have tarts.'

ENSA'S MISTAKE

ENSA had misjudged the situation – as had the USO – in thinking that the men wanted leg shows and displays of seduction on stage, all spiced with blue jokes and large helpings of smut. The reverse turned out to be the case. Soldiers in the desert or on any other battlefield were not that interested in sex symbols: they longed for reminders of home and family. Most carried with them photographs of their wives and children, much thumbed and tattered by constant viewing. Far from making passes at the ENSA girls, they used them as sounding boards for endless talk about home and the family lives they missed so much.

ENSA had misjudged the situation – as had the USO – in thinking that the men wanted leg shows and displays of seduction.

The fact that the ENSA girls were

Lilli Marlene

Lilli Marlene was the most unusual song of World War II. Starting out as a German poem written in 1915, it became a universal soldiers' favourite. The British 8th Army first heard it played and sung by the men of the Afrika Korps, and soon they adopted it in an English translation. The English *Lilli Marlene* became the signature tune for the popular British singer Anne Shelton, though the Americans preferred it as performed by the gravel-voiced, German-born actress and singer, Marlene Dietrich.

The reason *Lilli Marlene* transcended the hatred of war to acquire a universal appeal is evident from its lyrics:

Underneath the lantern by the barrack gate,
Darling, I remember the way you used to wait;
'Twas there that you whispered tenderly,
That you lov'd me, you'd always be
My Lilli of the lamplight,
My own Lilli Marlene.

Time would come for roll call, time for us to part,
Darling, I'd caress you and press you to my heart.
And there 'neath that far-off lantern light
I'd hold you tight, we'd kiss goodnight,
My Lilli of the lamplight,
My own Lilli Marlene.

Orders came for sailing somewhere over there,
All confined to barracks was more than I could bear;
I knew you were waiting in the street,
I heard your feet, but could not meet
My Lilli of the lamplight,
My own Lilli Marlene.

Resting in a billet just behind the line,
Even tho' we're parted, your lips are close to mine.
You wait where that lantern softly gleams,
Your sweet face seems to haunt my dreams,
My Lilli of the lamplight,
My own Lilli Marlene.

Film and cabaret star Marlene Dietrich worked diligently for the American United Services Organization during the war; she made numerous personal appearances, signed autographs and sang for the troops in a voice some people thought tuneless, but most regarded as irresistibly sexy.

from their own country was important to the men. The soldiers loved to hear the sound of a British woman's voice as she told them what was happening at home, how their children were faring without Daddy, how women were managing the rationing, the shortages, the air raids and the loneliness. With mail from home reaching them infrequently at times, their greatest worry was that *anything* might be happening and that, worse still, they didn't know about it. The ENSA girls, therefore, had to be much more than entertainers. They were patient confidantes and sympathetic listeners as well.

LUFTWAFFE INTRUSIONS

Aside from this, there were problems enough in taking entertainment out into the desert and close to the battlefront. For the performers, living conditions were necessarily primitive. The girls of the Hello Company were lucky enough to have a caravan as their quarters, but the men had to sleep in tents. Their open-air performances took place in daylight, for stage lighting at night would have drawn attacks from the Luftwaffe.

The singer Alice Delysia was performing at an ENSA show when an air raid began. She snatched up a Union Jack and waved it vigorously at the Luftwaffe aircraft overhead.

But even daylight was far from safe. More than once, the Hello Company's shows – consisting of variety, sketches, songs, comedy and conjuring tricks – ended suddenly when Luftwaffe fighters appeared overhead, swept the stage with machine-gun fire and dropped bombs on the audience. This was not an uncommon experience for ENSA entertainers in North Africa. On one occasion, the singer Alice Delysia was performing when an air raid began. She refused to stop singing, snatched up a Union Jack and waved it vigorously at the Luftwaffe aircraft overhead.

This showgirl is applying her make-up before a performance entertaining German troops in wartime France; by the standards of the time, she was quite scantily dressed.

YORKSHIRE COMES TO SICILY

The fighting in North Africa ended in June 1943, when the Germans surrendered and the men of the Afrika Korps, their greatest single fighting unit of the war, became prisoners. Three months later, the Allied campaign moved on to Sicily and Italy, and some of the big stars of ENSA went with it. On September 20, 1943, a month after the Allied conquest of Sicily, Gracie Fields, the Yorkshire lass with the soaring voice, arrived at a hospital there to entertain an audience of 800 wounded men and their nurses. There was a breathless pause when Fields was announced.

'They didn't know if it was true or not,' wrote Virginia Vernon, representing the Drury Lane Theatre in Sicily. 'A continuation of this breathless pause when she walked on stage. They couldn't believe their own eyes. Then applause. She made them roar with

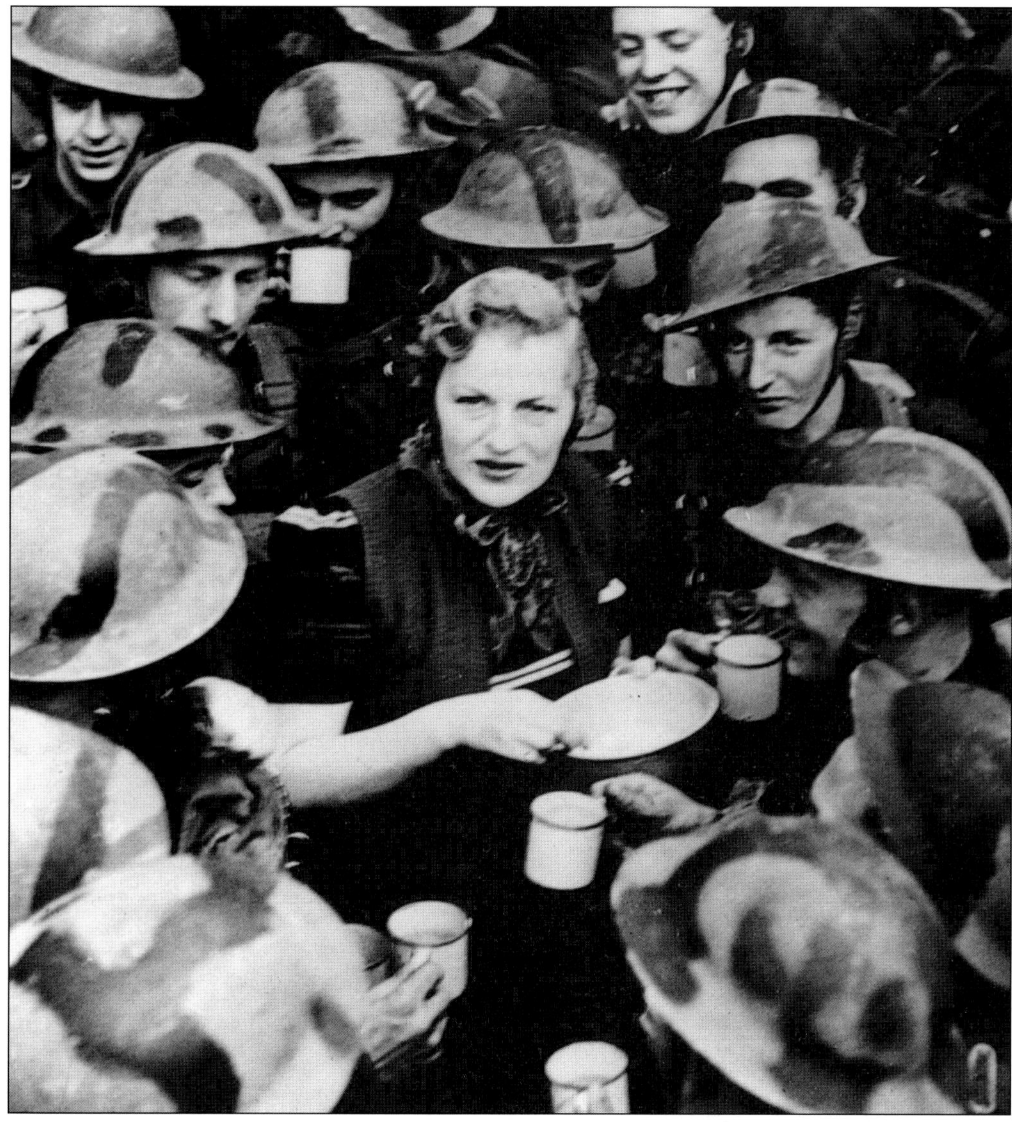

Singer Gracie Fields – 'Our Gracie' and one of the best-loved British entertainers – surrounded by men of the British Expeditionary Force during a visit to France in 1940.

laughter for half an hour, then sang *Ave Maria* and had us all in tears. Then, she gave them a laugh to finish. Those wounded boys and everyone there will always remember this Gracie Fields appearance.'

'[Gracie Fields] made them roar with laughter for half an hour, then sang *Ave Maria* and had us all in tears. Then, she gave them a laugh to finish.'

Fields, who was on a flying visit to Sicily, spent ten days on the island entertaining more than 60,000 men. She promised to remain with the troops of the 8th Army after the Allied invasion of Italy on September 3, 1943, but she had reckoned without her contractual obligations to a radio show in the United States. Fields was obliged to break her promise and depart for America, much to the men's disappointment.

THE BRILLIANT GRENFELL

Another much-admired British performer, Joyce Grenfell, was in a better position. Grenfell was a brilliant all-rounder – singer, actress, writer, painter, musician –

Joyce Grenfell, right, the British singer and comedy actress, who performed for troops in North Africa and the Middle East, was probably the greatest one-woman act in wartime entertainment.

Hollywood star Veronica Lake, pictured opposite, had originally worn her hair long and waved; in wartime she cut it short to encourage women to do the same, reducing the risk of entangling their hair in factory machinery.

which made her the ideal solo performer, particularly suitable for entertaining overseas. Early in 1944, with her accompanist Viola Tunnard, Grenfell began overseas tours that eventually took her across North Africa to Malta, Sicily, southern Italy, Cairo, Baghdad, Iraq, Persia (Iran) and India.

Grenfell and Tunnard first set out for North Africa and the Middle East on January 14, 1944. Some two weeks later, they were at a hospital in the Villa Desjoyeux, Algiers, coping with the difficulties of performing in a makeshift environment.

'Tuesday [February 1] was the hardest day we've done so far because of the tents,' Grenfell wrote in the journal of her tours. 'The courtyards...have enormous dark brown marquees in them, holding about 60 beds. They are narrow, ill-lit and their acoustic properties are exactly nil. However, the need for entertainment in these surroundings was obvious, and it turned out that no one [had sung] in tents, so we said we'd go. I tried standing in the middle, walking up and down, standing at one end. It was equally bad wherever we went, but even so the programme was welcomed and we got them singing....'

Grenfell was a huge success wherever she went. Robert Harbin, the ENSA organizer based in Baghdad, came to the conclusion that she was the greatest single artist he ever dealt with.

Grenfell was a huge success wherever she went. Robert Harbin, the ENSA organizer based in Baghdad, came to the conclusion that she was the greatest single artist he ever dealt with.

'If I had to give a medal, I'd give [it] to her,' Harbin commented. 'We used to strap a small piano on the back of a lorry, put her and Viola Tunnard...in as well, and off they went with just a sergeant [to guard them]. I never had any grumbling from them at all. Uncomplainingly, they went around the whole circumference of Paiforce [the troops in Persia and Iraq] and entertained one man, two men, hundreds. [Joyce] did an angel's job.'

THE USO'S ADVANTAGE

Gracie Fields and Joyce Grenfell were great artists whose stardom shone on long after the war was over, but the American USO had a far larger roster of

world-famous performers to bring to the business of entertaining their troops. The reason was Hollywood's grip on the global entertainment market. American movies of the 1930s had revolutionized the cinema, and top Hollywood film stars like Greta Garbo, Bette Davis, Olivia de Havilland, Betty Grable, Claudette Colbert and the vivacious 'Brazilian bombshell' Carmen Miranda were the new world-famous celebrities, setting a new standard of glamour, charisma and excitement on-screen. Clark Gable, James Stewart, Don Ameche and John Payne did the same for men.

The USO, established in February 1941 to set up social clubs and put on entertainment for the American forces, experienced a rush of big-name stars after the Japanese attack on Pearl Harbor ten months later. The stars volunteered to sell war bonds, enrolled in Civil Defense or joined an organization similar to the USO, the Victory Committee. Many male stars, like Stewart, Douglas Fairbanks Jr., and Robert Taylor joined the armed forces though they could have claimed deferment on grounds that they worked in the film industry, considered vital to the war effort.

Just how vital the film industry was – as a means of propaganda as well as entertainment – was soon proved not only by Hollywood but also by its British counterpart. The movies, British- or American-made, already exerted a powerful hold on mass cinema audiences in the 1930s; thus, in wartime, a propaganda message could be packaged as on-screen entertainment and have real impact.

WARTIME FILMS

In British wartime films, women were usually depicted as capable, making the best of difficult conditions, and remaining cheerful in the face of any and all problems. Fearful, jittery characters, always moaning and complaining, were included in the casts for contrast. Significantly, in the on-screen air raids it was the cheery types

Wartime Glamour

Pretty girls, scantily, but not scandalously, dressed, were regularly featured in wartime glamour photographs less as a means of sexual provocation, more as a reminder of home and the wives and girlfriends left behind. Few, if any, of these pictures were pornographic. The famous pin-up photograph of film star Betty Grable, so popular with American servicemen, showed off a neat little behind and plenty of leg but it was essentially innocent and had no obvious sexual connotations.

The military authorities were well aware how easy it was for young men, many of them away from home for the first time, to overheat and indulge in unrestrained promiscuity. As it was, venereal disease was a big problem in wartime. Glamour pictures, however, were intended to siphon off some of this sexual energy into harmless nostalgia.

Just like the girl next door. Slim, pretty, fresh-faced and smiling, this German wartime photograph typified the young wives and girlfriends waiting at home for their men to return from war.

army with rifles. The veteran actress Marie Lohr, playing the local lady of the manor, saves a group of children by throwing herself on a hand grenade. Muriel George, in the role of a local postmistress, kills a German with an axe, but does it sobbing wildly to indicate that it was done out of necessity, not brutality.

The famous film star Claudette Colbert is featured in this cigarette advertisement, which also managed to publicize not only her war work but also Paramount, the studio to which she was contracted, as well as her next movie.

FROM *MRS. MINIVER* TO MUSICALS

By contrast, the Oscar-winning *Mrs. Miniver* (1942), with Greer Garson in the title role, was made by the Metro Goldwyn Mayer studios in Hollywood

Brazilian film star Carmen Miranda, with her fruit-basket headgear, was widely imitated – here, in 1944, at London's Windmill Theatre, whose proud boast was that 'We Never Closed', despite air raids.

who survived, while the moaners were the ones who died in the rubble, their fears at last realized.

Film propaganda came in many different forms, however, and war era movies ran the gamut of stock situations, from the melodramatic to the domestic and the frankly escapist. One of the more melodramatic was the British-made *Went the Day Well?* (1942), with an almost completely female cast. Based on a story by prize-winning novelist Graham Greene, *Went the Day Well?* portrayed the situation that had faced Britain two years before the film was made, when a German invasion appeared imminent. In the story, the invasion – which never transpired in real life – has already taken place and its heroines perform extraordinary feats in their own personal defence of Britain. Thora Hird and Elizabeth Allen, playing two Land Girls, fend off the German

Betty Grable, with her dazzling smile and doll-like face, was the epitome of on-screen niceness. She appeared in 24 unremarkable films before rocketing to stardom during the war.

to show how the British defied the Germans and still came up with patriotism and fighting spirit intact. The film was set in the fictional London suburb of Belham. Pre-war life in Belham had been insular and complacent: which car or which expensive outfit to choose counted as a crisis decision in this self-absorbed environment, and the annual flower show was the great event of the year.

With the advent of war, everything changed, requiring the inhabitants of Belham to endure self-sacrifice, bereavement, air raids and a dire emergency when Germans appeared in the suburb. Mrs. Miniver, the eponymous heroine, found a wounded German pilot in the bushes and brought him home to tend his injury and, while

Mrs. Miniver, the heroine, finds a wounded German pilot in the bushes and brings him home to tend his injury and, while doing so, voices her defiance of Nazi Germany.

doing so, voiced her defiance of Nazi Germany, assuring the soldier that England would never yield to aggression.

Hollywood Canteen, a musical made in 1944 with songs by Cole Porter, was different. Set in a USO nightclub, the film combined the unabashed escapism at which Hollywood so excelled, with the participation of big-name film stars – Joan Crawford, Ida Lupino, Barbara Stanwyck, Roy Rogers – all of whom stepped down from normal top billing to play cameo parts. With ingredients like these, *Hollywood Canteen* appeared to be no more than a display of typical American gusto meant to take audiences' minds off the war. For all its vitality, though, the story was firmly rooted in wartime. It featured a young GI with a crush on film star Joan Leslie, who fulfils his personal dream by winning a night out on the town with her. Once the fun is over, there is an emotional farewell and the GIs depart for the war in New Guinea.

The rear view of the shapely Betty Grable smiling over her shoulder at the camera was the most famous photograph of the war. It was reproduced in the millions.

GRABLE THE PIN-UP

But the stars of Hollywood contributed a great deal more to morale boosting in the war than their on-screen roles. Some became icons for the U.S. forces, none more so than pretty, doll-like Betty Grable. Although Grable had featured in some 24 films before the war, she had made little impact in any of them. But with the war, Grable – with her long, beautiful legs, her air of wholesome American womanhood and her shiny, toothy smile – became the pin-up girl of the U.S. forces. The rear view of the

Betty Grable was not the only wartime pin-up; an off-duty submariner in the U.S. Navy relaxes in his bunk surrounded by several drawings of skimpily dressed glamour girls in provocative poses.

shapely Grable smiling over her shoulder at the camera was the most famous glamour photograph of the war. It was reproduced in the millions, to be stuck on walls and doors, inside lockers and above beds – not entirely for its sex appeal, but also to remind the troops of what they most longed for: home, the girl next door and Mom's apple pie.

In 1943, the Victory Caravan made a three-week tour of the States, with appearances by Claudette Colbert, Olivia de Havilland, Joan Bennett, Laurel and Hardy and Cary Grant.

SERVED BY THE STARS

American troops still in the United States, stationed there permanently or in transit to one of the war zones, received an extra treat in this context. In 1942, the Oscar-winning actress Bette Davis, together with actor John Garfield, opened the Stage Door Canteen in Hollywood, where servicemen experienced every film fan's dream – the stars were not only there in the flesh, they also cooked dinners, served them and danced with the men afterwards.

Sultry film star Marlene Dietrich worked in the Stage Door kitchen. Glamorous Hedy Lamarr, comedienne Betty Hutton, singer Judy Garland, and the comic duo Abbott and Costello waited on tables. Many a young GI had the thrill of actually dancing with Betty Grable. Entertainment was provided by singers Dinah Shore, Bing Crosby and Frank Sinatra.

Two shapely British girls put on a beauty show for American GIs stationed in Britain after 1942 in preparation for the D-Day landings in Normandy two years later.

Keeping the Servicemen Sweet

USO fare in World War II was about much more than appearances by established stars and professional entertainers. Social clubs set up by the USO were important as homes-from-home and places where American servicemen could talk and dance with local girls.

One of the best known was the USO club at Camp Kilmer, near New York City, the main staging area on the Eastern seaboard for men going overseas. Diplomacy, patience and plenty of feminine sympathy were needed when socializing with these men, who were facing imminent involvement in the deadly business of war. The girls met these criteria so successfully that they became known as the Camp Kilmer Sweethearts.

For the girls themselves, joining the USO and serving as hostesses reassured them that they, too, were contributing to the American war effort.

'After a year of just sitting around,' recalled Eleanore DeFellipo, 'my sisters and I joined the USO.... We would get on a bus that dropped us off right in front of the front door. We'd arrive with cookies and items we had baked, and we would serve hot dogs and sandwiches. And of course, we danced with the men.... You felt like the belle of the ball, one soldier after another would cut in to dance with you! [But] at the end of the evening, you got right back on the bus....'

Girls, dressed in official uniforms, provided companionship and served as dancing partners for U.S. Navy pilots enjoying a rest from combat at the Chris Holmes Rest Home in Hawaii.

Best Behaviour

Rules of behaviour were strict. The girls were forbidden to give out their telephone numbers and had to stay inside the canteen the whole evening. They were allowed to write to the servicemen, however, and Eleanore confessed, 'I knitted a lot!'

Eleanore's sister Paula wrote to so many of the men that she began to keep a map:

'Each time I received a letter, I placed a new star on the map; just nice, friendly letters to keep up their morale.... We also visited the wounded boys in the hospital...we mainly talked and wrote letters for them.'

These four WAVEs volunteered to be cheerleaders, rousing the spectators in support of the Ottumwa, Iowa, naval air station football team, during a game played there in October 1943.

It was a feast of stars that only the war could have produced, but there was more. In 1943 the Victory Caravan made a three-week tour of the States, with appearances by Claudette Colbert, Olivia de Havilland, Joan Bennett, Laurel and Hardy, and Cary Grant, among many others, all greeted by rapturous audiences. When the lushly beautiful Dorothy Lamour, star with Bing Crosby and Bob Hope in the Road

The famous wartime movie *Casablanca* (1942) tells the story of the cynical café owner Rick (Humphrey Bogart) who makes personal sacrifices to save Ilsa (Ingrid Bergman), the woman he loves.

films, visited a factory, she seemed to almost bring production to a halt.

STARS OVERSEAS

American stars' activities were mainly confined to the United States, leaving servicemen abroad without sufficient, or sometimes any, entertainment. But in April 1942 the first USO party of stars left the country to visit American troops in Britain. Merle Oberon, the regal, part-Sri Lankan actress, was with the company on this occasion, which proved a not entirely successful visit. Film star egos got in the way, and there was friction between the USO and ENSA, whose home patch had been invaded.

Outside the United States, Hollywood film stars remained generally hard to find. Two notable exceptions were Bob Hope and Joe E. Brown, who toured wherever U.S. troops could be found.

The USO faced a particular problem apart from this. It was one thing for big-name film stars to tour the States, where they could spend time entertaining the troops without infringing their studio contracts. It was quite another to go abroad, where the USO insisted on a minimum tour of three months. Actresses Ann Sheridan, Carole Landis and Paulette Goddard were among the few stars who made it overseas, but they came in for criticism from the U.S. Army's newspaper *Roundup* for failing to visit enough camps or, in Sheridan's case, cutting short their tours. They were even accused of shirking when the going got tough. Sheridan protested that she had to return to the United States to fulfil her contract and refuted the suggestion that she had gone overseas for the sake of publicity. 'If I'd wanted publicity,' she said furiously, 'I'd have stayed at home.'

Sheridan had, in any case, been kept

Ivy Benson

Yorkshire-born Ivy Benson was a highly accomplished musician, able to play the piano, the electric organ, the clarinet and the saxophone, but her chief fame in World War II centred on her all-female orchestra.

The war proved to be Benson's big opportunity. With so many male musicians in uniform, she received a flood of work offers. Ivy Benson's orchestra was hardly second best, despite critics' suggestions that a female band 'couldn't sound as good as a man's band'.

Mother Hen

The critics were wrong again – and Ivy Benson's professional approach was the main reason: she was a martinet, a strict disciplinarian who stood for no nonsense from her girls or anyone else. The band's signature tune *Lady Be Good* was meant to be taken literally. One girl called her 'a mother hen looking after her chickens'. Any girl not behaving according to Mother Hen's rules received a thorough dressing-down.

Ivy Benson's band played in ballrooms and theatres all over Britain, and appeared at the famous Palladium Theatre in London for 22 weeks straight. In 1943, the BBC chose Benson's as its official resident dance band – a decision which provoked much fury from other (male) bandleaders.

The all-girl band survived the war and played on until its last performance at the top-class Savoy Hotel in London in 1982. Its success and longevity were so renowned that male musicians applied to join, but Ivy Benson put them off with a single stipulation: she would accept only those who could fit into a suitable dress.

The wartime opportunity given to all-female bands was the basis for Ivy Benson's great success, which continued after hostilities ended. Here Benson and her band perform at Torquay, Southwest England, in 1953.

cooling her heels in New York for a month while the USO made up its mind about her tour. This sort of thing naturally deterred other stars from offering their services, although some were persuaded to change their minds after the Victory Committee staged a big rally where Gracie Fields and film star Kay Francis, among others, spoke about their experiences.

TOURING WITH BOB HOPE

Nevertheless, outside the United States, Hollywood film stars remained generally hard to find. Two notable exceptions were Bob Hope and Joe E. Brown, who defied the movie moguls to tour wherever U.S. troops could be found. Hope travelled tirelessly, starting in 1943 in Anchorage, Alaska, and going on to Europe, North Africa, the South Pacific and Iceland. He was accompanied by two lovely singers – his wife, Dolores, and Frances Langford, much acclaimed radio performer and star of 28 films. Langford became the most popular female star with the American forces in World War II.

CHAPTER 10

Aftermath

World War II gave women a unique opportunity to prove themselves beyond their traditional domestic roles; for them, the future was going to be very different from the past.

World War II was the most destructive and widespread the world had ever known. It wrought many permanent changes. For some women, it provided opportunities that would otherwise not have come their way. These were not only women who had gone into war work of various kinds, but also the brides of American and Canadian servicemen who left Britain to start a new life overseas after the war was over.

As well as the 70,000 brides who went to the United States, another 48,000 married Canadian ex-servicemen. After the war, most of them emigrated to Canada via Pier 21, the famous place of entry at Halifax, Nova Scotia.

After the rationing and shortages of the war, their most vivid memories of conditions on board ship naturally centred around food. For a start, they were amazed and delighted to find white bread and fruit served at meals.

Hilda Bradshaw, a bride who arrived on the *Aquitania* on July 28, 1946, took a white bread roll back to her cabin to show others who were too seasick to eat.

'We all gazed at it in wonder,' Bradshaw later recalled. 'We hadn't seen bread so white for a very long time.'

For Olga Rains, a Dutch bride, the Canadians were lifesavers. After the Nazi

World War II left much of Europe in rubble and ruin, presenting millions of people with the daunting task of rebuilding their lives and their cities, towns and villages.

Nagasaki was the second Japanese city to suffer the atom bomb, on August 9, 1945. At this single blow, more than 150,000 of the city's inhabitants were killed and injured.

invasion of the Netherlands in 1940, the Dutch were consistently starved, and many thousands died of cold and disease during the last winter of the war in 1944–1945.

'Then the Canadians came and liberated us,' Rains later recalled. 'The first month after the liberation, I was still too weak to do anything. In the first week in June 1945 I met Lloyd, my husband, one of the liberators.... It was love at first sight...on December 24, 1945 we were married with the permission of the Canadian Army in the beautiful old city hall in Haarlem.'

Olga Rains followed her husband to Canada in August 1946, sailing to Halifax and Pier 21 from Rotterdam on the *Lady Rodney*.

'I shared a cabin with three other brides....' she remembers. 'There was a bathroom in our cabin, which was a luxury we all enjoyed. The food served in the dining room was delicious, the crusty buns, bacon and eggs, oranges. Tears came into our eyes the first time we saw all this.'

Rescued by her Canadian marriage, Olga Rains was one of the very few lucky enough to escape a postwar Europe that had suffered monumental depredations for six long years. There had been too much destruction, too much killing, too much brutality, too much exploitation and far too many deaths – some 50 million in all – for the return of peace to smooth over the fundamental injuries civilization had sustained.

Much of Europe was a virtual wasteland. In Germany, occupied by the Allies until 1952, many families were destitute. Even in the capital, Berlin, women and children had become scavengers, picking over the rubble that lined the streets in search of some useful item of clothing, bed linen, utensils or food.

Millions of people, mainly women and children, had been displaced. Among them were Poles who had been used for slave labour by the Germans. More millions, especially Jews, were fearful of returning to their pre-war homes: despite widespread condemnation of Nazi anti-Semitism, hatred of Jews still existed in Europe, particularly in countries like Romania and Poland. Rather than face that again, many Jews preferred to become refugees in displaced persons (DP) camps, where they hoped for acceptance as immigrants in places outside Europe, such as the United States or Palestine. Millions of families had been separated during the war, and none of them knew which of their missing relatives were dead or where survivors were located.

There were nightmares for the families of men and women who had been prisoners of the Japanese. Their experiences had been so appalling that many were shadows of their former selves.

UNENDING NIGHTMARES

'Most Jewish families lost someone, or more than one, in the Holocaust,' concentration camp survivor Esther Psybysh recalled. 'There were many, many gaps in my own family – my parents, my brother, my cousins – not to mention several friends. But we didn't find anyone, even though we had help from the United Nations and the Red Cross. Our relatives and friends had vanished, and because we had no bodies to bury and make an end of it, we keep thinking of them dying in the gas chambers and being burned to ashes in the ovens. It's a

The French had virtually starved during the German occupation, when they were forced to subsist on a daily diet of only 1,000 calories. Here Allied convoys bring Parisians much-needed food.

nightmare that goes on and on....'

There were nightmares, too, for the families of men and women who had been prisoners of the Japanese. Though some survived better than others, their experiences had been so appalling that many returned home transformed into mere shadows of their former selves.

Millions of young women ended the war as widows. Fiancés killed in the war left behind women who had lost the prospect of marriage to the men they had loved.

Many German civilians were relieved when the British Army entered Berlin in 1945; what they had most dreaded was falling into the hands of the 'terrible' Russians.

Barbara Seymour, the daughter of British parents living in Singapore, was at school in Britain when the colony was captured by the Japanese in 1941. Her parents and several aunts and uncles became prisoners. All survived, but their return to Britain in 1945 was a great shock for their families.

'They were like strangers. Even my parents were like strangers,' Seymour recalled. 'It wasn't just that they were gaunt and pale after their experiences. They looked as if they were haunted. I remember my mother as a lively, cheerful woman, full of energy. But when she came home, all that had gone and she was silent and withdrawn. One of my aunts had nightmares for years, believing she was still in a Japanese prison. She'd wake up in the middle of the night screaming, get out of bed and search the house in case the Japanese were there. She found nothing, of course, but the nightmares didn't stop.'

NO HAPPY ENDINGS

Millions of young women ended the war as widows, faced with the task of bringing up children on their own. Fiancés killed in the war left behind young women who had lost the prospect of marriage to the men they had loved. Women like these had hoped for a resumption of family life, or the start of it, but instead were forced to go out to work to earn the living that had vanished when their men died. Some of them found it very hard to cope.

'There was a woman, Mrs. Murray, living a few houses away from us,' Patricia Albert remembered. 'She had lost her husband in the war and couldn't get over it. There was no money in the family, so she had to go out to work for the first time in her life and left her little boy with her mother. She felt terribly guilty, and to make up for it she spoiled the boy with daily presents which she couldn't really afford. He became quite impossible: if his mother didn't have the money or was too tired out to come home with a present every evening, he'd throw terrible tantrums. I once told him off when he tried to interfere with a game my friends and I were playing in the street. Would you believe that my mother actually punished me for that? The loss of his father, it seems, excused everything.'

Already relocated from the Anglo-Russian border zone, these Germans were being moved again, this time to a transit camp in the British zone, where they were housed in former stables.

RETURNING TO OLD ROLES

Work for the Mrs. Murrays of postwar Britain bore little similarity to wartime jobs, which had offered excitement and camaraderie and had given women new confidence in their abilities as they 'did their bit' for the war effort. It was inevitable, though, that these jobs would come to an end once the war was over. Employers had, quite rightly, promised men that they could have their jobs back when they returned. Once that happened, women who had replaced men in factories, government posts, technical establishments, on the railways or the buses were automatically dismissed.

Employers had promised the men they could have their jobs back when they returned from the war. Once that happened, the women who had replaced the men were automatically dismissed.

Unlike nurses or women who had served in uniform, they did not have the option of continuing in the service, so most of them returned home to become housewives again. Many were relieved: holding down a job and running a home at the same time had been exhausting. Some wanted to start families or go back to caring for their children themselves. Some had always been traditionalists at heart and believed firmly that a woman's place was in the home.

The mother of Barbara Presnall, a history professor at Texas Women's University, was one who found herself without a job at the end of the war.

'She worked at a shipyard in Long Beach, California,' her daughter remembered. 'She had given heart and soul to the job and had done a darn good job, but after the war she lost her position. Another woman [I know] had worked as a welder. She can't look at ornate welding now without thinking, "I could have done something like that." '

SPEAKING UP

Not all women laid off at the end of the war responded only with nostalgia.

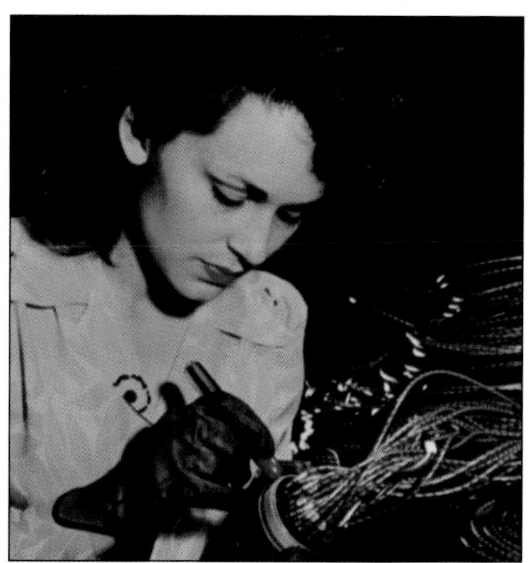

Women disproved the idea that they were the 'weaker' sex during the war, and although they afterwards returned to domesticity, it was not in their previous dependent frame of mind.

Several refused to accept what they saw as an unwarranted demotion. Ottilie Gattuss, who had worked at the Grumman Aircraft Engineering Corporation, wrote to U.S. President Harry Truman, setting out her protest:

'I happen to be a widow with a mother and son to support,' Gattuss told the President. 'I would like to know why, after serving a company in good faith for almost three-and-a-half years, it is now impossible to obtain employment with them. I am a lathe hand and was classified as skilled labour, but simply because I happen to be a woman, I am not wanted.'

Like Gattuss, Nona Pool wanted to continue work – in her case, as a welder – once the war was over.

'I said, "Hey, how about giving me a job welding?"' Pool remembered. 'And the guy, he turned around and looked at me and kind of laughed. He said, "Oh, I wouldn't doubt you're a good welder, but we don't have facilities for women." So I said, "I'll bring my own potty, just bring me a curtain." '

The 200 women who lost their jobs at the Ford plant in Highland Park, Michigan, went even further. They marched in protest in front of the Ford Building and carried placards with uncompromising messages: 'Stop discrimination because of sex' or 'How come no work for women?'

SEEDS OF CHANGE

Demonstrations like these were no real surprise. It had already been foreseen during the war that some American women would resist losing jobs that had brought them so much they had never known before: higher status as workers, wages that made them independent for the first time, and pride of knowing they had served their country.

However, the time had not yet arrived for their protests and demonstrations to change things. Effectively, what the war had done was to give women a certain period of leave from their traditional roles. Once there

VE – 'Victory in Europe' – Day, May 8, 1945; six WAAFs parade arm in arm down the Strand in London during the celebrations, which went on far into the night.

Postwar Japan

During the U.S. occupation of Japan, from 1945 to 1952, the Americans re-ordered Japanese life in the most fundamental fashion. Before the war, Japan had been a militaristic state, characterised by absolute obedience to authority and devotion to the 'divine' emperor, Hirohito. Women occupied a lowly, passive place in traditional Japanese society, and although 'Americanization' greatly altered Japan, their position was not essentially changed. Theoretically, the reforms brought about by the introduction of American democracy and a liberal scheme of education, including education for girls, gave Japanese women, as well as men, the same freedoms. The male-orientated culture of Japan was, however, so ingrained that few women, if any, attained high-ranking posts in business or government, advanced in the professions or enjoyed the personal freedoms American or British women could take for granted.

A Japanese girl meets her American boyfriend near U.S. commander Douglas MacArthur's headquarters in Tokyo. Fraternization was banned early on in the American occupation, but the ban was soon relaxed.

was no longer a war, their leave was up.

In these circumstances, it was not long before the pre-war situation reasserted itself in the workplace. The traditional woman's job had always been low-paying and low-status, with few, if any, opportunities for advancement. Thus it was inevitable that women war workers should find themselves downgraded. A wartime welder, for example, had to become a typist, a shipyard worker a grocery clerk. There was no chance that they could earn a 'man's wage' any more.

Women were not entirely back to square one, however. War work had enabled them to acquire expertise in very difficult, very demanding jobs, and their return to traditional roles could not negate the pride they'd felt as a result. In persuading women that they could be capable, skilled workers doing an important job, the U.S. Office of War Information had perhaps done its work too well: the women never forgot the compliment and resolved that prospects for their daughters were going to be a great deal better than their own. World War II, then, became an early combat zone for women in a separate struggle for equality in the workplace, even as they shared with men the burden of conquering Axis tyranny.

World War II became an early combat zone for women in a struggle for equality in the workplace, even as they shared with men the burden of conquering Axis tyranny.

Further Reading

BOOKS

Andrews, Maxene *Over Here, Over There: The Andrews Sisters and the USO Stars in World War II.* Zebra Books, New York, 1993.

Brayley, Martin *World War II Allied Womens Services.* Osprey Publishing Men at Arms series, London, 2001.

Carl, Ann B. *A Wasp Among Eagles: A Woman Military Test Pilot in World War II.* Smithsonian Institution Press, Washington and London, 1999.

Carson, Julia M. H. *Home Away from Home: The Story of the USO.* Harper & Brothers, New York, 1946.

Cole, Jean Hascall *Women Pilots of World War II.* University of Utah Press, Salt Lake City, 1995.

Colman, Penny *Rosie the Riveter.* Crown Publishers Inc., New York, 1995.

Cunningham, Cyril *Beaulieu: The Finishing School for Secret Agents.*

Leo Cooper, Barnsley, South Yorkshire, 1998.

Dundas, Barbara: *A History of Women in the Canadian Military.* Art Global, Montréal, 2001.

Fawkes, Richard *Fighting for a Laugh: Entertaining the British and American Armed Forces 1939–1946.* Macdonald and Janes, London, 1978.

Flanner, Janet *Paris Journal 1944–1955.* Harcourt Brace Jovanovich, New York, 1988.

Grenfell, Joyce *The Time of My Life: Entertaining the Troops – Her Wartime Journals.* Hodder and Stoughton, London, 1989.

Halter, Marek; Bernard, Michael (trans.) *Stories of Deliverance: Speaking With Men and Women Who Rescued Jews from the Holocaust.* Open Court Publishing Co., Chicago, Illinois, 1997.

Harris, Carol *Women at War 1939–1945 – The Home Front.* Sutton Publishing, Stroud, Gloucestershire, 2000.

Kaminski, Theresa *Prisoners in Paradise: American Women in the Wartime South Pacific.* University Press of Kansas, Lawrence, Kansas, 2000.

Keith, Agnes Newton *Three Came Home.* MacFadden-Bartell, New York, 1965.

Gossage, Carolyn *Greatcoats and Glamour Boots.* Dundurn P, Canada, 1991.

Kelsey, Marion *Victory Harvest: Diary of a Canadian in the Womens Land Army 1940–1944.* McGill-Queens University Press, 1997.

Land-Weber, Ellen *To Save a Life: Stories of Holocaust Rescue.* University of Illinois Press, Champaign, Illinois, 2000.

Litoff, Judy Barrett and Smith, David C. (eds.) *American Women in a World at War: Contemporary Accounts from World War II.* Scholarly Resources, Inc., Wilmington, Delaware, 2001.

McIntosh, Elizabeth P. *Sisterhood of Spies: The Women of the OSS.* Dell Publishing, New York, 1998.

Monahan, Evelyn M. and Neldel-Greenlee, *Rosemary All this Hell: U.S. Nurses Imprisoned by the Japanese.* University Press of Kentucky, Lexington, Kentucky, 2000.

Pawley, Margaret *In Obedience to Instructions: FANY and SOE in the Mediterranean.* Leo Cooper, Barnsley, South Yorkshire, 1999.

Rollyson, Carl *Beautiful Exile: The Life of Martha Gellhorn.* Aurum Press, London, 2001.

Rubin, Susan Goldman *Margaret Bourke-White.* Harry N. Abrams Inc., New York, 1999.

Sorel, Nancy Caldwell *Women who Wrote the War.* Arcade Publishing, New York, 1999.

Stoney, Barbara *Sibyl, Dame of Sark.* Hodder and Stoughton, London, 1978.

Tomblin, Barbara Brooks *GI Nightingale: The Army Nurse Corps in World War II.* The University Press of Kentucky, Lexington, Kentucky, 1996.

Virden, Jenel *Goodbye Piccadilly: British War Brides in America.* University of Illinois Press, Champaign, Illinois, 1996.

Wise, Nancy Baker and Christy *A Mouthful of Rivets.* Jossey-Bass Publishers, San Francisco, 1994.

WEBSITES

Please note that website addresses can change over time and some sites may become unavailable.

GENERAL

Reminiscences of American women, mainly on the home front, in World War II
- www.stg.brown.edu/projects/WWII_Women/

Women in the workforce during World War II
- www.u.arizona.edu/ic/mcbride/ws200/claud-petr.htm
- www.nara.gov/exhall/powers/women.html

Soviet women and World War II
- womenshistory.about.com/cs/warwwiisoviets/

Canadian women and World War II
- womenshistory.about.com/cs/warwwiicanada/

Rosie the Riveter and other female World War II heroes
- www.u.arizona.edu/~kari/rosie.htm

Women in World War II
- www.frontiernet.net/~pendino/World-War-II-Women.htm
- www.airmuseumca/waryears.html

Selected writings of Eleanor Roosevelt: American women in the war
- newdeal.feri.org/er/er14.htm

World War II in Ukraine: Ukrainian women at war by Andrew Gregorovich
- www.infoukes.com/history/ww2/page-11.html

INTRODUCTION

Oral histories of the Pearl Harbor attack, December 7, 1941
- www.history.navy.mil/faqs.faq663.htm

British Commonwealth Air Training Plan
- www.airmuseum.mb.ca/
- www.fleetairarmarchive.net/RollofHonour/TrainingCourses/BCATP_index.html

CHAPTER 1: GEARING UP FOR WAR

World War II posters
- www.nara.gov/exhall/powers/powers.html
- www.nara.gov/exhall/powers/nazi.html
- www.nara.gov/exhall/powers/watching.html

Women veterans of World War II
- www.pinn.net/~sunshine/essays/wwiivet.html

CHAPTER 2: LIFE ON THE HOME FRONT

Women's Land Army Corps and Emergency Farm Labor Service
- arcweb.sos.state.or.us/osu/osuwla.html

Life on the home front in Australia
- john.curtin.edu.au/manofpeace/homefront.html

Living through the Götterdämmerung of the Third Reich, 1945, by Ursula Grosser Dixon
- members.tripod.com/~Nevermore/gotter.html

Victory Gardens in the USA
- www.lib.ucdavis.edu/exhibits/food/panel8.html

Leni Riefenstahl biography
- www.leni-riefenstahl.de/eng/bio.html

Life on the home front in Canada
- peoria.k12.il.us/elmwood322/cwebber.html

CHAPTER 3: WAR WORK

Rosie the Riveter
- www.library.csi.cuny.edu/dept/history/lavender/rosie.html
- www.filmstransit.com/rosie.html

Rosie the Riveter memorial
- www.kcrt.com/series/rosie.html

Willow Run and the Arsenal of Democracy by Jenny Holan
- www.detnews.com/history/arsenal/arsenal.htm

Redstone Arsenal
- www.redstone.army.mil/history/women/welcome.html

German and American women working in factories
- theweboftime.com/Issue-1/Both-Sides/Rosies.htm

CHAPTER 4: THE ROLE OF NURSING STAFF

Letters from Sylvia Duke, Australian nurse in North Africa
- aaw.brainwaave.com.au/throughmyeyes/w2_wwp.asp

The Army Nurse Corps
- www.army.mil/cmh-pg/books/wwii/72-14/72-14.htm

CHAPTER 5: WOMEN IN UNIFORM

Women Air Force Service Pilots
- www.pbs.org/amex/flygirls
- www.wasp-WWII.org

Women and the military
- www.gendergap.com/military.htm

The Women's Army Corps: A Commemoration of World War II Service by Judith A. Bellafaire
- www.army.mil/cmh-pg/brochures/wac/wac.htm

Women's Marine Organisation
- www.womenmarines.org/con-join.html

Statue of 'Mollie Marine'
- www.womenmarines.org/history.htm

Amy Johnson biography
- www.raf.mod.uk/history/amyjohnson.html

Oveta Culp Hobby biography
- www.rice.edu/fondren/woodson/exhibits/wac/hobby.html

The Women's Auxiliary Ferrying Squadron
- www.nara.gov/exhall/people/women.html

Lilya Litvak, the White Rose of Stalingrad
- www.musketeers.org/Lilya.htm

Marina Raskova and Soviet female pilots by Harold Stockton et al.
- www.elknet.pl/acestory/raskov/raskov.htm

Nachthexen – Night Witches: Russian women pilots by Phyllis-Anne Duncan
- www.faa.gov/avr/news/Nexen.htm

WAVES
- www.womenofthewaves.com/profiles/

Women in uniform in World War II
- userpages.aug.com/captbarb/femvets5.html

The Coast Guard and the Women's Reserve in World War II
- www.uscg.mil/hq/g-cp/history/h_wmnres.html

Women in the Weather Bureau during World War II
- www.nssl.noaa.gov/~nws/women/history/ww2part1.html

Women of the CWAC
- www.ipsystems.com/powmia/WomenOfWar.html

Canadian War Museum: Canadian women in World War II
- www.earlofmarch.com/cwm/womenchart.html

Women's Royal Canadian Naval Service
- www.naval-museum.mb.ca/history/exhib10.htm

Canadian servicewomen
- www.cbc.ca/onair/specials/remembrance/symbols-servicewomen.html

CHAPTER 6: THE CLANDESTINE WAR – WOMEN AS SECRET AGENTS

Women spies
- www.undelete.org/military/spies.html

Women as partisans and members of the resistance
- www.interlog.com/~mighty/valor/history3.htm

Violette Szabo biography
- www.spartacus.schoolnet.co.uk/SOEszabo.htm

Virginia Hall biography
- www.spartacus.schoolnet.co.uk/SOEhall.htm

Women in intelligence
- www.gendergap.com/military/USmil9.htm#war-work

Nancy Wake biography
- www.spartacus.schoolnet.co.uk/SOEwake.htm
- nancywake.homestead.com/

CHAPTER 7: WOMEN AS PRISONERS

Holocaust rescue
- www.holocaust-heroes.com/villages.html

Concentration and death camps
- history1900s.about.com/cs/camps/

Jehovah's Witnesses and Nazism
- www.watchtower.org/library/g/1995/8/22/nazism_exposed.htm

Life in the Warsaw ghetto
- fcit.coedu.usf.edu/holocaust/resource/document/DocRing1.htm

***Porajmos:* genocide of the Roma gypsies in the Holocaust**
- www.philology.ru/liloro/letters.htm history1900s.about.com/library/holocaust/aa021099.htm

Sheila Allen in Changi Jail, Singapore
- www.english.upenn.edu/~scallen/
- www.abc.net.au/rn/history/verbatim/stories/s225023.htm

Displaced Jews in the United States Zone of Occupation, Germany
- www.ess.uwe.ac.uk/documents/harrison_report.htm

United States Holocaust Memorial Museum
- www.ushmm.org/dp/mapnew2a.htm
- www.ushmm.org/dp/intro.htm
- www.ushmm.org/dp/camp1.htm

Letter from President Truman to General Eisenhower concerning Jewish displaced persons
- www.ess.uwe.ac.uk/documents/Eisenhower_letter.htm

Museum of Tolerance Multimedia Learning Center
- motlc.wiesenthal.org/text/x33/xr3301.html

Displaced Jews in Europe 1945–1951
- geography.about.com/library/weekly/aa051898.htm

Australian nurses as prisoners
- www.angellpro.com.au/Wahsui.htm

Vivien Bullwinkel-Statham biography
- www.angellpro.com.au/Bullwinkel.htm

Women in Mauthausen concentration camp
- www.mauthausen-memorial.gv.at/engl/Geschichte/03.09.Frauen.html

Women in the ghettoes
- www.interlog.com/~mighty/valor/
- history1.htm
- www.interlog.com/~mighty/valor/history5.htm

Mona Louise Parsons biography
- www.athabascau.ca/wmst/november.html

CHAPTER 8: WOMEN REPORT AND PHOTOGRAPH THE WAR

Journalists, photographers, and broadcasters during World War II
- lcweb.loc.gov/exhibits/wcf/
- www.loc.gov/today/pr/1995/95-122

Martha Gellhorn biography and interview
- www.defenselink.mil/news/Mar1998/n03061998_9803063.html
- cci.wmin.ac.uk/pgjnet/gellhorn.html

Toni Frissell biography
- www.staleywise.com/collection/frissell/frissell.html

Clare Boothe Luce biography
- www.lkwdpl.org/wihohio/luce-cla.htm

Janet Flanner biography
- www.sbu.ac.uk/stafflag/janetflanner.html

Liberation of Paris, August 1944
- www.britannica.com/normandy/pri/Q00292.html

Helen Kirkpatrick biography and interview
- npc.press.org/wpforal/kirk3.htm www.spartacus.schoolnet.co.uk/2WWkirkpatrick.htm

Dorothea Lange biography and article
- www.vho.org/GB/Journals/JHR/7/3/Hummel285-317.html
- www.masters-of-photography.com/L/lange/lange.html

Women journalists covering World War II by Gerry J. Gilmore
- www.defenselink.mil/news/Feb2001/n02132001_200102135.html

CHAPTER 9: WOMEN AS ENTERTAINERS

Mrs. Miniver
- history.acusd.edu/gen/filmnotes/mrsminiver.html
- history.acusd.edu/gen/filmnotes/mrsminiver2.html

Tokyo Rose
- www.dyarstraights.com/orphan_ann/orphanan.html
- foia.fbi.gov/rose.htm

CHAPTER 10: AFTERMATH

Selected writings of Eleanor Roosevelt: woman's place after the war
- newdeal.feri.org/er/er15.htm

American Rosie the Riveter Association
- www.rootsweb.com/~usarra/

Canadian war brides
- www.cic.gc.ca/english/about/history/warbrides.html

Index

Note: page numbers in *italics* refer to illustrations